ECOLOGIES OF HARM

RHETORICS OF VIOLENCE
IN THE UNITED STATES

MEGAN EATMAN

THE OHIO STATE UNIVERSITY PRESS

COLUMBUS

Copyright © 2020 by The Ohio State University.
All rights reserved.

Library of Congress Cataloging-in-Publication Data is available online at catalog.loc.gov.

Cover design by Thao Thai
Text design by Juliet Williams
Type set in Adobe Minion Pro

To Beatrice, who showed up just in time, and Charlie,
who has been here every step of the way

ECOLOGIES OF HARM

NEW DIRECTIONS IN RHETORIC AND MATERIALITY
Barbara A. Biesecker, Wendy S. Hesford, and Christa Teston, Series Editors

CONTENTS

ACKNOWLEDGMENTS

I HAVE BEEN LUCKY to receive invaluable support at every stage of my writing process. The English Department and the College of Architecture, Arts, and Humanities at Clemson University provided resources essential for this project, including support for research-related travel. Lauren Gantz, Tekla Hawkins, Sarah Orem, and Michelle Smith read drafts and provided much-needed encouragement and constructive feedback. I am thankful that Tara Cyphers, the editors of the New Directions in Rhetoric and Materiality series (Barbara Biesecker, Wendy Hesford, and Christa Teston), and the anonymous readers all pushed this project in the best possible direction. Finally, in addition to the many other things they have done for me, my family members almost never asked, "When is your book going to be finished?" For that, I will always be grateful.

INTRODUCTION

Violent Rhetorical Ecologies

ON AUGUST 9, 2014, white police officer Darren Wilson shot Michael Brown Jr., an unarmed eighteen-year-old Black man, six times, killing him. Brown and his friend, Dorian Johnson, were walking together in Ferguson, Missouri, when Wilson approached in his police cruiser and told them to get out of the street. Wilson began to drive away, then backed up, after which an altercation ensued. Less than ninety seconds after he first encountered Wilson, Brown was dead. Subsequent criminal investigations cleared Wilson of wrongdoing, but a Department of Justice inquiry found that the Ferguson Police Department consistently overpoliced the city's Black population, and the city of Ferguson settled a wrongful death lawsuit filed by Brown's family (Hawkins). The shooting and aftermath inspired nationwide protests, many including the phrase "Hands up, don't shoot" to reflect the witness claim that Brown had his hands raised when Wilson killed him.

Understanding Brown's killing and the events that followed as rhetorical requires shifting common ways of thinking about the relationship of rhetoric and violence. It is not unusual for scholars to treat violence as communicative, but those examinations often focus on more carefully orchestrated violence.[1] Unlike acts of terrorism or state-run execution, Brown's murder was not planned for persuasive effect. Witnesses to Wilson shooting Brown did

---

1. As I will discuss below, scholars describe lynching, state-run execution, and torture as communicative acts.

not have advance notice of the murder, nor did Wilson engage in an elabo-
rate pre-killing ritual, as many lynch mobs did. When compared with these
other forms of violence, Brown's murder seems spontaneous. At the same
time, however, the killing shares "certain contagions and energy" with other
forms of white supremacist rhetoric and, through its violence, circulates them
further (Edbauer 14). Like lynching, of which it is a clear historical echo, Wilson shooting Brown constitutes Brown as a "black brute" and Wilson as a
noble savior. In his account of events, Wilson describes Brown as inhumanly
strong and angry, "like a demon" (Sanburn). The public discourse that circulated around Brown's murder transmits similar values. By reiterating the
topos that Brown was "no angel" and highlighting his alleged criminal actions,
distant rhetors constitute themselves, along with Wilson, as agents protecting
racialized "law-abiding citizens" from menacing "thugs."[2] Brown's murder thus
emerges from and continues a violent, white supremacist rhetorical ecology.
While Wilson never declared that he was "sending a message" by shooting
Brown, his actions reenergized existing white supremacist rhetoric, and the
fallout from the murder offered additional opportunities for white supremacist identity formation.

Ecologies of Harm examines how violent rhetorical ecologies constitute
public identity and structure surrounding debates. Viewing Brown's murder
as constitutive across modes—that is, constitutive in its direct violence, but
also through the rhetoric that surrounds it—makes its rhetorical force visible.
By "constitutive," I mean that Wilson killing Brown temporarily solidifies and
clarifies inherently unstable identities. While scholars do not always use the
word "constitutive," it is a commonplace that violence shapes the identities of
victims and participants. Violence clarifies the division of "us" and "them":
We are just and strong, they are dangerous and deviant. Violence is thus not
an interaction between discrete individuals, but a process that creates both
subjects. *Ecologies of Harm* builds on existing understandings of constitutive
rhetoric to map this process as it emerges through organized public violence.
Constitutive rhetoric is a process of interpellation; the text calls its audience
into existence and ties its members' shared identity to a particular belief or
course of action (Charland 137–38). While this process can be obvious—for
example, political speeches that constitute "real Americans" as white, working
class, and conservative—recent scholarship emphasizes that constitutive rhetoric can operate through an ambient, affective process, in which discursive
and nondiscursive elements combine to put people in place.[3] Wilson shooting

---

2. Commentators often use the phrase "no angel" to describe Black victims of police violence. For a Brown-specific example, see Eligon. For a detailed account of how "thug" is used
to describe Black victims of police violence, including Brown, see Smiley and Fakunle.

3. See Chaput; Edbauer; Gruber.

Brown articulates race relations and racial identity through a lens of threat, victimhood, and competing masculine strength, thus temporarily constituting the identities described above: Wilson as hero, Brown as monster. This constitutive rhetoric cannot function in isolation, however. It is impossible to separate the constitutive force of the murder itself from its surrounding rhetoric: portrayals of Black men and boys as threatening, of police officers as heroes, and of "good"/white citizens plagued by crime. Wilson's actions and their public significance emerge from and sustain these rhetorics. For that reason, I argue that rhetoric scholars should be attuned to the overall environments that violence's multimodal constitutive force can create. Brown's death is part of a violent rhetorical ecology that sustains some and harms others. Examining the rhetoric of his murder, then, requires addressing the practices that produce and maintain this violent ecology, as well as the options for resistance available in such a hostile environment.

I begin with Brown's murder because its apparent spontaneity makes it less legible as a communicative act, but more overtly rhetorical violent practices can also benefit from a focus on multimodal constitutive force. In addition to the killing of Black adults and children by police (with which the book begins and ends), *Ecologies of Harm* focuses on three interrelated violent practices: southern spectacle lynching, state-run execution, and torture in the War on Terror. Scholars describe all of these forms of violence as communicative. Lynching, for example, was carefully organized and publicly staged to send a white supremacist message to both white and Black audiences. As I will discuss in chapter 1, however, lynching's constitutive force does not stop with those audience members who saw the murder in person, nor with the distant spectators who received postcards of lynching victims after the fact (Wood 3). Absolute white supremacy was a foundation of white Southern identity, and its logic, in which Southern white men bore no obligation to "outsiders," permeated the rhetoric around lynching as well. Lynching, then, was a material rhetorical display, but it was also an essential part of a white supremacist ecology that preceded and exceeded the temporal boundaries of lynching as an event. Through its surrounding rhetoric, including discussions about whether and how lynching should be regulated, lynching offered multiple opportunities for white audiences to adopt its white supremacist philosophy and for Black audiences to be terrorized. Lynching, too, is constitutive across modes, but focusing too narrowly on one mode—public murder—can obscure some of the ways in which ostensibly nonviolent discourse mirrors lynching and furthers its white supremacist goals. Addressing surrounding rhetoric does not mean abandoning the rhetoric of physical violence. Instead, I discuss physical violence as one mode of constitutive rhetoric among others and map how these modes operate as part of a broader ecology.

While the practices I discuss are distinct in important ways, they share several structural characteristics. I refer to all of these phenomena as organized public violence. The violence is organized in that perpetrators actively plan it or follow a script established by previous incidents. For example, while lynchers did not always take time to plan their crime, even seemingly spontaneous lynchings followed patterns that distinguished them from other kinds of murders (Jean 355). Similarly, Brown's murder is startlingly familiar in comparison both to lynching (in which Black people were often killed for violations of decorum, like failing to walk on the sidewalk) and to the numerous more recent incidents in which police killed unarmed Black people. These patterns have rhetorical effects, even if perpetrators do not consciously imitate past violence. Through repetition, the forms of violence I discuss contribute to hostile physical and rhetorical environments in which only some subjects can thrive.

In analyzing rhetorical ecologies of violence, I also suggest a broad sense of violence's publicness. Even when physical harm is not widely visible, defenders frame the violent practices I discuss as acts by and for communities: for example, Southern whites, law-abiding citizens, or "America." That framing constitutes the community that authorizes or benefits from violence, as well as a community of "others": "black brutes," "superpredators," and "terrorists."[4] This framing is part of violence's constitutive function, and widely circulated narratives of identity allow community members to connect to violence, even when they cannot witness it. Community members can also recirculate narratives that facilitate violence: for example, when social media users or politicians portray Michael Brown as undeserving of life or insist that Black Lives Matter is a hate group.[5] This kind of participation is an essential part of violence's publicness, especially in an era in which most violence is only sporadically visible. Rather than focusing on the rhetoric embedded in highly visible violent spectacles, *Ecologies of Harm* traces how violence becomes sensible to a variety of audiences, even those that do not experience direct violence firsthand. How do community members participate in and resist violence that they never directly witness? How does violence affect available modes of being in a public space, and how do those effects manifest in public rhetoric?

By mapping the rhetorical ecologies around lynching, execution, torture, and police violence, *Ecologies of Harm* illustrates how ostensibly nonviolent rhetoric performs violence. Cultural and structural violence have material effects on perpetrators, victims, and spectators, even before and beyond an

---

4. In 1995, criminologist John DiIulio predicted a dramatic increase in crime by teen "superpredators." Crime did not increase, and his claims remain representative of alarmist rhetoric that fuels harsher policing strategies and prison sentences (Vitale).

5. For examples of this rhetoric, see Chumley; Jaffe; Economist Explains.

instance of direct physical harm. As an act of constitutive violence, Michael Brown's murder is *felt* on all sides. Wilson shooting Brown may not lead people to consciously change their views about crime or racism, but it draws on and reinforces existing cultural tropes that construct Black men and boys as dangerous others. White supremacist narratives of Brown's death *feel* right to people for whom these narratives are familiar, validating, and existentially important. The murder can thus serve as a comforting confirmation of white supremacist ideology. More obviously, the people constituted as violent others within this oppressive ecology can also feel the violence of Brown's death. One does not need to be a victim of direct violence to feel its possibility, especially when hints of that violence are present in everyday interactions. Violence's rhetorical power inheres in part in this sensibility, and careful attention to extended ecologies of violence can help rhetoric scholars discuss the force of violence in more nuanced ways.

This introduction will first situate my argument in the existing conversation about rhetoric and violence. I argue that rhetoricians should operate with an understanding of violence as direct, structural, and cultural, as well as constitutive across modes. This formulation requires thinking of rhetoric less as conscious and intentional persuasion than as the gradual shaping of public identity. I then explore the implications of a rhetorical ecology built on violence. Many uses of rhetorical ecology focus on the flow of rhetorical texts without addressing the constraints on or variable effects of that circulation. I argue that circulating violence produces violent rhetorical ecologies that facilitate some modes of being while foreclosing others. The cumulative effects of these ecologies are material, even though they are not as immediately, brutally material as direct violence. I then provide historical background on the interconnected practices of lynching, state-run execution, and torture. While each violent practice can be read as a rhetorical failure, I argue that all serve essential constitutive functions that proponents often obscure or disavow. Many justifications for organized public violence rely on well-defined, stable identities—the heroic in-group, the villainous out-group, the helpless victims—so advocates for violence must obscure violence's constitutive work.

RHETORIC AND/AS VIOLENCE

Even narratives that separate rhetoric and violence suggest an "intimate" relation between them (Crosswhite 134). Violence is often positioned as the precursor and alternative to rhetoric. Before there was rhetoric, there was violence, as in the myth of Prometheus recounted in Plato's *Protagoras*. Zeus gives warring humans an understanding of justice and a "sense of shame" so that they might regulate each other and themselves without turning to violence (136). Similarly, violence is often positioned as the consequence of rhetoric's failure. Claiming that certain audiences "won't listen to reason" is a common justification for violence. Implicitly, if this circumscribed version of "reason" cannot succeed, then violence is the only available persuasive technology. A similar narrative insists that violence is the condition for rhetoric—that is, that communities can only solve disputes with persuasion because their freedom to do so is secured with force (Crosswhite 150; see also W. Benjamin). In all of these cases, violence and rhetoric accomplish the same goal and are theoretically interchangeable; however, not everyone has the option to participate in nonviolent discussion. Individuals and communities who do not adhere to dominant values do not get to deliberate because, according to these narratives, allowing deliberation would be pointless or even dangerous (Roberts-Miller, *Demagoguery* 20). Instead, out-groups become targets for violence.

Given rhetoric's entanglement with violence, it is not a stretch to assert that violence could be rhetorical. While rhetoric scholars have been slower to address violence as rhetoric, interdisciplinary scholarship commonly describes violence as a tool for constituting an otherwise amorphous state power. Michel Foucault famously described public torture and execution as constitutive of sovereign power. If a crime, however minor, is an injury to the state, then public punishment "is a ceremonial by which a momentarily injured sovereign is reconstituted" (48). By proportionally harming the accused criminal's body, the sovereign (here, a prince or king) could reassert control over his subjects. In this version of violence as constitutive power, subjects need "to see the thing done" in order to participate in its constitutive economy (Wood 21). Other analyses of similar violence complicate this claim. Elaine Scarry describes torture as constitutive, explaining, "The physical pain is so incontestably real that it seems to confer its quality of 'uncontestable reality' on that power that has brought it into being" (27). Torture constitutes the otherwise unstable power of the state through the world-destroying pain it inflicts on the victim. Instead of a person, the victim becomes the pain, and that pain is evidence of the power of the torturer and the institution she represents (37, 56). In Scarry's framework, the impossibility of communicating pain, rather than the pain's public visibility, is key to torture's constitutive force.[6] The torture victim's unknowable pain is a source of either doubt or vague terror for those around her. In either case, she is constituted as an outsider, marked too fully by state violence.

---

6. Other scholars have contested Scarry's understanding of pain. See chapter 2.

These two versions of constitutive violence suggest the complexity of violence as rhetoric. While it is relatively easy to recognize an organized display of public harm as persuasive, the rhetoric of violence does not always—or even usually—work that way. Forms of violence that were once public, like state-run torture and execution, are now typically obscured. Violent spectacles that persist in the United States, like the public executions of Black men, women, and children by police officers, are more likely to be coded as spontaneous and detached from structures of power. Violence as rhetoric, then, is not confined to spectacles of violence like public execution and their immediate constitutive effects on victim, perpetrator, and audience. Violence as rhetoric is not even reducible to direct violence: a persons or persons inflicting physical harm on another person or persons, as in instances of killing or maiming (Galtung 292). Instead, addressing violence's rhetorical force requires an understanding of violence and rhetoric that recognizes their shared and varied materiality. In the discussions cited above, both Foucault and Scarry suggest that violent action makes an otherwise unseen power brutally "real" by inscribing it on the victim's body. Certainly, rhetorical performances of direct violence draw their force from the brute reality of human suffering, but that is only one version of violence's materiality. Pushing back on the notion of direct violence as a sudden materialization of power, *Ecologies of Harm* addresses the material rhetorical violence that exists before and after acts of direct violence. This violence, which dwells in quotidian structures and practices, can inflict harm differently than the more visible violence of killing or maiming.

Addressing the varied materiality of rhetoric and violence, then, begins with an expanded understanding of violence. In addition to direct violence, Johan Galtung identifies two other forms: structural violence and cultural violence. In the context of Michael Brown's murder, the direct violence is Wilson assaulting and shooting Brown. The surrounding circumstances and following events, however, involve structural and cultural violence, less obvious forms of harm that facilitate and emerge from each other and direct violence. Structural violence, Galtung explains, takes the form of exploitation and inequality, in which some individuals can live comfortably while others suffer (293). The overpolicing of Black neighborhoods in Ferguson, the laws adapted to allow it, and the economic inequality that fuels segregation are all forms of structural violence.[7] Cultural violence supports direct and structural violence. It "works . . . by changing the moral color of an act from red/wrong to green/right or at

---

7. A US Department of Justice investigation found that the Ferguson Police Department consistently overpoliced the Black community, often through "manner of walking" charges. Similar to "stop and frisk," manner of walking charges allow police to harass pedestrians (Hennessey-Fiske).

least to yellow/acceptable: an example being 'murder on behalf of the country as right, on behalf of oneself wrong.' Another way is by making reality opaque, so that we do not see the violent act or fact, or at least not as violence" (292). Responses to Brown's death that described him as a "thug" undeserving of life are forms of cultural violence, as are similar, long-circulating narratives of Black criminality. While direct violence is sometimes more visible because it is legible as an event, structural and cultural violence are pervasive and, over time, similarly affecting (294).

Describing all of these practices as violent emphasizes violence's widespread and varied materiality. It is not just that, as others have discussed, spoken or written rhetoric supports violence.[8] Nor is it that all language is violent through its symbolic substitution.[9] Rather, in the circumstances I discuss, spoken, written, and otherwise performed rhetoric *is* violence in that it affects material harm. Its materiality is different from that of direct violence, but it is no less felt, both for its victims and the people who benefit from it. As Sara Ahmed explains, circulating feelings "create the very surfaces and boundaries that allow all kinds of objects to be delineated," including "self" and "other" (*Cultural Politics* 10). For example, the cultural violence of the word "thug" attaches negative feelings (fear, anger) to Brown and other young Black men, and as that rhetoric circulates in discourse (whites and authority figures using the term to demean) and action (treating Black men as criminals), the attachment gets stronger. This rhetorical pressure is cumulative and felt, especially for those who are constituted as other. Direct violence, then, is only one part of a violent rhetorical ecology. Structural and cultural violence also have material, constitutive effects.

Recognizing a wider variety of violent practices allows for a more nuanced understanding of violence's constitutive force and the relationship between violence and rhetoric. Organized public violence is rhetorical because it shapes relationships among people and affects possible modes of public participation. It does not determine these relations, but through repeated circulation in multiple forms, tropes of organized public violence and the identities they construct can come to seem natural. In many of its instantiations, the violence I discuss is a kind of semi-ambient rhetoric: only sometimes legible as violence, but always present as atmosphere. Rhetorical violence shapes versions of the world, but slowly, through processes of accretion. Occasional

---

8. Burke's "The Rhetoric of Hitler's 'Battle'" is a prominent example of this approach to violence and rhetoric. For more recent work, see Engels and Saas; Roberts-Miller, *Demagoguery*; Towns.

9. See Haynes.

spectacles of controversial direct violence can obscure this slower but equally damaging process.

Ecologies of Harm uses a cultural rhetoric methodology to build theory from the practices being examined (Bratta and Powell). When I began researching violence, I was interested in why communities continued to use and defend obviously ineffective violent practices. As I discuss below, lynching, execution, and torture all fail at their alleged purposes (punishing and deterring crime and extracting intelligence). Rather than assuming that ineffective violence is pointless or vestigial, my research begins with the assumption that ongoing violence does significant cultural work. While violence can have other rhetorical tasks, organized public violence in the United States almost uniformly maintains dominant identities perceived to be at risk: white, masculine, Southern, "American." *Ecologies of Harm*'s theory of violent rhetorical ecologies and violence as constitutive rhetoric emerges from the study of these practices. Each chapter examines how the rhetoric of and around practices of direct violence constructs the parties involved. While my analysis is structured around practices of direct violence, I focus on the intersections of direct, structural, and cultural violence and the cumulative effects of their overlapping operations. My analysis of resistant practices, present to varying degrees in all chapters, addresses how rhetors constitute communities and reality differently, even as they are operating from within oppressive rhetorical ecologies.

FROM ECOLOGY TO THE WEATHER

To address the cumulative effects of direct, structural, and cultural violence, *Ecologies of Harm* also adapts an understanding of rhetorical ecology. An ecological framework tracks rhetoric's motion, including the changing status of ostensibly static elements like audience and text (Edbauer 9). *Ecologies of Harm* addresses how violence circumscribes this movement. A rhetorical ecology produced by practices of direct, structural, and cultural violence is hospitable to only certain identities and practices. In this way, violent rhetorical ecologies mirror features of a biological ecosystem that many discussions of rhetorical ecology do not address. Ecosystems are not blank spaces through which all creatures can move with ease. Instead, they allow some groups to flourish, others to die, and many to struggle in a liminal space. Rhetorical ecologies, violent or not, have similar limits and affordances. Mapping what a rhetorical ecology allows or disallows and how rhetors resist those limits is key to understanding violent rhetoric's diffuse operations of power.

The term "rhetorical ecology" emphasizes the mobility and mutability of rhetorical terms, even in a seemingly static rhetorical situation. Noting that elements of rhetorical situations—speakers, texts, audiences—cannot be separated from their constitution within it, Jenny Edbauer argues for treating "rhetoric both as a process of distributed emergence and as an ongoing circulation process" (13). The concept of rhetorical ecologies allows rhetoricians to map this emergence and circulation, tracing how persuasive texts transform over time. Within this formulation, circulation is a source of power. Catherine Chaput uses the example of the Confederate flag, a "deeply affecting sign for many rural, white Southerners, who identify their patriotism and history through it" (14). Through circulation, the flag has accrued additional and modified meanings that build on, rather than erase, its initial association with regional rebellion and chattel slavery.[10] Its power comes from this circulation, which explains why attempts to make it less visible—for example, removing the flag from the South Carolina State House—are met with virulent opposition.[11] Threats to the Confederate flag's ongoing visibility *feel* existentially threatening for its proponents because, in terms of a white Southern identity that inheres in Confederate symbolism, they are. White Southern identity emerges in relation to the Confederate flag and its attendant philosophies—white supremacy, the "Lost Cause"—and can thus be reasserted and defended through it. The flag must keep circulating in order to continue to reiterate that identity.

While rhetorical ecologies are always in motion, then, the example of the Confederate flag shows how that motion can fuel an oppressive stasis. The "flow" within rhetorical ecologies may be in the service of blockage—that is, a maintenance of the status quo (Mays). Using systems theory, Chris Mays argues that rhetorical ecologies sustain themselves through circulation such that even systems that seem intractable are in constant motion, often shifting in minor ways to compensate for new developments. This continual movement is necessary because the systems involved are "inherently unstable" (Mays). For example, the Confederate flag's constitution of white Southern identity requires continued circulation because the identity it represents is fragile. White Southern identity cannot sustain itself; if the flag does not cir-

---

10. I differ from Chaput on this point. While Chaput writes that the flag's connection to slavery "does not penetrate" the positive affective energy around the flag, I argue that the flag's appeal inheres in part in its reinforcement of an oppositional white supremacist identity (15).

11. The Confederate flag at the South Carolina State House was temporarily removed in 2015, shortly after white supremacist Dylann Roof killed nine people at Mother Emanuel African Methodist Episcopal Church in Charleston. The legislature began flying the flag again in 2018 (Marchant).

culate, individuals who claim that identity will need other affectively saturated texts to reinforce their shared existence. While violence does not typically factor into discussions of rhetorical ecology, practices of direct, structural, and cultural violence function similarly. Repeated police shootings of unarmed Black men, women, and children reinforce an atmosphere of terror and grief as well as a shared understanding of white victimhood and heroism. The multimodality of this violence—that it is reiterated in traffic stops, social media arguments, viral video footage of people suffering and dying—can be considered a form of circulation that maintains the status quo.

Many discussions of rhetorical ecology foreground flow without addressing how power allows or disallows movement.[12] I argue for a version of rhetorical ecology that traces the cumulative effects of circulating violence, including how that circulation reinforces existing structures of power. I trace the constitutive rhetoric of violence to map how rhetorical ecologies become and remain inhospitable and the effects of that inhospitality. This approach addresses how power inheres in everyday practices and is reinforced at multiple levels and through varied systems. Many discussions of violence suggest a top-down version of power: that is, a "state" (usually constructed as federal) imposing its will on a population.[13] Racist violence in the United States complicates this hierarchical understanding. While the violence I discuss often benefits state and federal governments, none of it is universally avowed by those governments. All of the practices of direct violence in *Ecologies of Harm* are sites of occasional controversy and (sometimes cursory) debate, and some, including lynching and certain versions of state-run execution, draw their rhetorical power from opposing formal structures of authority. The term "state violence," while accurate, risks masking the nuances of how these violent practices operate.[14] While they reinforce existing power structures, their power is not solely in the force of the state, even as it is exerted through its citizens. If violence's power is in part its proliferating, constitutive force, then the everyday practices of viewing, sharing, arguing about, and reinforcing violence are essential.

---

12. Chaput is a notable exception. Edbauer's original discussion of rhetorical ecologies emphasizes the power of circulation but does not address constraints on who and what can circulate.

13. Foucault is a paradigmatic example of this version of power, but even recent adaptations of biopolitics often emphasize the state (for example, Mbembe; Puar, *The Right to Maim*).

14. Lauren Berlant describes similar issues with the concept of sovereignty. She writes that sovereignty "is inadequate for talking about agency outside of the power of the King's decree or other acts in proximity to certain performances of law. . . . It is also a distorting description of the political, affective, and psychological conditions in which the ordinary subjects of democratic/capitalist power take up positions as agents" (97–98).

It is this perpetual circulation of violence that maintains a hostile rhetorical ecology.

Attention to inhospitable rhetorical ecologies allows for a consideration of quotidian violence that, as I noted above, is less visible as violence. Recent scholarship on biopolitics and power provides tools for addressing harm that is not reducible to a single event. The cumulative effects of direct, structural, and cultural violence create debility, a liminal state of perpetual physical struggle. Jasbir Puar coins the term "debility" to address "injury and bodily exclusion that are endemic rather than epidemic or exceptional" (*The Right to Maim* xvii). Like Lauren Berlant's "slow death," debility marks "the physical wearing out of a population" (95).[15] Puar contrasts the event of disabling injury, after which the disabled person can use the injury as a basis for compensatory claims, with the long-term debility that one incurs from ongoing circumstances like overwork, improper health care, and toxic-but-legal living conditions (*The Right to Maim* xvi–xvii). Conditions of debility maintain power structures but have few spaces of public recognition; they can be more challenging to contest than practices of direct violence. Direct violence often obscures debility by drawing attention and energy away from ongoing harmful conditions (24). Distant audiences may perceive direct violence as more visceral and affecting; in fact, a great deal of human rights rhetoric assumes that they will. The slow grind of debilitating conditions like underemployment and inadequate housing is harder to represent as a crisis, in large part because this kind of suffering is often coded as normal or deserved. Debility's cultural violence manifests in the repeated insistence that people experiencing endemic injury do so as the result of personal weakness, rather than as the result of a structurally violent system.

The concept of debility draws attention to how all forms of violence, including structural and cultural, are material conditions that wear on body and mind. Discussing the aftermath of slavery, Christina Sharpe describes felt conditions of ongoing oppression:

> In what I am calling the weather, antiblackness is pervasive *as* climate. The weather necessitates changeability and improvisation; it is the atmospheric condition of time and place; it produces new ecologies. *Ecology: the branch of biology that deals with the relations of organisms to one another and to their physical surroundings; the political movement that seeks to protect the environment, especially from pollution.* (106)

---

15. For a discussion of the slow violence of environmental destruction, see Nixon.

Along with debility, the weather is an important counter to an understanding of rhetorical ecology that elides how ecologies produce cumulative material effects and sustain structures of power. The ecology Sharpe describes grows from slavery and continues the objectification and oppression of Black people; it is "slave law transformed into lynching law, into Jim and Jane Crow, and other administrative logics that remember the brutal conditions of enslavement after the event of slavery has supposedly come to an end" (106). As the weather, oppression is a constant sensory presence. Its version of power relies on direct, structural, and cultural violence that both continue through history and remain in the cultural memory of oppressed people. Sharpe explains that even if a landscape could be totally transformed, the weather can never be erased (105). It persists "*as* climate," defining the conditions of possibility for those dwelling within it.

Ecologies of Harm traces the elements of violent rhetorical ecologies that produce and resist a hostile, debilitating climate. I argue that rhetorical ecologies are more than collections of shifting, circulating elements; they also produce moods, dispositions, orientations toward people and the surrounding environment. They have (and are) cumulative effects. This is one way of understanding the cooperation of direct, structural, and cultural violence. Each is more than the sum of its parts because, through continued circulation, these forms of violence are world-making. *Ecologies of Harm* addresses the components of this world, their constitutive effects, and the strategies rhetors use to disrupt them.

OBJECTS OF ANALYSIS: A BRIEF HISTORY OF ORGANIZED PUBLIC VIOLENCE

While the forms of violence addressed in *Ecologies of Harm* are distinct, they emerge from and sustain related rhetorical ecologies. Their overlapping histories provide insight into how US communities have historically practiced violence as rhetoric. Proponents of lynching, state-run execution, and torture all claim that these practices "send a message" to recalcitrant others.[16] Advocates claimed that lynching was the only appropriate response to the rape of white women by Black men, death penalty retentionists have long claimed that the death penalty deters crime, and torture supporters insist that torture convinces its victims to share life-saving intelligence. While all of these claims are demonstrably untrue, this rhetoric is part of violence's constitutive func-

---

16. I discuss this phrase in more detail in the conclusion.

tion. Despite its pervasiveness, direct violence in the United States requires some justification, however flimsy. Supporters justify violence by constituting its targets as both dangerous and inherently unreasonable. This narrative allows supporters to hedge their bets; even if the violence in question isn't effective, they can claim that it was the only option for convincing an irrational audience.

Constituting the community that performs the violence has proven more complicated. Authorities and practitioners have adapted practices of execution and torture over time to ensure that their violence could be distinguished from the "uncivilized" violence it purports to punish. As Wendy Hesford explains, human rights rhetoric often revolves around the idea that when it comes to distant suffering, "seeing is believing" (29). Hesford describes the primal scene of human rights as a visual and affective encounter in which the viewer will "(1) recognize the other as a human rights subject; (2) identify with the other through an awareness of one's own vulnerability; and (3) be moved to act on his or her behalf" (48). Human rights organizations thus work to make suffering visible to spectators who have the power to act against it.[17] Communities practicing violence, on the other hand, work against this assumed ocular epistemology of suffering. As practitioners decreased the visibility of execution and torture, they increased their rhetorical control. The function of each form has shifted along with those changes. A hidden, clinical execution cannot communicate the same values as a hanging in the public square, nor can torture that few see or know about.

These transformations and the justifications that authorities offer for them are an important part of violent rhetorical ecologies. In briefly mapping rhetorical transformations of lynching, execution, and torture, I argue that even proponents have treated these violent practices as primarily communicative. Proponents' consistent focus on encouraging "appropriate" community reactions suggests that all of these forms of violence are designed to communicate to and about the communities that authorize them, rather than to the avowed audience of dangerous outsiders. This focus explains, in part, why practices like execution and torture persist even though they are ill-designed to accomplish their alleged goals. While their key communicative function fails, they constitute communities in evidently appealing ways.

---

17. I will return to Hesford's concept of the ocular epistemology and her associated critique in chapter 2 and the conclusion.

"Civilized" Killing

Modern execution procedure is perhaps best understood as a response to the rhetorical problems of public hanging, the primary execution method in the colonies and the early United States. Of these rhetorical problems, publicness was the easiest to solve. Before the mid-nineteenth century, publicness was an essential part of execution procedure, and viewing an execution was not considered shameful. People from surrounding communities would travel to witness the multi-hour ceremony, typically held in a venue that could accommodate a crowd. Executions served a pedagogical function. As Stephen John Hartnett explains, "physical punishments and the death penalty were employed as public spectacles of seeing and knowing, as means of drawing clear lines to demark values, identities, and the cost of transgressing community norms" (5). To reinforce these messages, hangings were typically accompanied by gallows speeches, sermons, or pamphlets warning the spectators against a life of crime and its supposed precursors, like alcohol or idleness. That hanging was also a form of entertainment, and that the audience sometimes sided with the condemned, did not initially threaten the institution. The death penalty's didactic potential appeared to outweigh concerns that the crowds might get the wrong message (Banner 28).

The move to private executions was motivated in part by changing conceptions of what constituted appropriate viewing for civilized people. David Garland notes that men and women of taste were supposed to "draw back in disgust at the sight of vulgarity or unpleasantness, above all from scenes of violence or brutality"; he quotes John Stuart Mill's statement that "it is in avoiding the presence not only of actual pain, but of whatever suggests offensive or disagreeable ideas, that a great part of refinement consists" (*Peculiar Institution* 145). Hanging was frequently gory; sometimes the condemned died instantly and sometimes she strangled over the course of several minutes, and no one was sure how to guarantee the former instead of the latter (Banner 170). However, Banner notes that "before the last third of the nineteenth century, accounts of bungled or obviously painful executions contain no indication that spectators found them too troubling to bear" (172). New attitudes about violent spectacle complicated public execution. Given that civilized people were not supposed to see gore, it seemed increasingly unlikely that public execution would sway audiences in a moral direction. Elites began to worry that public executions were corrupting the poor and working-class audience members—thought to be highly susceptible to negative influence—rather than persuading them to avoid crime. As a Massachusetts newspaper put it, "An hundred persons are made worse, where one is made better by a public execution" (qtd. in Banner 150).

The easiest way to deal with the crowd's reaction was to eliminate the crowd. Authorities began building walls around scaffolds, hiding hanging from the public, "as a means to impose efficiency, order, and the semblance of respectability" (Wood 23). The pool of witnesses was narrowed by race, gender, and class to avoid "any semblance of an unruly or impressionable crowd," and some states went so far as to ban press from the gallows to prevent sensationalism in the news (Wood 28). These actions suggest that the audience was considered a large part of the problem. While the text of execution would need modifications, limiting the audience to people who would interpret the event "correctly" would improve the death penalty's rhetorical effects. Presumably, the intention was that the observations of elite witnesses would be transmitted through newspapers and oral accounts to the larger population, thereby structuring the would-be crowd's understanding of the death penalty. Elite viewers could mediate the potentially corrupting spectacle for an audience perceived as vulnerable.

As hanging's variability became too troublesome for Victorian mores, states sought new methods of execution. In 1886, New York created a commission to replace hanging as the state's primary method of execution (Sarat, *Gruesome Spectacles* 63–64). While the committee was charged with finding a humane alternative to hanging, its reasons for rejecting several potential methods suggest that painlessness was not a primary concern. The guillotine, while thought to be painless, had problematic associations. The committee's report noted that the guillotine was associated "with the bloody scenes of the French Revolution" and that audiences would find it "totally repugnant to American ideas" (qtd. in Banner 180). The committee was also concerned about the audience's comfort, rejecting the guillotine in part because "the profuse effusion of blood which it involves . . . must be needlessly shocking to the necessary witnesses" (qtd. in Banner 179). The firing squad, on the other hand, was rejected because it required too many executioners and had a "tendency to encourage the untaught populace to think lightly of firearms" (qtd. in Banner 180). Hanging, which the committee reviewed once more to ensure that they wanted to make a change, was rejected in part because of its association with Southern spectacle lynching. One committee member mentions that "cultured or high-minded persons" have a prejudice against execution based on "the multitudes of accounts which have been published of such scenes which have occurred, not necessarily associated with the death penalty" (qtd. in Garland, *Peculiar Institution* 119). The ideal method of execution was not simply painless. Rather, it would make a positive argument about the community as a whole by discouraging crime and demonstrating the state's ability to conduct an execution without traumatizing audience members.

The committee's reasoning provides two important details about execution as a rhetorical practice. First, what counted as "humane" execution was based on audience experience rather than the experience of the executed person. The method the committee chose, electrocution, had never been used to execute a human, so there were no assurances that it would provide a humane experience. In lieu of demonstrable humaneness, electrocution offered sophisticated machinery that marked the community as technologically advanced and, implicitly, "civilized."[18] Second, by functioning as its uncivilized other, extralegal violence shaped state violence. As the committee tried to find a new way to execute, they were concerned with distinguishing the state's violence from the extralegal violence of lynching. The committee positions lynching, at its peak frequency at the time of the committee's decision, as the other of state-run execution. Execution needed to send the "right" message about state authority and constitute a civilized community, and dissociation from lynching was a part of the commission's rhetorical strategy. Electrocution and subsequent methods of execution (the gas chamber and lethal injection) thus emerge from an existing ecology of concern about decorous ways of killing. Lethal injection, as discussed in chapter 2, is the culmination of this logic. Through multiple levels of obfuscation, lethal injection kills without the appearance of killing. Lethal injection's civilized appearance fuels its rhetorical and legal positioning as the most humane method of execution.

As I will discuss in more detail in chapter 1, lynching's rituals were similarly intertwined with state-run execution. The South was slower than the North to abolish public executions, and lynchers adapted features of the still-familiar ritual to grant authority to their violent spectacles (Wood 23–24). As Wood explains, "Lynch mobs even appropriated many rituals of public executions—the declarations of guilt, the confessions, the taking of souvenirs and photographs—to confer legitimacy on their extralegal violence" (24). Similarly, lynching drew its legitimacy in part from the presence and behavior of the crowd. Just as public executions were supposed to be didactic and solemn, lynching was constructed as an act of popular justice that required witnesses to function appropriately (24–25). The presence of a large, white

---

18. Speaking to the legislature just before the formation of the Gerry Commission, Governor David Bennett-Hill suggested that a more technologically advanced method of execution would also be more humane. He stated that hanging had come down "from the dark ages" and asked "whether the science of the present day cannot provide the means for taking the life of such as condemned to die in a less barbarous manner" (qtd. in Sarat, *Gruesome Spectacles* 63).

crowd testified to popular support for white supremacy and its performance through violence.

While lynching adapted rituals of public execution, lynchers' actions were also *against* the state, even as they operated with tacit or explicit state approval. Lynching's proponents constructed it as an act of popular justice that expressed the will of the people, even when that expression was *technically* illegal. State law was effectively suspended in these instances because "local norms of justice contradicted state law and interrupted its operation" (Garland, "Penal Excess" 810). While state law could punish a Black person accused of a crime, lynchers often wanted torture as well, something that even a public state-run execution could not offer (813). Lynchers used "methods that would most forcefully convey the hatred and contempt they felt for the supposed perpetrator and his unspeakable crimes" (814). Their anachronistic violence sent a message that state-run execution could not and, in doing so, constructed the lynch mob as the true authority. While some measure of punishment could come from the state, real "justice" had to come from the mob.

Even though authorities designed state-run execution to be different from lynching, the "tough on crime" rhetoric on which the death penalty relies reinforces a similar investment in decisive violence. A story from Texas, long-standing leader of executions in the United States, illustrates this point ("Number of Executions"). In 2010, during the Texas gubernatorial primaries, Senator Kay Bailey Hutchison was exploring Governor Rick Perry's political vulnerabilities. Hutchison's staff asked focus groups about the near certainty that Perry had allowed the execution of an innocent man, Cameron Todd Willingham, and impeded inquiries into the investigators' conduct. Multiple reports stated that these events improved Perry's standing in the eyes of at least one focus group member, who stated, "It takes balls to execute an innocent man" (Burns and Haberman). Perry won the primary and the election. Nine years later, he is the US secretary of energy.

The focus group member's statement highlights the importance of violence as constitutive rhetoric. As I noted above, both lynching and state-run execution are designed in ways that counter their avowed purpose of deterring crime. Because lynching often targeted Black people at random or for minor violations of the racial order, it communicated that even law-abiding Black people were subject to death according to the whims of white community members. In Hutchison's research, the focus group member similarly privileges ethos over the administration of careful, measured justice on which state-run execution is supposedly based. In this version of the death penalty, executing the innocent is manly; thus, judicial safeguards like due process and appeals are feminine and weak. The speaker values execution's perceived ability to constitute those who authorize it as strong over its avowed retributive function. This understanding surfaces in a great deal of "tough on crime" rhetoric, linking contemporary punishment to lynching's obviously expressive brutality. The Trump administration's advocacy of oppressive and ineffective carceral practices is one example of this rhetoric's persistence (Lopez).

Lynching and state-run execution, then, are both part of the rhetorical ecology of "punishment." In punishing, whether for an actual crime or a violation of decorum, communities constitute themselves as righteous and strong; in punishing through technological mediation, communities that use the death penalty constitute themselves as civilized as well. In both practices, the experience of the person being lynched/executed is important only insofar as it communicates something about the authorizing community. Lynching and execution are for the living.

Torture as Constitutive Rhetoric

Interrogational torture shares several characteristics with lynching and state-run execution. Like lynching and execution, torture is supposed to "send a message" to its victims. Like lynching and execution, torture is remarkably ineffective at its purported purpose. Experts have repeatedly noted that torture does not produce accurate intelligence and that other methods, like building rapport with detainees, work better.[19] Torture's primary utility is not as an interrogational method but as a multiply constitutive rhetoric. Torture constitutes large-scale problems of violence as solvable through the application of violence to individual bodies. It suggests that the body contains data that can be extracted through the correct application of violence. Perhaps most importantly, torture reinforces the boundaries between in-groups and out-groups and defines the in-group's values. This function holds even, and perhaps especially, if torture does not work. Like executing the innocent, torture for torture's sake can make a claim about the torturer's willingness to act decisively and disregard consequence.

As Darius Rejali explains, the torture of choice for modern democracies is "clean" or stealth torture (8). Stealth torture is physical torture that does not leave marks on the body, for example, waterboarding, stress positions, or electroshock (4). Democracies may be more likely to use this form of torture because of concerns about international monitoring and their professed commitment to human rights (8). To keep their international reputation and

---

19. See Shermer; Bohannon; "Former FBI Agent."

power, democracies that rely on physically coercive techniques have to ensure that their techniques do not leave physical evidence. Even if a victim speaks out later, stealth torture operates on the assumption that without visual evidence of wounding, no one will believe the victim's story. In this way, stealth torture is based on an ocular epistemology nearly identical to the one that Hesford describes in relation to human rights rhetoric (and that structures the history of execution). Torture in democratic states is designed to thwart the human rights spectacle.

Anti-torture law in the United States punishes only a narrow version of torture, effectively permitting a variety of stealth practices. Michael Vicaro explains that the US anti-torture statute "codifies as law a specific model of subjectivity—ontologically and epistemologically isolated private individualism—and torture—intense physical pain purposefully administered with affective cruelty" (408). This limited understanding exempts a variety of torture methods. A focus on physical and psychological tortures does not account for the ways in which torture could harm "the detainee's selfhood or world" (409). This kind of lasting harm, demonstrated in the CIA's cultivation of "learned helplessness" through "enhanced interrogation techniques," does not readily sort into the statute's definition of pain.[20] The definition also requires that torturers torture deliberately and out of enjoyment (412). The law codifies the cultural belief that only bad people torture, as well as the belief, visible in the rhetoric of state-run execution, that "good" violence is detached from personal feeling. Along with stealth practices, this legal framework complicates many efforts to make "enhanced interrogation" publicly legible (and legally actionable) as torture.

Compared to scarring torture, which sends a message to all those who would resist government control, the messages of stealth torture are less clear. Since stealth torture is hidden, its opportunities for direct address of the general public are limited. Within its users' vernacular, however, and within a broader context when it is exposed, stealth torture makes claims about the community that authorizes it. Like lethal injection and lynching, stealth torture constructs its users as restrained. Within torture's logic, the exigence for violence always comes from the victim; if she would simply share information, then there would be no need for torture. By choosing to administer a carefully orchestrated repertoire of stealth techniques, the torturers mark themselves as "civilized," particularly when compared with the "unreasonable" victim and the affective cruelty that the torture statute requires. As my discussions in the

---

20. For more on this process, see the discussion of *Salim v. Mitchell* in chapter 3.

chapters to follow will indicate, many communities do not find it challenging to do violence while preserving a beneficent ethos. Stealth torture offers an opportunity to use violence while remaining above it.

Additionally, willingness to torture, like support for the death penalty or a counterfactual defense of lynching, establishes a persona for the torturer, supporter of torture, or torturing community. There are a few versions of this ethos. In one version, the rhetor is so angry that she will do anything, even if her actions are illegal or immoral. Support for torture becomes a statement of passion for the cause rather than a thoughtful policy decision. Another reinforces a (usually racist) division between "criminal" and "noncriminal" by assuming that torture victims deserve torture, even if they are innocent of the particular crimes of which they are accused.[21] Relativist narratives draw on a similar rhetoric of division, excusing moral concerns by asserting that "enemies" would do worse to "us" or to the victims of torture.[22] Recent history suggests that these arguments are not really about policy, since they mostly emerge after torture has already been exposed or on the campaign trail as candidates establish their personas. Arguing for torture allows speakers to establish their allegiances. Like supporting lynching or the death penalty, supporting torture also means supporting a suite of other assumptions about the world. Speakers can use support of any of these forms of violence as shorthand to show their audiences who they are.

Torture, then, illustrates the complex circulation of violence as an object of feeling and attachment. Much of this circulation occurs in the aftermath of violent spectacle or in more mundane interactions, distant from direct physical harm. Its rhetorical functions, like the audience-focused constitutive functions described in the prior section, largely erase the experience of the victim of violence. While torture in particular is framed as a message *to* a recalcitrant other, it is instead a message *about* them (that they are dangerously other) and about the community that authorizes torture (that its members are vulnerable but strong). This message circulates further when rhetors allege, in spite of evidence, that torture "works." When rhetors make these arguments, torture *is* working—just not in the way that its proponents claim.

---

21. Donald Trump provides another example. On the campaign trail, he stated that waterboarding works, and "if it doesn't work, they deserve it anyway for what they do to us" (Jacobs).

22. The post–Abu Ghraib argument that Iraqis would have experienced worse abuse under Saddam Hussein is an example of this logic. See Markman et al. for a psychological perspective on how these claims persuade.

PLAN OF THE BOOK

The chapters in *Ecologies of Harm* focus on how violent rhetorical practices constitute both proponents and victims of violence. My analysis focuses on how this constitutive force operates across modes—through direct, structural, and cultural violence—to produce a violent rhetorical ecology. Chapter 1, "Habits of Violence: Lynching as Anti-Deliberative Epideixis," uses an epideictic frame to address the cultural functions of Southern spectacle lynching and its supporting rhetoric. A growing body of scholarship has focused on lynching's spectacle, particularly as it circulated and circulates in photographs. "Habits of Violence" moves beyond a focus on spectacle to address the habits of public behavior that lynching suggested and how they manifested in public discourse. Using research from Southern newspapers and early twentieth-century debates over federal antilynching legislation, the latter of which has received little scholarly attention, I argue that Southern spectacle lynching functioned as epideictic and constitutive rhetoric, clarifying the terms of white supremacy and instructing viewers on appropriate ways of being in the community. Lynching's supporting rhetoric cited and extended lynching's values by insisting that only white Southerners could interpret lynching accurately and labeling all other interpretations presumptuous and offensive. This pervasive rhetorical refusal forced antilynching activists to either accept the premise that white Southerners were virtuous and law-abiding, thereby replicating lynching's cultural violence, or address their appeals to outside audiences.

Chapter 2, "'There Must Be a Way of Carrying It Out': Ideal and Real in Lethal Injection," examines how rhetors materialize pain in lethal injection. Compared to more controversial execution methods (for example, electrocution), lethal injection receives little scholarly attention, even within the extensive interdisciplinary conversation about the death penalty. The rhetoric around lethal injection is of interest, however, because of how lethal injection complicates abolitionist rhetorical strategies that rely on revealing hidden pain. Both sides of the death penalty debate invest in an ocular epistemology of suffering: States attempt to obscure signs of suffering, and anti–death penalty activists attempt to reveal them. Drawing evidence from two US Supreme Court cases concerned with the constitutionality of lethal injection, I argue that lethal injection's capaciousness complicates the dissociations of appearance and reality and ideal and real on which many anti–death penalty arguments rely. While petitioners in these cases attempt to reveal lethal injection as cruel rather than humane, the state's and Court's responses suggest that lethal injection can be both. This chapter's insights into lethal injection's cultural work and the limits of revealing pain as a rhetorical strategy can be helpful in addressing other ostensibly nonviolent punishments.

Chapter 3, "Spectacular Violence, Mundane Resistance," attends to underexamined archives of torture and other carceral violence in the War on Terror. Vernacular and scholarly narratives around torture in the War on Terror tend to focus on the initial impact of the torture photographs from Abu Ghraib prison and the subsequent lack of prosecution or substantive policy change.[23] This chapter examines two sets of institutional texts from the American Civil Liberties Union (ACLU) to highlight the possibilities of dwelling with violence after the shock of its initial revelation has passed. While it is necessarily limited by "what the law can name," the rhetoric of and around *Salim v. Mitchell,* a civil suit against the psychologists who developed the CIA's torture program, also highlights the limits of retributive justice (Michelle Brown 976). These limits are even clearer in *Did You Kiss the Dead Body?,* a project by the ACLU's first artist-in-residence that critiques an oppressive medical gaze by adding visuals to the autopsy reports of detainees who died in US custody. These texts, each of which attempts to build a narrative of torture from an obscured archive of carceral violence, are shaped around what cannot be said or seen within institutional frameworks. While neither is the revolutionary answer that torture merits, these texts suggest options for working within and against the grain of retribution.

Chapter 4, "Loss and Critical Memorialization," analyzes critical memorial practices as a way of addressing historical and contemporary violence. I examine how two texts addressing past violence deploy memorial's epideictic function to critique dominant narratives of violence and norms of memorialization and suggest alternative ways of being in a community. The Texas After Violence Project's interviews with people affected by the death penalty make visible an involuntary community shaped by violence and structural exclusion. Interviews with the family of Charles Brooks Jr., the first person to be executed by lethal injection, provide narratives of culpability and mourning that contradict the precise moral calculus that execution ostensibly offers. The Moore's Ford Memorial, an annual memorial and lynching reenactment in Georgia, contests both lynchers' claims about lynching and the limited lynching memorial archive. While photographs of Southern spectacle lynching have become important resources for public memory, their perspective is necessarily limited, highlighting the destruction of Black bodies and excluding the vic-

---

23. See Sontag, "Regarding the Torture," as well as Butler; Grusin; Puar, *Terrorist Assemblages.*

tim's life and the community's mourning (Mitchell 7). Repeated performance can emphasize the perpetual nature of community trauma and complicate (as lynching did) the separation of spectator and participant. The memorial reclaims lynching's spectacle to reinforce a community bound by resistance and survival. Together, these two memorial practices refuse a dominant notion of memorialization that situates violence, especially violence against marginalized communities, in the past. Instead, each memorial extends grief and mourning into the present, indicating that the violence they document is not over.

The conclusion reflects on issues raised throughout the book by asking what forms rhetorical scholarship can and should take when scholars are working within violent rhetorical ecologies. In part, this is a question specific to scholarship on rhetoric and violence, and the conclusion will return to the common claim, discussed above, that violence is a failure of rhetoric. More importantly, however, *Ecologies of Harm* as a whole operates on the assumption that all rhetors are affected by violence, albeit to different degrees and in different ways, such that violence is always relevant to rhetorical scholarship. Violence is not the other of rhetoric but rather a constant copresence that rhetoric scholars must negotiate. In addition to providing approaches for addressing multimodal constitutive violence, *Ecologies of Harm* argues for an understanding of violent rhetorical ecology as pervasive, even in ostensibly nonviolent spaces. The conclusion provides examples of how attention to pervasive violence can challenge existing rhetorical concepts and how rhetoric scholarship can adjust to reflect these challenges.

CHAPTER 1

Habits of Violence

Lynching as Anti-Deliberative Epideixis

DEFENDERS OF SOUTHERN SPECTACLE lynching typically claimed that lynching was a necessary response to Black men raping white women. This claim was false—most lynching victims were not even accused of rape, and existing accusations were highly suspect.[1] The intensity with which lynching supporters deployed this defense, however, suggests that its falsehood didn't matter. In 1892, Ida B. Wells wrote an editorial in the Memphis *Free Speech* decrying this flimsy justification. Wells's editorial responded to the People's Grocery lynching, in which a mob tortured and murdered Black business owners Thomas Moss, Calvin McDowell, and Henry Stewart (Goldsby 43). This lynching deviated from lynchers' standard crime-and-punishment narrative, as Moss had likely been targeted because his business was in competition with a white-owned grocery store. Wells famously wrote, "Nobody in the section of the country believes the old thread-bare lie that Negro men rape white women," suggesting instead that Black men were often lynched for having consensual relationships that their white lovers later denied. In *Southern*

---

1. Wells mentions the lynching of Edward Coy, a man whose white partner was likely pressured into accusing him of rape. Before she applied the match to burn him at the stake, Coy "asked her if she would burn him after they had 'been sweethearting' so long." Wells notes that the woman "was publicly reported and generally known to have been criminally intimate" with Coy.

Horrors: Lynch Law in All Its Phases, Wells documented a response published in Memphis's *Daily Commercial*:

> The fact that a black scoundrel is allowed to live and utter such loathsome and repulsive calumnies is a volume of evidence as to the wonderful patience of Southern whites. But we have had enough of it. There are some things that the Southern white man will not tolerate, and the obscene intimations of the foregoing have brought the writer to the very outermost limit of public patience. We hope that we have said enough.

This piece was not the only threat Wells received, but it is notable in that its insistence on the rape justification forces the authors to make a contradictory argument. The letter implies that Wells could be lynched for disputing the authors' narrative of lynching and, by doing so, verbally attacking white women's honor. In other words, Wells deserved lynching not because she had committed a crime, but because she had an "incorrect" and therefore offensive interpretation of lynching.

It is not surprising that lynching advocates refused to address Wells's argument, opting instead for threats that contradicted their own claims. While readers would not have initially known Wells's identity, the *Free Speech* was a paper run by African Americans, and addressing critiques levied by a Black author would be far beyond what an ecology of white supremacy and a persistent Southern honor culture would allow. Within the terms of Southern honor culture, white men were expected to defend contested claims with force, or threats of force, rather than evidence. The truth, as Kenneth S. Greenberg explains, was less important than the passion with which a man of honor would defend his claims (62). The rush to duel in response to insult was an affirmation of honor, even if the claim that the man fought to defend—for example, that lynching was a response to rape—was untrue. The need for violence would be even stronger when the accusation came from a person of color, although, as the response to Wells indicates, it would take a different form. While white men of honor would duel, the editorial team at the *Evening Scimitar*, reprinting the letter above, suggested a different sort of violence for the then-unknown author of the offending editorial. Evidently assuming that the author was male, the *Evening Scimitar* stated that "it will be the duty of those whom he [the author of the editorial] has attacked to tie the wretch who utters these calumnies to a stake at the intersection of Main and Madison Sts., brand him in the forehead with a hot iron and perform upon him a surgical operation with a pair of tailor's shears" (qtd. in Wells).

This contradictory lynching defense demonstrates lynching's multimodal constitutive work. Lynching both was embedded in and reinforced habits of public life that were connected to a narrow version of white Southern identity. This identity, characterized by an emphatic refusal to compromise or acknowledge competing interpretations of Southern life, is consistent with but not reducible to the antebellum honor culture that Greenberg describes. A furious refusal to deliberate and insistence on counterfactual interpretation of lynching's purpose allowed speakers to reconstitute the Southern white supremacist identity that lynching stages, but without immediate need for direct violence. Speakers could even perform a lynching ethos when they were not discussing lynching. In any argument about Southern autonomy or race relations, a refusal to engage constituted the speaker within an oppositional and violent regional identity.

This chapter examines how lynching and its supporting rhetoric constituted and reinforced a white, Southern, and largely masculine ethos. Lynching was a form of epideictic rhetoric that clarified white supremacist values and reinforced the rules of public life for both white and Black Southerners. While epideictic rhetoric was long dismissed as ornamental oratory detached from public life, scholarship in the late twentieth and early twenty-first centuries reevaluated the role of epideixis, repositioning it as "that which shapes and cultivates the basic codes of value and belief by which a society or culture lives" (Walker 9). Examining lynching as epideixis draws attention to how the values and beliefs it shaped manifested in other areas of public life. In its fundamental excess, lynching told white Southern men that their power over Black people was limitless; anything less than murder was restrained. Lynching advocates reinforced this identity by refusing to deliberate over lynching and insisting, as the authors above did, that any critique of lynching was a challenge to the core of Southernness. The resulting rhetorical ecology offered few options for contesting lynching, and even antilynching arguments often included problematic validation of the South as victim.

To map lynching's rhetorical ecology, I analyze defenses of lynching in relation to the rhetoric of lynching itself, as well as broader constructions of post-Reconstruction Southern identity. I focus in particular on defenses of lynching that take place after the rape defense has fallen out of favor to better illustrate how a lynching-related ethos persisted in ostensibly nonviolent rhetoric. In addition to drawing on a well-established body of interdisciplinary lynching scholarship, I use changing newspaper coverage from the *Atlanta Constitution* to demonstrate changing public discourse around lynching.[2] I will begin by discussing lynching's constitution of white supremacist identity. Scholarship on lynching describes it, contra lynching apologists, as an expres-

---

2. Access to the *Atlanta Constitution* digital archives was provided by the University of Georgia. My trip to the University of Georgia was funded by a Lightsey Fellowship from the Clemson College of Architecture, Arts, and Humanities.

sive practice.[3] Lynchers did not have to lynch in order to punish or deter crime, but the regular performance of mob murder and torture terrorized Black people and reinforced white solidarity. I will argue for reading lynching's expression as a form of epideictic rhetoric that clarified the nature of white supremacy and reinforced shared values. I will then examine the 1935 Senate filibuster of the Costigan-Wagner Bill, a proposed federal antilynching law, a moment of public controversy around lynching that shows how speakers practiced an oppositional Southern identity even when direct violence was unavailable. This filibuster was the second of three filibusters of similar legislation, and it provides the opportunity to examine a sustained and calculated public performance of pro-lynching identity. Unlike the first filibuster, that of 1922's Dyer Bill, the Costigan-Wagner filibuster contains little explicit deployment of the rape defense or open praise of lynching. Instead, the form and content of Southern Democrats' arguments reinforce white Southern values and identity in a subtler way. When lynching apologists could no longer count on widespread acceptance of openly pro-lynching tirades, their rhetorical refusal and reservation of interpretive rights extended the ethos that lynching constituted for the white Southern community.[4] Refusing to consider the legislation demonstrated a commitment to a version of Southern white supremacy that included but was not limited to the power to kill.

LYNCHING AS EPIDEIXIS

As I noted in this book's introduction, lynching was carefully crafted for communicative purposes. Its public display clarified what it meant to be white or Black in the South: the right to kill with impunity and an irresolvable vulnerability to violence, respectively. Framing lynching as epideictic emphasizes this function and situates ritual violence as a core part of dominant narratives of Southern identity. Lynching emerges from a perceived crisis of white supremacy to reinforce shared values and model appropriate behavior for community members. Those community members can then practice lynching's version of

---

3. See Garland, "Penal Excess"; Goldsby; Tolnay and Beck; Wood.

4. I use the term "interpretive rights" somewhat hesitantly, more as a description of a dominant understanding of interpretation than as a reflection of how interpretation always works. In using the term "interpretive rights," I draw on Miranda Fricker's concept of testimonial injustice, in which "prejudice on the hearer's part causes him to give the speaker less credibility than he would have otherwise given" (4). Speaking from a place of privilege, the rhetors I will discuss claim that they are the only ones who can understand a text or a community's needs. Other opinions are either invalid because of the speakers' identities or, in a slightly different structure than what Fricker describes, the speakers' opinions mark them as "other."

Southern identity in other ways, thereby reinforcing its core values. Thinking of lynching as epideictic rhetoric, then, requires attention to the role of epideixis in constructing communities and the multimodal processes of citation by which those communities can be reconstituted and associated identities performed. I will draw on both traditional and posthumanist understandings of epideixis to explain the relationship between lynching's spectacle and related practices of white supremacist Southern identity.

Lynching has a long history in the United States, but what Philip Dray calls "Southern spectacle lynching" emerged as a distinct form in the 1880s and 1890s (47). For much of early American history, lynching "was understood to exist in lieu of established systems of justice": for example, on the frontier, where settlers might choose to execute an alleged criminal themselves rather than waiting weeks for a traveling judge to arrive (18–19). Southern spectacle lynching, on the other hand, was a preferred alternative to an established criminal justice system. Lynching was not the only way to ensure that an accused criminal would be put to death. A Black person accused of a serious crime in the South was likely to be executed quickly, and the states with the highest rates of lynching also had the highest rates of execution (Wood 25–26). Lynching, however, offered expressive and constitutive possibilities that state executions did not. Lynching did not require that the victim be accused of a capital offense and was usually more public and more brutal than state-sanctioned execution. Additionally, lynching located the power to exact justice in "the people," allowing white Southern communities to "[claim] the sovereign power to manage their own affairs, defeat their own enemies, and assure their own security" (Garland, "Penal Excess" 822). These affordances made lynching an effective way to clarify and reinforce white supremacist values.

Southern spectacle lynchings had a relatively consistent order of events. A Black man or woman was accused of a crime or breach of decorum. Offenses ranged from murder and rape to "being disreputable" and "throwing stones" (Tolnay and Beck 47). The accused was then apprehended, from jail if necessary, and murdered in a public place, typically one with significance for the community (such as a town square) or in relation to the alleged crime (such as the crime scene or the victim's home). Lynch mobs sometimes tortured their victims into "confessing" their crimes or asked the alleged victim to identify her assailant.[5] Many lynchings had large audiences, and sometimes

---

5. I use "her" here because this part of the ritual was often gendered, with a woman being asked to confirm the identity of her attacker (and thus, implicitly, that she had been attacked). The alleged victim would also be given the option to participate in the lynching but was usually represented by a male relative (Dray 11).

there would be enough notice of an impending lynching to allow people from neighboring towns to attend.[6] The publicity and the crime-and-punishment narrative were important. Mob killings that did not meet these standards—that were too secretive or that failed to frame their actions as punishment of a "black brute"—were more likely to be condemned in local newspapers (Jean 355). Controlling what was labeled a "lynching" was an important way of preserving the practice's acceptability (353–54).

Like other forms of epideictic rhetoric, lynching emerged from a moment of community crisis, but its most obvious functions in this crisis were pragmatic (Condit 289). Lynching was part of a larger, evolving campaign to undo any gains that African Americans had made during Reconstruction and reestablish white supremacy in all areas of Southern life. While lynching records before 1880 are sketchy, there is evidence that mob lynching of Black people became common during Reconstruction, as the South attempted to "win the peace by thwarting in any way it could the Northern efforts to reconstruct the South" (Dray 39, 47–48). The first chapter of the Ku Klux Klan formed shortly after the end of the Civil War, and Klansmen's whipping and terrorizing of Black Southerners extended some of slavery's terror into the postbellum period (Dray 39–44). After Reconstruction, lynching played an important part in reestablishing white supremacy in government as well, with groups of white Southerners attacking and intimidating Black voters and politicians. Lynching was "a more intensified, more public, and hence more political ritual of race terror" designed to scare Black Southerners into total submission (Garland, "Penal Excess" 799). Because lynchers often killed people who had committed minor crimes or no crime at all, lynching sent the message that there was little that people of color could do to keep themselves safe.

Lynching also sent messages to whites that would have been especially compelling in light of changing economic and social conditions. As David Garland explains, the "structural transition from one mode of race control (slavery) to another (Jim Crow segregation) was at the time experienced by many white communities as a new vulnerability to crime and an intolerable threat to the status and authority of white Southerners" ("Penal Excess" 799). Urbanization added to a sense of instability. The rural economy had faltered in the postwar years, but Northern investment in Southern industries was increasing, and by the turn of the century, white and Black Southerners were moving to urban areas for work (Wood 5). This changing social world could

---

6. For example, the *Atlanta Constitution* and other papers publicized the lynching of Sam Hose (referred to as "Sam Holt" in other reports) sufficiently that the train schedule could be altered to bring spectators to Newnan, Georgia (Dray 11–12; Tolnay and Beck 23, 52).

feel threatening even to those newly urbanized middle-class whites not threatened by Black labor. For middle-class white Southerners, it was "moral propriety and self-discipline, as well as a sense of authority over their households," that separated them from poor whites and Black Americans (Wood 7). Lynching allowed whites to perform this kind of moral superiority and strength by eliminating a perceived threat to their way of life.

In this changing social context, lynching served an epideictic function. Like any structuring ideology, white supremacy was always unstable, requiring rituals to reinforce its values and interpellate whites into a group that defined their shared interests, but a combination of actual changes and perceived threats from "masterless" Black men would have made the late nineteenth and early twentieth centuries seem especially treacherous. As Wood explains, "white supremacy and white solidarity were . . . ideologies that needed to be constructed and established and that required constant replenishing and constant reenvisioning" (8). Lynching could replenish and reenvision white supremacy by staging it as the public destruction of a Black body by whites. By bringing people together as part of a mob, it constituted a white supremacist community. Even if some white audience members were disgusted, their presence in the group contributed to the white supremacist spectacle.

Lynching's white supremacist spectacle necessarily made claims about the nature of white supremacy and the appropriate behavior of its adherents. This kind of clarification is an important feature of epideictic rhetoric. In a reading of Aristotle, Gerard Hauser suggests that epideixis could equip audience members to make better decisions through a modeling of practical wisdom or prudence (*phronêsis*) (12). He explains that "epideictic occupies a unique place [in public discourse] in celebrating the deeds of exemplars who set the tone for civic community" (14). Epideictic rhetoric could help people make better decisions by highlighting model citizens' good choices. Because epideictic speeches did "not seek to *tell* what a person did, but to *display* nobility at the level of praxis," they helped audiences understand how ideals like prudence or bravery could manifest in their day-to-day behaviors (15). It is in this didactic function that many scholars have located epideictic rhetoric's previously overlooked importance. Jeffrey Walker writes that epideictic rhetoric "shapes the fundamental grounds, the 'deep' commitments and presuppositions, that will underlie and ultimately determine decision and debate in particular pragmatic forms" (9). Epideictic rhetoric, these arguments suggest, is an important part of who people are.

Lynching's clarification of white supremacist values can be read as similarly didactic and constitutive. In the years following Reconstruction, many whites adopted white supremacist practices that masked economic divisions to unite under the banner of race. Uncertainty around post-Reconstruction white supremacy posed a particular problem for whites in power. The Populist Party had drawn attention to economic inequality among whites, and economic insecurity combined with circulating populist ideas could lead poor whites to think that they deserved more from their wealthy white employers (Garland, "Penal Excess" 800). Lynching erased economic inequality among whites, creating a unified mass all purportedly linked by their physical and moral strength. Lynching illustrated that white supremacy meant killing in public, in a group, with impunity. This version of white supremacy did not, however, require sacrifice from other whites. Wealthy whites, for example, were not required to take action to reduce income inequality. Instead, shared violence and a narrative of strength and victimhood formed the core of white Southern identity, concealing other possible understandings of what being a white Southerner could mean.

The sort of decision-making that lynching suggested, then, was distinct from the prudent and considered process that classical epideictic was supposed to model. While lynching had an epideictic structure, the ways of being in a community that it modeled were essentially the opposite of what Aristotle describes. Lynching was an anti-deliberative epideictic, one that reinforced "'deep' commitments" that are antithetical to what many classical and contemporary audiences would think of as healthy democracy (Walker 9). Of course, in a traditional understanding of violence as the other of rhetoric, all violence is anti-deliberative because it substitutes force for discussion. Lynching's rhetorical force complicates this division. Embedded in a history of white Southern resistance and performed in spite of a functioning legal system, lynching's anti-deliberative performance is itself constitutive; its anti-deliberative form is part of its argument. Lynchers chose to band together and murder their victims, even in cases when the state would have done it for them, and this choice suggests a community bound only by its shared values and responsible only to its members. Lynching was a choice that communicated to and about white Southerners that they need not accept any version of reality that did not support this version of white supremacy. Lynching was, in part, communication about how and why white Southerners shouldn't communicate.

This version of white supremacy, and thus the white supremacist community it constituted, was reinforced through citation, with performances accumulating meaning through the repetition and reinvigoration of similar messages. E. Johanna Hartelius and Jennifer Asenas suggest the concept of citational epideixis as a way of thinking through epideixis (and the concept of "the rhetor") in a posthumanist mold. Combining work on posthumanism and citationality, the authors argue for thinking of epideictic rhetoric as a rein-vigoration of circulating tropes rather than the work of a single author (365–67). They note, importantly, that this concept does not eliminate the speaker's accountability for her words. Quoting Judith Butler's work on citationality, they explain that "removing authorship does not entail relief of accountability; there is no reason why one who 'renews the linguistic tokens of a community' should not be held responsible for doing so" (375). They also note that cita-tional epideixis allows for a broader sense of accountability. If the rhetor origi-nates her claims, then she is solely responsible, but in Hartelius and Asenas's posthumanist approach, "responsibility is instantly dispersed into a collective of language users" (375). This dispersed responsibility connects to the ways in which language accrues meanings through circulation. One person cannot control which meanings precede her or which meanings spread and "stick," to use Sara Ahmed's term, though she is in control of which of the avail-able meanings she re-presents (Ahmed, *Cultural Politics* 11–12). Hartelius and Asenas suggest that all community members are responsible for considering which claims proliferate and why.

Like the other forms of violence discussed in this book, lynching cites existing forms of structural and cultural violence. As I described in the intro-duction, lynching's ritual drew heavily on the procedures of state-run execu-tion while relocating the power to punish in the local community rather than in state officials (Wood 24). Periodic inclusion of witnesses and "confessions," often obtained through torture, linked lynching to the more familiar spec-tacle of public execution. Lynching's version of white masculinity was also anchored in existing practice. As Gail Bederman explains, Victorian culture positioned manliness, whiteness, and civilization as articulated categories. Being a "civilized" man required restraint of the passions, and white men were assumed to have superior self-control; to lose control would be to become "as savage as the negro" (qtd. in Bederman 52). Manly men were supposed to have exceptionally strong passions, so restraining them showed particular strength. Particularly when paired with the claim that lynchers were civilized, lynch-ing's performance of brutal violence constituted lynchers as both manly and appropriately moved by a violation of the racial order. Lynching performed the idea that "there are some things that the Southern white man will not tol-erate" (qtd. in Wells). By positioning violations of the racial order as the limit of white men's patience, lynching brought an already racist understanding of masculinity into a new white supremacist context.

Community members could practice this version of white supremacy and cite its structuring values without participating in a lynching. Like ancient audiences who incorporated the virtues of heroes into their everyday lives, white Southerners could practice a white supremacist and anti-deliberative ethos in habitual and quotidian ways. It was by adapting these virtues that citizens could practice lynching's lessons on "how to *be* in a community" (Hartelius and Asenas 369). Lynching's construction of white supremacy meant that direct violence was always an option but only sometimes a requirement. Instead of inflicting direct physical harm, white Southerners might simply refuse to acknowledge or support any version of the world that contradicted their preferred white supremacist version. Because lynching suggested (as the *Daily Commercial* editorial indicates) that anything less than murder was tolerant, white Southerners could cite lynching's values by both demanding total submission and performing anger and offense when that submission was not forthcoming or did not meet their standards. Being in this Southern white supremacist community meant always behaving as if murder were a valid option.

In addition to sustaining existing structures of power, the repeated citation of white supremacist identity likely offered affective benefits. The prevalence of lynching and parallel rhetorical habits (discussed below) suggests that lynching's version of white supremacy appealed to audiences. While I have described historical and cultural reasons for this appeal above, it is also likely that lynching, like other forms of epideictic rhetoric, was fun. Discussions of epideictic rhetoric often mention the pleasure rhetors and audiences experience through the virtuosic performance of an epideictic speech as key to its persuasive force. Hartelius and Asenas note that "the pleasure experienced by audiences as a result of epideixis is powerfully instructive. It is conducive to absorbing substantive lessons of vice and virtue" (371). For both classical audiences and lynching attendees, some of this pleasure may come from feeling a connection to a larger community forged through shared values. Lynchers did not kill in isolation. Instead, they could see their actions situated in relation to a larger practice and concept of white supremacy, getting the enjoyment that comes from "stretch[ing] their daily experiences into meanings more grand, sweet, noble, or delightful" (Condit 290). When individual white Southerners attended a lynching, looked at a lynching photograph, or refused to engage with an antilynching argument, they put white supremacist ideals into practice and connected with a shared identity. These circulating texts and repeated practices reinforced a positive experience of whiteness. The more pro-lynching rhetoric circulated, through speech, images, or direct violence, the more familiar—and thus stronger and more pleasant—this constitutive force became.

Scholars commonly discuss lynching as a constitutive force for white supremacy, but thinking of it as an epideictic display clarifies the connections between everyday practice and lynching's spectacle. Lynching constituted a

Southern white supremacist identity that extended beyond the site of direct violence and was practicable in a variety of circumstances. Adapting the posthumanist connection of epideixis and citation highlights how lynching's violence and related discursive practices transformed and reinvigorated existing understandings of white supremacy. It was through this repeated multimodal citation that lynching created an atmosphere of terror that persisted even when lynching ceased to be a preferred tool of racial oppression.

CHANGING RHETORICAL PATTERNS

As I noted above, lynching's supporting rhetoric was an essential part of its cultural and constitutive work. The rape justification constructed lynchers as threatened men of honor who were driven to kill by an unbearable crime, and defending that interpretation was a way of performing an oppositional Southern white supremacist identity. During lynching's peak, Southern newspapers also highlighted this narrative, often describing the alleged crime and subsequent lynching in detail in order to thrill readers. As antilynching activists gradually persuaded white Americans to see lynching as a shameful threat to civilization, public discourse shifted, but the oppositional Southern white supremacist identity did not disappear from public life. Instead, as open defenses of lynching and the rape justification in particular fell out of favor, lynching supporters performed Southern white supremacist identity in subtler ways.

This change in the public rhetoric around lynching is apparent in the *Atlanta Constitution*'s lynching coverage. According to the Tuskegee Institute's records, Georgia had the second most lynchings of any state, 531—of which 492 were of Black victims—between 1882 and 1968 ("Lynching, Whites and Negroes"). The *Constitution* was for years an enthusiastic supporter of these lynchings, particularly during their national peak in the 1890s. The paper even offered a $500 award for the capture of alleged murderer and rapist Sam Hose, then paid it after he had been captured, tortured, killed, and dismembered in front of a large crowd in 1899. The paper commented, "The *Constitution* never issued a check with greater pleasure" (Dray 8). It was not until after Leo Frank, a Jewish factory superintendent accused of raping and murdering a thirteen-year-old employee, was lynched in Atlanta that the paper began to tone down its enthusiasm (Wood 182–83). Frank's murder drew attention from a national community increasingly cognizant of lynching as a serious social problem, and the *Constitution,* like other Southern papers and communities around this time, began to treat lynching differently.

Even lynching reportage from a more enthusiastic era, however, showed an awareness of audience and the importance of reinforcing an understanding of lynching as honorable, civilized, and uniformly supported. Some articles contain a combination of lurid detail and assurances that the mob was orderly and dignified; others treat lynching only briefly, as a routine occurrence about which no one should be overly concerned. An article entitled "Another Lynching" (1893) noted that in the course of the lynching, "not a loud noise was heard, and not a shot was fired." "A Double Lynching" (1895) made the similar claim that "not a shot was fired and few loud words were spoken." This pairing—no shots fired, no loud noises—paints a picture of strength and control. The mob is allegedly overcome by emotion in response to a horrific crime, but not to the degree that it would disturb nearby community members.

This combination of strong feeling and restraint was a feature of Victorian masculinity, which was itself an important site for policing racial boundaries and reinforcing the meaning of whiteness. According to Victorian understandings of gender, all men were beset by powerful sexual urges, but white men's ability to control those urges made them "manlier" than men of other races (Bederman 48–49). As Gail Bederman notes, these norms were an essential part of lynching's narrative: The "black beast rapist" was a monster, while white men were beacons of restraint and civilization (49–50). News coverage that describes the lynch mob as calm in the face of horrifying crime reinforced this narrative and preserved the men of the lynch mob as civilized, manly, and white.

Part of the newspaper's emphasis on civilization was the frequent claim that participants and audience members were highly regarded within the community. An account of "A Kentucky Lynching" states, "The lynching was conducted with as much order as was possible considering the business in hand. Those who took part were evidently reputable people, and so sure were they that they were doing it for the good of the county that they only [t]ook partial precautions to conceal [t]heir identity." "Another Lynching," cited above, is more specific in identifying reputable attendees:

> The crowd was thoroughly representative and included many of the best citizens of Laurens [South Carolina]. The scene of the lynching is less than a mile from the home of Senator Irby, who is said to have been a spectator, and to have addressed some remarks to the crowd, urging them to be temperate and orderly and not to fire into the body. He said that the country was opposed to lynch law and deplored the circumstances that sometimes made it necessary for the protection of the virtue of women and children.

This image—men opposed to vigilante justice but driven to it by horrifying crime—was common in defenses of lynching. It also suggests, importantly, a separation of action and essence and a reservation of interpretive rights that corresponds to Southern honor culture. This newspaper coverage claims that while lynching may look barbaric to outsiders, the people involved were civilized, and thus the proceedings were as well. The privileging of a community's judgment of itself, led by "elite" community members, appears frequently in the filibusters discussed below, but with a focus that elides rather than openly justifies lynching's violence.

Lynching was so acceptable, according to this news coverage, that even Black Southerners approved. It was relatively common for lynching reportage to include an assessment of the Black community's opinion of the murder. A piece entitled "A Sunday Lynching" states, "A large crowd of people, both white and black, are going out to see the body. The blacks seem to think that Lewis [the victim] met his just dues. Lewis confessed that he had been in almost every jail in the state." Claims like this contribute to a monolithic image of a South that supports lynching, one that subsumes Black communities' opinions within a larger narrative that justifies violence against its members. In an extension of the paternalistic racism so common in defenses of slavery, white speakers are assumed to know what members of the Black community think and feel. Lynching, this coverage suggests, is good for everyone.

The emphasis on decorum and calm community acceptance contrasts the sensational tone of much of the coverage, which also often includes a great deal of detail about the crimes of which victims were accused. In his recounting of Sam Hose's lynching, Philip Dray cites congressman James M. Griggs's "much-reprinted account of the Cranford murder," the crime of which Hose was accused. Griggs's account puts particular emphasis on the alleged assault of Mattie Cranford. Griggs describes how the perpetrator "carried [Mattie Cranford's] helpless body to another room, and there stripped her person of every thread and vestige of clothing, there keeping her till time enough had elapsed to permit him to accomplish his fiendish offense twice more and again!" (4). An example from "A Sunday Lynching" is similar, dramatizing a woman's fight with her alleged assailant, the eventual lynching victim. The author writes that the lynching victim "rushed in and grabbed the lady by the throat" and "threatened to shoot her if she resisted," but was so frightened by his victim's screams that "he only succeeded in scratching up her throat and made quite a bruise on her face with the end of the pistol" (2). The attention to these women's alleged plights both contributed to lynchers' justification for violence and provided entertainment for readers in the form of "folk pornography" (Hall xx).

Even when the coverage did not provide detailed narration of the attack, the narration of the mob's movements and actions could give the coverage a breathless tone. For example, May 1892's "A Triple Lynching" begins with a large headline, then has several subheadings that describe the scene before the main text. Together, the headline and subheadings read: "A TRIPLE LYNCH- ING / Takes Place Up in the Hills of Habersham, / AND THREE NEGROES DANGLE / [At] The End of Long Heavy Trace Chains, / LOCKED TIGHTLY ABOUT THEIR NECKS. / The Sheriff Overpowered, the Jail Broken Open and Three Negroes Journey Toward 'The Beautiful Shore'" (1). Having several sub- headings is not uncommon for front-page news. The content and formatting of these, however, suggest that audiences should be titillated by this news and specifically the description of the lynching. The portions printed in all capital letters highlight the image of the victims' corpses, with details about the mur- ders positioned as second-tier information. The article goes on to provide a detailed description of how the lynch mob kidnapped and murdered the three victims. It also recounts the victims' last words and their respective modes of death (one of a broken neck, two of strangulation).

This detailed and sensational reportage highlights the mob's impunity and provides an opportunity for vicarious enjoyment. The level of detail raises questions about the article's final statement that the coroner has labeled these murders "death from unknown hands" (1). While the article describes the mob's leader as "heavily masked," the amount of information provided sug- gests that the reporter was either present for all portions of the lynching or heard a detailed account from someone who was (1). The fact that the *Consti- tution* could print so detailed a story and end it with an indication that no one will be prosecuted is not surprising, given that prosecution for mob members was extremely uncommon. A reminder of the mob's impunity, illustrative of its power, could also give an additional thrill to the readers who did not attend the lynching or who wanted to relive the events through reading the newspa- per. The article's breathless tone constructs these events as exciting and fun, and the ending of the article makes it clear that there will be no consequences.

Coverage of this kind had dissipated significantly by the mid-1930s. Decades of antilynching activism had contributed to the shift away from thrilled narratives of grotesque crime and righteous punishment. Beginning in the mid-1910s, the NAACP circulated lynching photographs to a national audience to expose lynching's horrors on a broad scale (Wood 183). These pamphlets helped to shift public discourse around lynching by presenting it as shameful rather than triumphant. Images of mutilated Black bodies contested lynchers' claims of civilized restraint. Increasingly, many white Southerners began to treat lynching as a "regional embarrassment" to be hidden or even stopped (Wood 185). A decrease in lynchings may have also affected newspaper coverage. Whereas 230 people were lynched in 1892 and 64 in 1922, 1932 was the first year that lynching fell into the single digits since before the Tuskegee Institute began keeping records ("Lynching, Whites and Negroes"). Lynching had become less routine, and while they were still unlikely to be prosecuted, lynchers could no longer be certain that their actions would be met with uniform praise.

The *Atlanta Constitution*'s coverage of lynching in the years surrounding the Costigan-Wagner Bill is sparse, with a significant number of articles focusing on the conversation around antilynching legislation and relatively few documenting recent lynchings. The changing coverage reflects changes in public discourse and circumstances more broadly: fewer lynchings and increased public opposition to them, within and outside of the South. An article from 1933 reports on the Georgia Council of Southern Women for the Prevention of Lynching's discussion of federal antilynching legislation, and another from 1934 reports on a meeting of the Federal Council of Churches in which members spoke about the need for federal antilynching legislation (W. F. Caldwell; "Anti-Lynching Laws Urged"). There are articles about the filibuster of the Costigan-Wagner Bill, including some that reproduce portions of filibuster arguments. These articles, unlike earlier pieces on lynching, suggest minimal investment in the outcome of the debate. Coverage of actual lynching focuses on a few well-publicized incidents in Kentucky, Maryland, Florida, and California and typically lacks the thrilled tone of earlier coverage. In at least one case, the paper even refers to a lynching victim as having been "accused" of a crime, rather than presenting him as presumptively guilty ("Reward Offered"). These pieces suggest a different sort of public relationship with lynching: careful, less emotional, more detached. While ongoing use of public torture lynching indicates that individuals and communities were still invested in lynching, the degree to which that enthusiasm could manifest in public had changed.[7]

This is not to say that the *Constitution* and other Southern newspapers had completely transformed. An article in the *Constitution* claims that "everything was calm in Marianna" after the lynching of Claude Neal, thereby reinforc-

---

7. Community behavior after public torture lynchings also showed awareness of the changing public perception of lynching. Citizens of Waco, Texas, who had gathered by the thousands to mutilate, burn, and photograph the corpse of lynching victim Jesse Washington were also eager to "undo the damage to their national reputation" once those photographs began to circulate beyond the town's borders (Wood 181). An NAACP investigator dispatched to the city shortly after the lynching had an unusual degree of trouble getting information about and acquiring photos of the murder and aftermath, with her interview subjects indicating that they were concerned about bad publicity (Wood 181–82).

ing an image of the civilized lynch mob that contrasts sharply with the widely circulated details of Neal's murder and dismemberment ("Two States"). Similarly, an editorial from early 1934 insists that a too-slow justice system and the possibility of criminals being pardoned are the true causes of lynching, so a law allowing for emergency trials would do more to stop lynching than antilynching legislation. The author speculates that "when our courts awake to the fact that they are in part responsible for many lynchings surely some kind of emergency trial law would be welcome" (Woodall 5C). While this editorial does not explicitly deploy the rape defense of lynching, the suggestion that some crimes will "dethrone reason" and thus require rapid punishment would have been legible as a reference to rape. The tone, however, is still notably less sensational, and the author positions himself as antilynching even as he supports some of its underlying claims about crime in the South.

This gradual shift away from open deployment of the rape justification and enthusiasm for lynching is important context for the arguments within the filibuster of the Costigan-Wagner Bill. Defenses of lynching and white supremacy were often obvious: for example, Rebecca Latimer Felton's famous assertion that "if it needs lynching to protect woman's dearest possession . . . I say 'lynch' a thousand times a week if necessary" (qtd. in Whites 369). Less obvious iterations of white supremacist identity are still damaging, however, and perhaps more so because of their subtlety. Looking to the filibuster speeches in the context of this broader shift shows how speakers could perform a Southern white supremacist identity that is intimately tied to lynching, even without explicit narratives of crime and punishment.

PRACTICING RHETORICAL REFUSAL

Discussion of Senators Edward P. Costigan (R-Colorado) and Robert F. Wagner's (R-New York) "bill to assure to persons within the jurisdiction of every state the equal protection of the laws by discouraging, preventing, and punishing the crime of lynching" occurred in this changed and changing public atmosphere around lynching ("Punishment for the Crime"). Introduced in Congress in January 1934, the Costigan-Wagner Bill proposed federal penalties for state officials who failed to protect victims from lynching or apply due diligence to prosecuting the offenders (Dray 341). The bill describes the violence with which it is concerned:

> The phrase "mob or riotous assemblage," when used in this Act, shall mean an assemblage composed of three or more persons acting in concert, without authority of law, for the purpose of killing or injuring any person in the

custody of any peace officer or suspected of, charged with or convicted of the commission of any crime, with the purpose or consequence of preventing the apprehension and/or trial and/or punishment by law of such person or otherwise of depriving such person of due process of law or the equal protection of the laws. ("Punishment for the Crime")

The bill justified its proposed federal intervention through the Fourteenth Amendment guarantee of equal protection under the law. It was a slight revision of 1922's Dyer Bill, which passed the House of Representatives but was removed from the Senate agenda after a filibuster. Twelve years later, the Costigan-Wagner Bill's chances seemed better, in part because the Southern press was more "sympathetic to the idea of some kind of federal antilynching penalty" (Dray 343). Its eventual failure was due in part to President Roosevelt's reluctance to either support the bill at its inception or intervene in the filibuster and risk angering the Southern Democrats whose votes he needed to pass New Deal legislation (Dray 356–57). Like the Dyer Bill, the Costigan-Wagner Bill passed in the House of Representatives but never came to a vote in the Senate.

The form and content of these filibusters reproduce the white supremacist Southern identity that lynching suggests. Like lynching, the filibusters were instrumentally unnecessary. The legislation almost certainly would not have passed if it came to a vote, so the commitment to preventing formal discussion of the bill makes a statement about the Southern Democrats' values. The choice to filibuster antilynching legislation suggests an identity consistent with lynching's anti-deliberative values. Like lynching itself, the filibuster speeches are epideictic, and their identity performances reinforce lynching's values in both dramatic and subtle ways. Both the Dyer Bill and Costigan-Wagner Bill filibusters insist on sole interpretive rights, building a narrative of "the South" as simultaneously fragile and all-powerful. The filibuster of the Dyer Bill does this in large part through reiteration of the rape justification. With open use of the rape justification less available, the filibuster of the Costigan-Wagner Bill relies on subtler manifestations of Southern white supremacist ethos.

Speakers in the filibuster of the Dyer Bill insist on the rape justification for lynching implicitly and explicitly. For example, when Senator James Watson (R-Indiana) contests Senator Kenneth McKellar's (D-Tennessee) claim that lynchings "are getting to be more prevalent in the North, in comparison to total population, than in the South," McKellar clarifies that he meant not overall population, but "colored population" (Congressional Record, 29 Nov. 1922, 398). The assumption, of course, is that states only lynch in response to crimes committed by Black people, so a state with a larger Black population would naturally have more lynchings. McKellar goes on to insist that this understanding is the only reasonable one. When Senator Frank Willis (R-Ohio) pushes McKellar to admit a deliberate misrepresentation of facts, reading his original statement back to him from the prior page of the Congressional Record, McKellar responds, "I was talking about the colored population and everybody understood it that way. Nobody took exception to it, and nobody takes exception to it now, I am sure, except the Senator from Ohio [Willis]" (398). McKellar not only refuses to admit that his claim was misleading but insists that Willis is the only person who would misunderstand it. The "true" nature of lynching, he implies, is clear to everyone, except for the occasional troublemaker.

Senator Thaddeus Caraway (D-Arkansas) is more explicit in his deployment of the rape justification for lynching, but his argument echoes McKellar's in his refusal to consider interpretations or opinions other than his own. Referencing the bill's provision that the mob must capture an individual "as a punishment for or to prevent the commission of some actual or supposed public offense," Caraway states, "Here is a bill which undertakes to punish a mob if they lynch a man guilty of an offense, however heinous it may be" (NAACP; Congressional Record, 29 Nov. 1922, 400). He goes on:

> I am sure, although I have no way to substantiate it, that a society known as the society for the protection of the rights of colored people wrote this bill and handed it to the proponents of it. These people had but one idea in view, and that was to make rape permissible, and to allow the guilty to go unpunished if that rape should be committed by a negro on a white woman in the South. (Congressional Record, 29 Nov. 1922, 400)

Caraway, presumably misnaming the NAACP, constructs the Black community as both sophisticated enough to write a credible bill and animalistic enough to want nothing but rape. Many audience members within and outside the Senate would have recognized this accusation as ludicrous, since antilynching activists had been publicly debunking the rape justification for decades. Caraway's acknowledgment that he has no evidence, however, suggests that the truth is not important. His certainty needs no substantiation, because his claim illustrates a commitment to a shared white supremacist world view. In this context, Caraway's claim becomes challenging to refute. Once Caraway has declared the bill a conspiracy, he and others who share his world view can reject any claims to the contrary as attempted cover-ups.[8]

---

8. Patricia Roberts-Miller identifies this impossibility of invalidating evidence as a key part of conspiracy rhetoric. She notes that when evidence in support of a conspiracy or fringe political or social position disappears, its adherents "simply find new support" ("Conspiracy Bullshit" 466).

McKellar's and Caraway's insistence on their perspectives, even in the face of contradictory evidence, has several rhetorical functions. One is the affective display of party loyalty, something that Southern rhetors had long performed through absurd counterfactual statements. As Patricia Roberts-Miller explains, proslavery rhetors often performed party loyalty through blatantly false claims (*Fanatical Schemes* 40). These statements demonstrated an intense emotional attachment to the cause. Speakers said these absurd things—for example, that the antebellum State Rights party was "actuated by as much purity of purpose, and true love of country, as ever inspired the bosoms, or directed the movements, of any men on earth"—not because they were true, but because the speakers were so devoted to the cause that truth did not matter (qtd. in Roberts-Miller, *Fanatical Schemes* 40). Caraway's conspiracy theory can function in this way. The conspiracy that Caraway describes is unlikely, but that unlikelihood may only amplify his performed devotion to white supremacist ideals. Caraway's readiness to see a racial threat anywhere suggests a strong adherence to a white supremacist world view.

These rhetorical tactics also reflect a way of being in the community, a fundamentally anti-deliberative stance that the speakers perform as a part of white Southern identity. This performance involves a constitutive rhetorical refusal. It is a "rhetorical refusal" both in that it is a refusal of deliberation, a foundation of classical understandings of rhetoric as a civic art, and in that the refusal has its own rhetorical and constitutive force. John Schilb uses the term "rhetorical refusal" "to denote an act of writing or speech in which the rhetor pointedly refuses to do what the audience considers rhetorically normal. By rejecting a procedure that the audience expects, the rhetor seeks the audience's assent to another principle, cast as a higher priority" (3). The "higher priority" here is the maintenance of Southern white supremacist identity and the opposition of all federal actions positioned as threats to the Southern states. In refusing to deliberate with "outsiders," the senators may persuade each other and anyone reading the newspaper coverage of the filibuster that the senators are a part of this Southern white supremacist group.

In the Costigan-Wagner filibuster, the deliberate misreadings through which rhetors perform an oppositional identity do not usually include references to rape, but they serve a similar provocative purpose as earlier deployments of the rape justification. There are a few consistent tropes that suggest this powerful victim identity, in which the South's constant victimization requires Southern speakers to exert as much control as possible over the conversation. The Costigan-Wagner filibuster contains several incidents of what seems to be willful misreading and misinterpretation, both of the bill itself and of what its framers have said about it. Speakers also make blatantly false and highly suspect statements about the South, insisting that it has long been free of racial discrimination and that legislation will only cause problems. Additionally, these speakers' performances reinforce self-serving standards of decorum, often taking offense at the very suggestion that the South is not a racial utopia.

A common mischaracterization frames the bill as a federal penalty for murder that senselessly separates murder by three or more people from murder by one or two. These arguments ignore that the bill requires demonstrable negligence at the state level before the federal government will intervene. Senator Hugo Black's (D-Alabama) speech is one of several that include this element. Black states that "every time a prisoner escapes, somebody may have the Governor tried; it means that if the prosecuting attorney fails to prosecute he may go to the penitentiary; and the trial is taken away from the State where the crime was committed and is conducted by the Federal court" (Congressional Record, 29 Apr. 1935, 6528). Black's speech repurposes Reconstruction-era anxieties about federal intervention. The hypothetical interventions Black describes—for example, trying the governor after a prisoner escapes—omit the state complicity that the bill requires, as well as the mob violence that the bill is designed to address. While Black states that "every time a prisoner escapes," the federal government may step in, the bill itself has a much narrower scope. Only if there was evidence that the governor was complicit in the prisoner's escape, and the prisoner was imprisoned for a lynching, would the Costigan-Wagner Bill apply. Black's more radical interpretation of the bill highlights his refusal to understand the text or concede the sponsors' intentions.

Other speakers focus on the definition of lynching, refusing to acknowledge it as a distinct form of violence that may require targeted intervention. Senator Tom Connally (D-Texas), for example, asks, "Mr. President, is it not just as great a violation of the rights of the person involved whether he be murdered by three men or one man?" Senator James Byrnes (D-South Carolina) has a similar claim: "I believe that lynching is murder whenever the victim of the mob dies at their hands. It is impossible for me to understand how men, and particularly lawyers, can make a distinction between lynching a human being when that crime is participated in by three persons, and the murder of a human being by an individual." These claims elide the particularities of both lynching and the bill. The bill provides penalties for state actors' criminal negligence, thus distinguishing between a murder in which no state officials were involved and one in the sheriff delivers the victim to the mob. The failure to acknowledge this difference allows speakers to hide the official complicity and widespread involvement that distinguishes lynching from other forms of murder. In their repeated condemnation of murder and purported concern about what is fair to murder victims, the speakers also perform a moral clarity consistent with lynching's ethos. Within this narrative, the difference between right and wrong action is clear to members of the Southern in-group, but outsiders are attempting to cloud that distinction.

An exchange between Wagner and Byrnes highlights the anti-deliberative nature of this rhetorical pattern. Byrnes has been discussing the circumstances under which the bill would apply, arguing that the "person" within the bill could also be a corporation, and thus the bill could be used for anti-union purposes (Congressional Record, 29 Apr. 1935, 6541). Wagner, one of the bill's sponsors, objects to this line of argument, saying, "Instead of dealing in technicalities, as it is so easy to do if one seeks reasons for opposition, why not face the facts? Is it not generally known what lynching is and how it takes place, so that when we talk about it we confront not some imaginary situation but something which everybody knows and recognizes? We know how lynchings occur and what they are" (6541). Byrnes, however, does not admit to understanding lynching, even when Wagner notes that Byrnes has been discussing lynching. When Byrnes asks Wagner to define lynching, he gives the following definition:

> One is charged with a crime—and by the way, it is not always rape. As a matter of fact, the records show that offenses other than rape are charged most generally. Some very trivial offenses have been charged, usually against persons of a certain race. When a suspect is apprehended, and the community is aroused, and three or more persons go into the jail and take the victim from the custody of a sheriff and string him up to a pole, or do something like that, that is called a lynching. When that occurs, either with the connivance of the sheriff or other official or through his neglect—and we know exactly what that means—then not only is the officer in such a case guilty of a crime but the county should pay by way of liquidated damages for his offense. (6541)

Wagner is looking for stasis, suggesting that regardless of disagreements about specific policy, senators can agree that they know what a lynching is and what it means to be complicit with one. But neither Byrnes nor anyone adhering to lynching's version of Southern white supremacy could grant that point, as it would indicate deliberation with someone who has been constructed as a hostile outsider. Byrnes laments that the definition Wagner gives is not in the bill, stating that Wagner "now says that his definition of 'lynching' is that two men must go into a jail, pull a man out, and hang him to a telegraph pole" (6543). Wagner protests the problematic interpretation, stating, "Mr. President, the

Senator asked me what the ordinary case of lynching was. The Senator must not make misstatements of fact" (6543).

Heated exchanges and bad faith arguments are not uncommon in the US Senate, particularly during a filibuster. As a part of lynching's rhetorical ecology, however, these misreadings of both the bill itself and lynching as a cultural practice have a particular resonance. Lynching forged a community identity based on violent control; rather than modeling prudence, it advised the opposite, a mode of community participation focused on bending reality to the will of in-group members. Repeated insistence on counterfactual inter-pretations of lynching and antilynching legislation thus reinforces lynching's work and suggests allegiance to the community that lynching creates.

Consistent with antebellum and Reconstruction rhetorics, these rhetors also posit the South as a constant victim of unnecessary Northern and fed-eral intervention. Senators repeatedly claim that the bill unfairly targets the South. As Senator Ellison Smith (D-South Carolina) argues, "There is no use for us to try to disguise anything. This bill is aimed at the Southern States. Read the letters in the newspapers about our barbarity and our lack of civili-zation" (Congressional Record, 25 Apr. 1935, 6371). Smith, who later refers to the antebellum South as "the finest civilization America ever saw," suggests that malicious misrepresentation gives many Americans the wrong impres-sion of the South (6616). Senator Josiah Bailey (D-North Carolina) makes a similar claim in his extended defense of the South, stating, "All of this suspi-cion is not founded, I think, on prejudice, but founded upon an ignorance for which I blame no man, upon an ignorant belief that the Southern States and the southern counties and the southern courts are not quick to execute the law" (6371). Bailey's argument suggests that the South has an undeserved bad reputation on which this legislation draws and to which it contributes. In this frame, the proposed legislation continues a legacy of malice toward and ignorance of the South that only Southerners are well equipped to recognize.

Along similar lines is the *tu quoque* argument related to crime and anti-lynching laws in other states. Senators critique the bill's sponsors for not implementing similar laws in their respective states, as well as for allegedly ignoring urban crime that occurs outside the South.[9] Wagner points out that the law would apply to all states, but to no discernible effect (Congressio-nal Record, 29 Apr. 1935, 6544). Connally asks, "Why has the great sovereign State of New York, standing with its shoulders high above the other States in wealth and population, under its acknowledged powers at the present time

---

9. For example, from Senator Connally: "Mr. President, why should the criminals in Chi-cago, who lined up some seven or eight other gangsters against a brick wall and shot out their lives, go free of this measure?" (Congressional Record, 25 Apr. 1935, 6366).

enacted no antilynching law? Is it any less a crime if the act should be committed in New York than if it should be committed in the State which I, in part, represent?" (Congressional Record, 25 Apr. 1935, 6365). Senator Bailey also takes exception: "I resent the imputation on the face of this bill that my State is not capable of executing judgment in righteousness with respect to the humblest, the most miserable representative of either the white or the colored race" (6369). Bailey notes that South Carolina has a law similar to that proposed in the Costigan-Wagner Bill, but "the State of New York and the State of Colorado do not have such laws" (6369). The implication is clear: People from other regions are content to ignore their own problems, but want to meddle in Southern affairs.

A key part of this victim construction is the claim that the South is free of racial animosity and any effort to curb lynching is likely to reawaken bad feeling and cause racial violence. Black's argument is representative:

> Is it right, is it fair, is it just to the thousands of Negroes who do not feel disgraced when we mention the name of their race, but who, instead, have a feeling of pride that it is their race, is it right to them or is it right to us, who live there side by side, whose destiny must be inseparably linked the one with the other, for political advantage or any other motive, to enact legislation which drives a wedge between the races . . . ? Is it fair to us at this time, when we are working in peace and harmony the one with the other, to do something which will bring about again the spread of the flame of race antagonism, and instill prejudices which, thank God! have been stifled in the hearts of most of the people of Alabama and of the other States of the South? (6533)

Black's argument is familiar in many ways, reinvigorating both a long tradition of paternalistic racism and a Reconstruction-era disdain for "outsiders." Both are common in the filibuster, with speakers repeatedly insisting that they "have nothing but good will for the colored people" and that Southerners will resolve any lingering racial problems "if [they] may be let alone" (respectively, Bailey, Congressional Record, 25 Apr. 1935, 6369; Byrnes, Congressional Record, 29 Apr. 1935, 6539). Black's argument is also typical in its implication that antilynching legislation may cause lynching by "driv[ing] a wedge between the races." Black presents a unified South and projects racial hatred onto self-hating Black Americans and politicians seeking "advantage" in elections. Black's argument deflects problems of racism and racist violence and insists on an interpretation of Southern life that many people, including many Southerners, would view as false.

Black's argument is dramatic, and the expression of strong feeling through-out the filibuster highlights victim identity and suggests self-serving standards of decorum. In addition to insisting that only Southerners can know the South, these speeches also indicate that outsider interpretations are presump-tuous, rude, and sometimes deliberately malicious. Senator John Bankhead (D-Alabama) asks, "Why does the Senator from Colorado think he knows more about the race situation in the South than do those of us who live there? Does he impugn our sincerity in saying that we are friendly to the colored race?" (Congressional Record, 30 Apr. 1935, 6627). Importantly, this claim constructs Costigan's antilynching stance as an affront to Southern identity, particularly the hospitality that Bankhead's and other paternalistic versions of racism claim. This narrow version of "those of us who live" in the South erases the many Southern experiences and opinions that contradict the dominant account. It also makes this argument personal: It's not just that people mis-understand or misrepresent the South, but that they do so in a hurtful way. As Senator Connally puts it, "Those of us who come from a certain section of the country deserve the sympathy of Senators and Representatives from other sections rather than their attitude of hostility" (Congressional Record, 25 Apr. 1935, 6366).

Linking "lynching" and "the South" too closely can be problematic. Racially motivated lynching happened elsewhere in the country, and even lynching in the South was not solely a Southern problem. Jacqueline Goldsby points out that lynching flourished in the South in part because it was easy for other Americans to dissociate it from national culture (27). Even as they attempt to highlight violence in other parts of the country, however, these fili-buster participants tie support for lynching to Southern identity. The filibuster highlights how lynching and an imagined version of the South and Southern identity were intertwined, encouraging "outsiders" to think of this violence as none of their business. Filibuster speakers' rhetorical refusal, connected to Southern white supremacy, constitutes a Southern identity that is intimately connected with support of lynching.

CONCLUSION: HABITS OF VIOLENCE

The repeated citation and reiteration of a violent white supremacist identity had cumulative effects. As the examples above show, Southern white suprem-acist identity—often articulated as the only correct Southern identity—was practiced in part through a violent refusal to address outsider perspectives. Unsurprisingly, this practice narrowed the available ground for antilynching arguments. In an argument before a subcommittee of the Committee on the Judiciary on behalf of his bill, Wagner illustrates the hazards of adopting, deliberately or not, the norms that structure lynching and its surrounding rhetoric. While Wagner is emphatic about the horrors of lynching, he suggests that "the poisonous effects" of lynching affect not just the victim, his or her family, and the Black community, but also the lynchers and spectators. He explains, "There are thousands of people, swept into the current by the frenzy of the moment, who suffer a moral relapse from which recovery is almost impossible" (4). According to Wagner, lynching defenders may not actually support the practice, but could, instead, be engaged in a sort of boosterism:

> A lynching is such a horrible strain upon the repute of a section that every effort is made to efface it. And the only method of effacement is apology. These apologies include a mass of dogmas, prejudices, and falsifications that exercise a pernicious effect upon the public welfare. It is a tragic spectacle to watch people who abhor lynching forced by the pressure of events to make extenuating pleas for the evil in their midst. (4)

Wagner's characterization of lynching defenders is telling. According to this argument, individuals who defend lynching are not guilty of any wrongdoing. Rather, concern for their region's reputation forces them to make arguments that they would not otherwise make. In this argument, lynching defenders are victims of lynching as well because lynching forces them to use damaging rhetoric. That Wagner does not explain what the "pernicious effect" of this rhetoric is means that he could be discussing the ways in which this rhetoric supports future racial violence, but he could also or instead be following abolitionist arguments and previous antilynching arguments by drawing attention to the moral damage that whites incur from supporting a violation of human rights. Within the context of this paragraph, it seems more likely that audiences would perceive the latter meaning. After all, Wagner describes watching people defend lynching as a "tragic spectacle," a phrase that could just as easily describe what happens to a lynching victim.

Wagner's position as an antilynching activist makes it likely that he is engaging in cunning identification. Burke suggests that a rhetor can align himself with the interests of a hostile audience, even as he critiques that interest, by "using terms not incisive enough to criticize [the interest] properly" (*A Rhetoric of Motives* 36). In other words, while Wagner criticizes lynching, he aligns himself with pro-lynching interests by accepting the rhetoric of misrepresentation and victimization prominent in pro-lynching rhetoric. In suggesting that the individuals defending lynching are only trying to support their region, Wagner implies that the "dogmas, prejudices, and falsifications" that appear in these lynching defenses are a secondary effect. The true purpose of lynching defenses is to help mitigate the damage that lynching does to the region's reputation, and the preservation of lynching is an unintended consequence. This argument is problematic because Wagner attempts to dissociate lynching and Southernness in a way that, however unfairly to Southerners who oppose or are targets of lynching, cannot be done. As we have seen, lynching and its supporting rhetoric helped reinforce a regional identity based on the violent practice of white supremacy. Wagner's argument falls short as antilynching rhetoric because it incorrectly assumes that lynching is divorced from broader understandings of community and can therefore be dissociated from arguments that purport to be concerned about reputation.

Wells's more successful arguments also show the marks of a dominant, anti-deliberative Southern identity. Her initial antilynching editorial, cited above, constitutes Southernness differently. By including the claim that "nobody in the section of the country believes the old thread-bare lie that Negro men rape white women," Wells disrupts the foundation of supposedly righteous white masculine anger that formed an important part of Southern white supremacist identity. She claims a knowing, antiviolence Southern identity and argues that white male lynching supporters are similarly knowledgeable but lie to protect white women from disrepute and themselves from consequences. Obviously, this argument hit a nerve; the immediate turn to threats of violence required Wells to flee the region. The pervasive linkage of white Southern identity and violent refusal—rhetorical or otherwise—puts this response in context. A critique of lynching was, for some white Southerners, an existential threat, because the core of white Southern identity was bound up in lynching and associated practices of white supremacy.

As this example suggests, Wells's transformation of the lynching conversation did not center on persuading white supremacist Southerners. Instead, Wells expanded lynching's ecology, appealing to middle-class Northern whites and constructing lynching as a national shame rather than a quaint regional quirk (Bederman 45). By directing the majority of her antilynching arguments to audiences outside the South, Wells performs her own rhetorical refusal. There is no space for her argument, nor for a version of Southernness that includes people of color, within lynching's rhetorical ecology, so Wells looks elsewhere. Her efforts could not stop lynching; it seems unlikely that any one person's rhetoric could. By constructing lynching as a social problem rather than a benign regional idiosyncrasy, Wells transformed the terms of national discussion, thus paving the way for proposals like the Costigan-Wagner Bill.

It is a commonplace that lynching was both spectacular and ordinary. In contemporary discussions, lynching's ordinariness becomes a part of the spectacle. Recirculated lynching photographs often direct attention to the lynching spectators, positioning their apparent comfort with public murder as an indication of the pervasiveness of racial violence and hatred (Wolters 399–400). Understanding lynching as an epideictic that clarified community values is another way of mapping this ordinariness and its consequences. The comfortable atmosphere of white supremacist violence visible in lynching photographs did not just appear; it required building and frequent reinforcement. Southern white supremacists maintained a pervasive atmosphere of racial violence in part by building the principles of lynching into everyday life.

CHAPTER 2

"There Must Be a Way of Carrying It Out"

Ideal and Real in Lethal Injection

THE DEATH PENALTY in the United States centers on appearances. States have spent more than a century trying to obscure pain in execution. As Stuart Banner notes, colonists and early US audiences found little objectionable in a public hanging, even though hanging was unpredictable and often grotesque (146–48). By the mid-nineteenth century, however, Victorian understandings of decorum and medical advances in pain management made painless execution before a sedate crowd seem necessary (Garland, *Peculiar Institution* 145; Banner 170). Communities modified their methods of execution, many ultimately moving to the electric chair and, in the late twentieth century, to lethal injection, and restricted the number and kind of witnesses allowed at executions. By avoiding methods that visibly mutilated the body and staging executions before limited audiences, authorities could control audience reaction and differentiate state-run execution from both the crimes it punished and the extralegal executions of Southern spectacle lynching. The rhetoric of the death penalty is thus centered on strategic concealment. As spokesperson C. J. Drake said of Florida's lethal injection protocol, "the point is to make what you see as uneventful as possible" (qtd. in Kaufman-Osborn 179).

To oppose this logic of concealment, anti–death penalty activists have often tried to reveal the hidden suffering that people experience during execution. The electric chair, which was hidden from the public and often mutilated condemned prisoners, was particularly conducive to this approach. For example, when Florida inmate Thomas Provenzano challenged the state's use of the electric chair, his case included evidence from the prior "botched" execution of Allen Lee Davis. While the Florida Supreme Court found the electric chair constitutional, Justice Leander J. Shaw appended images of Davis's corpse to his dissent so that they would be made public (Supreme Court of Florida; Kaplan). Florida phased out the electric chair soon after the court's decision.

These arguments about execution's cruelty rely on the dissociation of appearance and reality. As Chaïm Perelman and L. Olbrechts-Tyteca explain, the dissociation of philosophical pairs allows rhetors to cope with seemingly intractable contradictions (416). An anti–death penalty argument, for example, may state that while a method of execution *appears* humane, it is actually cruel, either because the condemned person's pain is hidden from the audience or because cruelty goes beyond the immediate suffering that execution entails. This argument allows audiences to reconcile their perception with a contradictory stance: Everything seems fine, but it is not. The related dissociation of ideal and real functions similarly. In many anti–death penalty arguments, including some of those discussed below, rhetors concede that the death penalty is fine in theory, but argue that it cannot be practiced in a constitutional or humane manner. Revealing suffering is often a part of these arguments as well. By highlighting execution's grim realities in contrast to its impossible ideal, stakeholders can construct the death penalty as cruel without addressing its morality.

Lethal injection complicates this concealing/revealing dynamic. Lethal injection is designed to eliminate the visual horrors associated with earlier methods, and since the condemned person is unlikely to be decapitated or catch on fire, there are fewer resources on which anti–death penalty rhetors can draw to show the death penalty's cruelty.[1] The rhetoric of lethal injection, however, goes beyond concealment. Even as it kills, lethal injection is a display of conspicuous nonviolence that reinforces the authorizing community's "civilized" identity. Compared to older methods and to the crimes it punishes, lethal injection can represent the community as restrained and even merciful. For this reason, exposing the possibility or actuality of suffering during lethal injection may not jeopardize lethal injection's status as "humane." Situated in the ecology of lethal suffering, lethal injection looks good, even when it goes wrong.

In this chapter, I examine two legal arguments about lethal injection's possible cruelty. US Supreme Court cases *Baze v. Rees* (2008) and *Glossip v. Gross*

---

1. Hanging mishaps sometimes caused partial decapitation (Banner 173). Pedro Medina caught fire during his execution in Florida's electric chair (Associated Press).

(2015) each revolve around the constitutionality of a lethal injection protocol. I focus on legal contexts because, as I discuss below, the US Supreme Court has been a primary site for contesting the death penalty since the mid-twentieth century. *Baze* and *Glossip* are both pivotal cases in death penalty jurisprudence and the first two Supreme Court cases to deal with lethal injection. Historically, lethal injection in the United States has involved three drugs, injected consecutively: one to render the prisoner unconscious, one to paralyze the prisoner, and one to stop the prisoner's heart. Both *Baze* and *Glossip* focus on the first drug, which parties in both cases agree must function correctly to ensure a humane execution. If the first drug does not adequately anesthetize the prisoner, then she may be conscious but paralyzed during the painful administration of the second and third drugs. In *Baze,* the petitioners argued that Kentucky's lethal injection protocol, while constitutional if done correctly, violated the Eighth Amendment because the risk of error in administering the first drug was too high. In *Glossip,* the petitioners argued that Oklahoma's lethal injection protocol was fundamentally unconstitutional because the first drug was pharmacologically incapable of rendering the prisoner insensate. In both cases, the US Supreme Court upheld the lower courts' rulings and the state's lethal injection procedures.

These cases are of interest in part because of how the petitioners materialize pain in the absence of conventionally recognizable evidence. Their arguments both complicate and reinvest in an ocular epistemology of suffering, a "seeing-is-believing paradigm" common in many arguments about human rights (Hesford 29). Because even "botched" lethal injection does not typically offer the visual horrors of older execution methods, revealing pain becomes more complex. Petitioners in both *Baze* and *Glossip* capitalize on the uncertainty associated with the use of a paralytic drug, arguing that we may not know, now or in the future, how many people have suffered unconstitutionally during their executions. In *Baze,* the petitioners use a cumulative version of harm, measured over time rather than through individual experiences, to argue that the possibility of error in administering the first drug will *eventually* and *inevitably* result in unconstitutional pain. In *Glossip,* the petitioners use medical evidence about midazolam's pharmacological properties to complicate the humane ethos that lethal injection draws from its quasi-medical procedures. In both cases, petitioners argue that people are suffering, even though it is not visible to observers. Whereas lethal injection's lack of spectacle typically serves as assurance of painlessness, these petitioners argue that its calm facade masks terrible pain.

The response to and ultimate failure of these arguments also highlight the limits of revealing pain as a rhetorical strategy. To varying degrees, the petitioners' concepts of harm are intertwined with a desire for the death penalty to be the "best"—the least painful, the most consistent—that it can be. Alongside their dissociation of appearance and reality, the petitioners attempt to reconcile the preexisting separation of ideal and real, arguing that available modifications can bring the death penalty closer to perfection. Importantly, though, the arguments and ultimately the decisions in *Baze* and *Glossip* show how lethal injection resists the binary logic on which many anti–death penalty arguments rely. In its material practice and written and spoken defenses, lethal injection is both ideal *and* real, as well as medical and nonmedical, obscure and commonsense, and violent and nonviolent. While these dualities could seem like a source of weakness, I argue that lethal injection's durability as a method of execution stems in part from its capaciousness. Arguments that rely on the audience's separation of these philosophical pairs are less effective if lethal injection is built on compatible contradictions.

Unlike lynching and torture, lethal injection has received little attention in rhetoric scholarship, perhaps because its material rhetorical processes are harder to pin down. It is both the culmination of a progressive process of concealment and a seeming outlier, detached from the death penalty's ostensible rhetorical purposes. Within an ecology of punishment that centers on concerns about appropriate violence and the appearance of humaneness, however, lethal injection's constitutive force is apparent. Lethal injection constitutes a "civilized" community because of, rather than despite, its near invisibility. In this way, lethal injection more closely mirrors the overall constitutive rhetoric of the carceral system than visible practices like lynching. In the contemporary United States, punishments that do not *seem* violent are the norm.[2] Debates around lethal injection offer insight into the cultural functions of these "civilized" punishments, as well as the rhetoric that contests and supports them.

First, I will describe the rhetoric of lethal injection, arguing that lethal injection's medicalized procedures allow the state and the authorizing community to construct themselves as both merciful and "tough on crime." I then situate the arguments in *Baze* and *Glossip* within the history of Eighth Amendment challenges. Judicial rhetoric around cruel punishment tends to emphasize the state's intent and a teleological narrative of social progress, and these facets make challenging a method of execution more difficult. I examine the rhetoric of *Baze* and *Glossip* in turn, focusing on how petitioners in each case attempt to dissociate appearance and reality to reveal hidden pain, as well as the respondents' and Court's competing understandings of what punish-

---

2. As of mid-2017, the number of executions in the United States has dropped each year since 2012 ("Executions by Year").

ment should be. I conclude by reflecting on the implications of these arguments for other, more common forms of ostensibly nonviolent punishment.

THE RHETORIC OF LETHAL INJECTION

Lethal injection is multiply invisible. Like most state-run executions since the early twentieth century, lethal injection takes place inside a prison before a limited group of witnesses. Its procedure limits visible indicators of possible distress, including convulsions, bleeding, and swelling. Compared to public hangings, in which both the execution method and the audience could create an unexpected spectacle, or the frequent horrors of electrocution, lethal injection is predictable. A lack of spectacle within the execution also contributes to a broader invisibility. Executions are rare, and only particularly controversial executions receive national news coverage. If an execution goes as planned, then there is little to report about it. The public narrative of execution often stops at the death sentence, and in the intervening years of appeals, even community members may think little about the prisoner's eventual death (Garland, *Peculiar Institution* 295).

This invisibility is an asset and limit of lethal injection. As I noted above, lethal injection's visual innocuousness can make it difficult to verify or draw attention to the condemned person's suffering according to dominant norms, thereby making it more difficult to argue that the death penalty is cruel. Lethal injection relies on a dominant understanding of pain as an objective reality with a location in the body. This understanding constructs pain as both accessible through appropriate tools and expertise and "radically solipsistic" (Kaufman-Osborn 139).[3] As Elaine Scarry explains, "To have pain is to have *certainty*; to hear about pain is to have *doubt*" (13). This tension makes talking about the pain of others more challenging. Within this logic, understanding the pain of others requires some access to the site of harm: a visible sign of injury (like a burn) or a weapon through which the viewer can imagine the wound (like the electric chair) (Scarry 16). Lethal injection is crafted to avoid these suggestions of pain and, through that absence, to seem painless.

This understanding of pain often structures anti–death penalty arguments. An ocular epistemology of suffering assumes that audiences do not perceive or

---

3. Kaufman-Osborn explains that the modernist view of pain is historically specific and internally fraught (138–41). It is not the only way to think about pain, nor is it necessarily the most productive for antiviolence work. The modernist view of pain has long structured conversations about cruel execution, however, and its values underlie the conversations in *Baze* and *Glossip*.

understand pain until it is made visible; then, once they see it, they will act on it. This ocular epistemology is intertwined with the modernist understanding of pain, since the pain of others must be processed through external visual evidence (like a wound or weapon). In this understanding, pain is something within the sufferer that must be made visible to outsiders who have the power to help. Witnesses or other stakeholders who share accounts or images from executions participate in this logic. Justice Shaw's choice to make images of Allen Lee Davis's execution public is one example. Importantly, states' gradual moves toward obfuscation also participate in this logic, albeit to opposite ends. With nothing to see, there are presumably fewer opportunities to draw attention to possible suffering.

Lethal injection's erasure of bodily damage can also seem problematic for the state because of how it shifts the rhetoric of execution. Publicly destroying a body sends a message about community power. Lynching, as I described in the previous chapter, sent a message of deliberate excess: Not only could whites kill, but they could torture and mutilate joyously, publicly, and with impunity. Lethal injection refuses that excess and thus sends a different message, but the effectiveness of that message is disputable. Kaufman-Osborn describes the lack of obvious physical harm as a problem for governments that draw power from execution's violence. He writes, "Precisely because it remains unmarked, precisely because it bears no signs of the violence done to it, the lethally injected corpse resists its incorporation within tales of political signification regarding sovereign authority far more effectively than does the body produced by hanging or electrocution" (214). Instead, he argues, lethal injection can "communicate, construct, and validate only those meanings that are suggested by the paradigm of waste disposal" (214). In this understanding, only "botched" lethal injections would send a strong message, because they "make palpably real the embodiment of the person being executed" (214).

I argue that lethal injection's attempted erasure of the body is more complex than the model of "waste disposal" would suggest, although the idea of purging the community of a negative force is certainly an element of death penalty rhetoric. Lethal injection's simultaneous violence and nonviolence constitutes a community that can and does "have it all." This constitutive feature is more visible when we think of execution as multimodally constituted, drawing on and reinforcing a variety of cultural values as part of the "capital punishment complex" (Garland, *Peculiar Institution* 14). Viewing lethal injection primarily in relation to traditional goals of public execution misses the ways in which punishment can be adapted to new circumstances and group identities. Lethal injection's different materialization offers a flexibility: It is violence and nonviolence, action and inaction. While lethal injection may not offer as obvious a display of state or community power, its performance holds the contradictions of modern capital punishment together in a relatively cohesive way, allowing communities to be both "tough on crime" and merciful. The cases below illustrate how the states involved manage these dualities to maintain a usable version of the death penalty.

While I provide more detail about Kentucky's and Oklahoma's lethal injection procedures below, I will give a basic overview of the lethal injection process here.[4] Witnesses are in a separate viewing area and can watch the lethal injection through a one-way mirror. The condemned person is strapped to a gurney. Within or just outside of the execution chamber, execution team members set an intravenous (IV) line through which to inject the drug or drugs used in the execution. Often, the team establishes two lines in case a backup is needed.[5] The team can then inject the drugs into the IV line from an adjacent room or other space out of sight of the witnesses. Witnesses are typically not permitted to see the execution chamber until the IV is set and functioning properly. Once both the IV and the witnesses are in place, the execution begins. Witnesses can hear the prisoner's last words and see his or her death. A medical professional verifies death before the prisoner's body is removed from the chamber.

While lethal injection does not always go as planned, the overall procedure suggests a (relatively) calm and "civilized" death, distinct from the crimes that lethal injection punishes. Its deliberate disproportion reflects the common claim that execution should be about retribution rather than revenge. Arguing against Connecticut's proposed death penalty repeal in 2012, State Representative Lawrence Cafero describes the difference between these terms:

> Vengeance is an emotion. Government does not have the luxury of having emotions, whether that be compassion or vengeance. Government has to seek justice. Justice is the core definition behind retribution. I am for the Connecticut death penalty because it is retribution which accomplishes justice. . . . I am not for the Connecticut death penalty because it is revenge.

---

4. Some states do not make their lethal injection procedures public, and while most states retain lethal injection as their primary method of execution, few of those states use the death penalty regularly ("Number of Executions by State and Region"). This overview of the process is synthesized from the protocols of Kentucky and Oklahoma, discussed below, and from states (1) for which details of the lethal injection protocol are publicly available and (2) that executed at least one inmate using lethal injection in 2016: Florida, Georgia, Missouri, and Texas. All protocols were collected from the Death Penalty Information Center's "State by State Lethal Injection" page.

5. Georgia, Missouri, and Florida all specify that the execution team should establish two intravenous lines.

Oh, we have those emotions. We hear details of these heinous crimes and our blood boils. Our thoughts sometimes get away with us of what we would do to those individuals, but we don't have that luxury collectively. (House of Representatives)

Cafero suggests that it is natural to want to harm people who commit violent crimes, but that voluntary repression of those feelings is an essential part of contemporary execution. Right feeling, as reflected in part in methods that minimize suffering, separates government violence from the violence it punishes. Compared to the acts of which some death row inmates were convicted, lethal injection can seem merciful. The community *could* demand a more exact eye-for-an-eye accounting—for example, an execution that involves torture—but they instead settle (according to this perspective) for lethal injection.

Lethal injection's comparatively innocuous appearance also obscures causality, contributing to a narrative of a civilized and merciful community. As I noted above, it is unlikely that witnesses will see blood, a wound, or convulsions. Lethal injection also involves less execution-specific equipment than electrocution or hanging. Federal Circuit judge Stephen Reinhardt described lethal injection as "terminating life through appropriate medical procedures in a neutral, medical environment" (qtd. in Garland, *Peculiar Institution* 52). The euphemistic "terminating life" and the fantasy of neutrality are consistent with the narrative of lethal injection as distinct from more visibly violent acts of killing. With the execution team out of sight and the condemned person in a quasi-medical environment, it may seem as if the prisoner just dies rather than being killed by the state. If the person being executed were in a cot rather than strapped to a gurney, she might appear to be dying in a hospital. The gurney is essential, however. In addition to securing the prisoner, the straps serve as a visual reminder that the prisoner is dangerous. A vacuum of visible responsibility—no tool for killing, no visible people using it—helps to position the prisoner as responsible for her death. The state carries it out, but she causes it.

Lethal injection, then, allows a community to kill without feeling like killers. It is not that the community must visibly exert its will on the condemned person's body *or* lose the ability to show power. Rather, communities can exert their will through the performed refusal of visible harm, thus allowing them to have violence *and* nonviolence in the same ritual. The community is powerful but humane and, importantly, its violence is distinct from that of the person being executed. Community members may even feel merciful, since they chose the "civilized" route of retribution rather than revenge.

Contesting lethal injection often involves disrupting its vision of neutrality and rational retribution. The petitioners in *Baze* and *Glossip* attempt to upset the balance between violence and nonviolence by recoding seemingly innocuous elements of execution as harmful. The US Supreme Court, however, has repeatedly indicated that the standard for cruel punishment is less connected to the victim's suffering than to the punishing government's intent. Just as lethal injection protocol allows a community to be both violent and nonviolent, Eighth Amendment jurisprudence indicates many ways in which a punishment can be both cruel and constitutionally acceptable.

CRUEL AND UNUSUAL

Baze's and *Glossip*'s focus on revealing unconstitutional pain is typical of modern anti–death penalty arguments, but the courts were not always the primary venue for death penalty challenges. Until the mid-twentieth century, death penalty debates in the United States centered on moral questions. The NAACP's Legal Defense Fund (LDF) shifted that ground when it began litigating death penalty cases as an extension of its civil rights work (Garland, *Peculiar Institution* 218). The death penalty's racial bias, particularly its similarities to race-based lynching in the South, brought the LDF into the abolition business (218–19). The organization's "moratorium strategy" "involved litigating in all the nation's death penalty jurisdictions with the aim of producing a nationwide suspension of executions pending a decision by the Supreme Court" (219). In this litigation, the LDF claimed that the death penalty's infrequent use made it an inherently "unusual" punishment and suggested that it was falling out of favor as the country's "standards of decency" changed. These arguments also relied on a dissociation of ideal and real: While capital statutes may have *seemed* unbiased, Black defendants with white victims were far more likely to be sentenced to death (220). These arguments were most successful in *Furman v. Georgia* (1972), in which the US Supreme Court found that death sentences in Georgia and Texas (and, by extension, any state with similar policies) were, at best, problematically arbitrary (219–20). For the first and only time in US history, the Court suspended executions until states improved their sentencing procedures.[6]

---

6. The Court evaluated these procedural improvements in *Gregg v. Georgia* (1976). Many of the changes that states made in response to *Furman* remain standard in capital proceedings, including bifurcated trials (one phase to determine guilt or innocence and one phase for sentencing) and sentencing guidelines (Garland, *Peculiar Institution* 258–60).

While *Furman v. Georgia* was an ostensible victory, procedural challenges to the death penalty have been largely unsuccessful in its wake. While the US Supreme Court has determined that some once-common practices are cruel and unusual, method-of-execution challenges, like the cases I discuss below, have little chance of success.[7] The US Supreme Court has never ruled that a state could not use its preferred method of execution (*Baze* 9). This is due in part to the way the law defines cruel punishment. In Supreme Court Eighth Amendment jurisprudence, the definition of "cruel" punishment favors the state. A "cruel" punishment must be both inherently and intentionally cruel; accidental cruelty or cruelty that is not directly attributable to the tools of punishment does not qualify. Additionally, examples of cruel punishment suggest that it must be extremely cruel, beyond what a state attempting to adhere to contemporary standards of decorum would choose. In many cases (including *Baze* and *Glossip*), the Court indicates that if a state is *trying* to execute its prisoners humanely, the results need not be perfect to be constitutionally acceptable. This emphasis on intent renders the ideal/real binary problematic. If the state's *effort* is ideal, then the result does not have to be.

Early method-of-execution cases provide information about what constitutes cruel punishment. In *Wilkerson v. Utah* (1878), the Court held that execution by firing squad did not violate the Eighth Amendment, in part because the method was commonly used by the military and thus not "unusual" (99). Writing for the Court, Justice Nathan Clifford provides examples of what would constitute cruel punishment. Referring back to a commentator who mentioned historical methods of punishment including "public dissection" and "burning alive," Clifford writes, "Difficulty would attend the effort to define with exactness the extent of the constitutional provision which provides that cruel and unusual punishments shall not be inflicted; but it is safe to affirm that punishments of torture, such as those mentioned by the commentator referred to, and all others in the same line of unnecessary cruelty, are forbidden by that amendment to the Constitution" (99; citation omitted). The *Wilkerson* Court thus indicates a vast gray area between obviously cruel punishments and acceptable punishments. It is unclear if punishments that do not include torture could be unconstitutionally cruel; the only test of cruelty offered is that of proximity to the severe and deliberate cruelty of these historical methods.

---

7. Post-*Furman,* the Court has held that it is unconstitutionally cruel to execute defendants who are legally "insane" (*Ford v. Wainwright,* 1986), defendants with "mental retardation" (*Atkins v. Virginia,* 2002), and defendants who were under the age of eighteen at the time of their crimes (*Roper v. Simmons,* 2005).

In re Kemmler (1890), which addresses New York's adoption of the electric chair, provides similar examples. The Court declined to hear William Kemmler's case, but did offer a brief comment to explain why it would not overturn the lower court's decision. The Court's comment quotes the state supreme court's opinion, in which Judge Charles C. Dwight wrote that courts would be obligated to condemn a punishment that is "manifestly cruel and unusual" such as "burning at the stake, crucifixion, breaking on the wheel, or the like" (136). The US Supreme Court's comment notes that while electrocution was unusual, "it could not be assumed to be cruel in the light of that common knowledge which has stamped certain punishments as such" (136). Here, as in *Wilkerson,* the Court suggests that cruel punishments will be obviously unacceptable. The Court also references New York's intent in choosing the electric chair, noting that the lower courts understood that the legislature chose the electric chair because they felt it was humane, and "the courts were bound to presume that the legislature was possessed of the facts upon which it took action" (136). The lower and ultimately higher courts assume that the state was well-intentioned and knew what it was doing; thus, the punishment it chose could not be unconstitutionally cruel.

The judicial rhetoric in these two cases suggests that cruel punishment is obvious, intentional, and unlikely in the United States. The examples that the *Wilkerson* and *Kemmler* Courts give were not feasible options for states in the late nineteenth century, as changing beliefs made painless execution seem both possible and necessary. Instead, these examples evoke older British practices (as the *Wilkerson* opinion mentions) and contemporary Southern spectacle lynching.[8] The *Kemmler* comment similarly elevates contemporary state-run executions by assuming that the state government's professed interest in humane execution can only produce humane results. The Court dismisses the possibility that, despite the state's intentions, the then-untested electric chair could be cruel.[9]

Wilkerson and *Kemmler* also identify "unnecessary" cruelty as a key feature of cruel punishment. This idea is important in *Baze* and *Glossip,* as the Court reiterates in both cases that the death penalty need not be painless to be constitutional. The line between necessary and unnecessary cruelty is blurred,

---

8. Describing expert testimony on cruel punishments, the Court notes that execution with pain "superadded" was evident in "the early history of the parent country" (*Wilkerson* 135). The expert also notes that while these punishments were legally permissible, "the humanity of the nation by tacit consent allowed the mitigation of such parts of those judgments as savored of torture or cruelty" (135).

9. According to witnesses at Kemmler's execution, the electric chair was cruel. See "Far Worse Than Hanging."

but often connected to the state's intent. *Louisiana ex rel. Francis v. Resweber* (1947) highlights the problems with an understanding of cruel punishment that requires deliberate, unnecessary cruelty. Willie Francis, sixteen years old and Black, was sentenced to death by electrocution, but the electric chair did not function properly during his execution. Electric current passed through Francis's body, but he did not die, and prison officials took him back to his cell to await a rescheduled execution. The electric chair had to be repaired before they could try to execute Francis again. Francis tried to stop the execution, arguing in court that a second execution violated the Fifth Amendment prohibition of double jeopardy and the Eighth Amendment prohibition on cruel and unusual punishment. The Court found, however, that the second execution could proceed:

> The cruelty against which the Constitution protects a convicted man is cruelty inherent in the method of punishment, not the necessary suffering involved in any method employed to extinguish life humanely. The fact that an unforeseeable accident prevented the prompt consummation of the sentence cannot, it seems to us, add an element of cruelty to a subsequent execution. There is no purpose to inflict unnecessary pain, nor any unnecessary pain involved in the proposed execution. The situation of the unfortunate victim of this accident is just as though he had suffered the identical amount of mental anguish and physical pain in any other occurrence, such as, for example, a fire in the cell block. (*Louisiana ex rel.* 464)

Because state officials did not intend to inflict unnecessary pain on Francis, and the electric chair itself was not inherently cruel, Louisiana was permitted to execute Francis.

The Court's reasoning in the above decision illustrates the problematic and state-serving logic of cruel and unusual punishment. As the example of "a fire in the cell block" suggests, there are many ways in which the state could be responsible for harm without specifically intending it. A fire in a cellblock has a cause, and even if no state actor is directly at fault, the fire may be more or less damaging due to the actions of state officials. Neither a fire nor a botched execution just "happens." The assumption that such events are outside of the state's responsibility relies on a dissociation of real and ideal that maintains narrow standards for culpability. While the *Furman* petitioners argued that the death penalty must be shut down because, while it worked in theory, it was not fair in practice, the decision in *Francis* is anchored in a more "realist" attitude. A realist political style dismisses opposing arguments that are deemed too idealistic or theoretical, insisting instead on planning for a cut-throat and ethically imperfect "reality" (Hariman 42). Along similar lines, the Court suggests that perfect executions are a fantasy, and it is unrealistic to demand them.

Like most modern arguments about method of execution, *Baze* and *Glossip* also address "evolving standards of decency." In the opinion in *Trop v. Dulles*, Chief Justice Earl Warren wrote that "the [Eighth] Amendment must draw its meaning from the evolving standards of decency that mark the progress of a maturing society" (US Supreme Court, *Trop*). In death penalty cases, this standard is usually connected to consensus: Is this practice common, or are there indications that the country has already largely abandoned it (Bessler 16–18)? Justices look for signs of "progress," and if they are present, may hold that a punishment is out of step with contemporary mores.[10] Like the criteria discussed above, the "evolving standards of decency" test constructs the institutions and communities that conduct executions generously. The concept of evolving standards of decency invests in a positive cultural teleology. As I discuss below, this, too, creates issues for the dissociation of real and ideal on which *Baze* and *Glossip* rely. If communities are always improving, then lethal injection, the most recent execution innovation, is necessarily the best.

These cases involve additional uncertainty in that they center on the *risk* that an execution will be cruel. Both *Baze* and *Glossip* require the Court to determine whether their respective lethal injection protocols present "a substantial risk of serious harm." The "substantial risk" standard appears in *Farmer v. Brennan* (1994), in which the US Supreme Court held that "a prison official may be held liable under the Eighth Amendment for acting with 'deliberate indifference' to inmate health or safety only if he knows that inmates face *a substantial risk of serious harm* and disregards that risk by failing to take reasonable measures to abate it" (*Farmer*; emphasis mine). Through this standard, a punishment need not be consistently cruel to violate the Eighth Amendment; instead, it needs to present a "substantial risk" of cruelty, even if that cruelty is not present in every application of that punishment. Materializing a risk, though, is challenging, particularly given the infrequency of executions and a limited range of analogous situations. Determining "substantial risk" in this context requires stakeholders to grapple over what kind of evidence of potential pain is appropriate and how much of it the parties need.

---

10. For example, justices discussed the infrequency of the practices in question in both *Atkins v. Virginia* and *Roper v. Simmons* (Bessler 18).

These legal conditions create particular challenges for arguments, like those of the petitioners in *Baze* and *Glossip,* that dissociate appearance and reality or real and ideal. Because cruel punishment has been described as both deliberately cruel and unlike modern punishment, lethal injection is almost inherently outside of what the Eighth Amendment can recognize. It is inherently "ideal," despite its imperfections, because it marks the accepted stopping point of a progressive telos.

BAZE V. REES: OPTIMIZATION AND "COMMON SENSE"

Introduction and Background

The petitioners in *Baze v. Rees* argue that Kentucky's lethal injection protocol must be optimized through procedural changes. While they concede that the execution protocol is constitutional if performed correctly, they argue that the possibility of human error creates a "unnecessary risk" of serious pain (Barron et al. 38). Their argument reinforces a modernist understanding of pain as located and potentially observable in the body while also troubling dominant understandings of harm in execution. The respondents and ultimately the Court disagree with the petitioners' assessment, arguing that Kentucky's safeguards already go beyond what is required and no further optimization is necessary. Read together, these arguments illustrate how lethal injection complicates arguments that rely on a binary between real and ideal. Legal and cultural standards for cruelty allow lethal injection to be "ideal" even and perhaps because it can involve suffering.

When the US Supreme Court ruled on *Baze v. Rees,* thirty states used the same three-drug protocol for lethal injection: sodium thiopental, to induce unconsciousness; pancuronium bromide, to induce paralysis; and potassium chloride, to induce cardiac arrest (*Baze* 1). Kentucky's lethal injection protocol, the subject of *Baze v. Rees,* was typical. A phlebotomist and an emergency medical technician (EMT) would have "up to one hour to establish both primary and secondary peripheral intravenous sites in the arm, hand, leg, or foot of the inmate" (*Baze* 6; note omitted). The phlebotomist and EMT then left the room to observe the execution through a one-way mirror. A separate execution team, responsible for mixing the drugs and putting them in syringes, would then inject the drugs through those intravenous lines, flushing the lines with saline after each drug to prevent clogs. While the execution team administered the drugs from a separate room, the warden and deputy warden remained in the execution chambers with the inmate, where, through visual inspection, they would determine whether the first drug had rendered the inmate unconscious. If the inmate did not appear unconscious, the execution team would administer another dose of sodium thiopental. Otherwise, the execution would proceed, and the warden and deputy warden would continue to observe the inmate for any signs of distress (*Baze* 6). A physician was present in case the prisoner needed to be revived for a last-minute stay of execution, and the state used an electrocardiogram (EKG) to confirm death (6–7).

Petitioners Ralph Baze and Thomas C. Bowling, both sentenced to death in Kentucky, did not argue that this protocol was inherently cruel. Rather, they argued that the risk of error in mixing and administering the drugs was "unnecessary," given the options of a single-drug protocol or changes to protocol to better monitor anesthetic depth. If the first drug was not mixed or administered correctly, an inmate could be inadequately anesthetized and experience pain with the administration of the second and third drugs (*Baze* 8). The petitioners "argue that the courts must evaluate '(a) the severity of pain risked, (b) the likelihood of that pain occurring, and (c) the extent to which alternative means are feasible, either by modifying existing execution procedures or adopting alternative procedures'" (*Baze* 8; citation omitted). According to the petitioners, if a state can reduce the risk of severe pain with a procedural change, it is responsible for doing so.

The Court ultimately sides with the state, which argues that focusing on unnecessary risk—rather than unnecessary cruelty—places an undue burden on the state (*Baze* 8–9). In a December 3, 2007, brief, the respondents argue that "petitioners' 'unnecessary risk' standard places the states under a continuing obligation to adopt the 'lowest risk' alternative that is 'reasonably available,' even if the risk being avoided is insignificant" (Middendorf et al. 18). Allowing petitioners to challenge execution protocols based on the existence of a "marginally safer alternative," the Court's majority opinion explains, could lead to chaos:

> Permitting an Eighth Amendment violation to be established on such a showing would threaten to transform courts into boards of inquiry charged with determining "best practices" for executions, with each ruling supplanted by another round of litigation touting a new and improved methodology. Such an approach finds no support in our cases, would embroil the courts in ongoing scientific controversies beyond their expertise, and would substantially intrude on the role of state legislatures in implementing their execution procedures—a role that by all accounts the States have fulfilled with an earnest desire to provide for a progressively more humane manner of death. (*Baze* 12; citation omitted)

A version of the death penalty that requires this level of attention to cruelty, the state and the Court suggest, is neither legally required nor sustainable. An optimized death penalty amounts to no death penalty at all.

Optimizing Lethal Injection

The petitioners attempt to make a procedurally optimized death penalty seem necessary and achievable. To combat the visual innocuousness of lethal injection, the petitioners conceive of harm differently. Rather than locating the harm of lethal injection in specific bodies, the petitioners focus on how "unnecessary severe pain may be inflicted on inmates in the aggregate" (Barron et al. 42). In a brief to the Court, they write, "When a method of execution is administered in a flawed manner that creates a foreseeable danger of inflicting severe pain, that method, performed repeatedly over time, *will inflict* unnecessary pain on a subset of executed inmates" (35). The same brief argues that the lower courts erred in ignoring the long-term effects of Kentucky's protocol. The petitioners write, "Moreover, the courts below were able to characterize the risks as insubstantial . . . only by myopically focusing on Petitioners' individual executions considered in isolation from the inevitable consequences of the repeated use of the protocol being used to execute them" (42). According to the petitioners, attention to the visible evidence associated with individual bodies cannot provide an accurate assessment of the risk of harm. Instead, the courts must view harm on a larger scale, viewing execution as a practice in which harm inheres over time.

While their version of harm requires speculation, the petitioners anchor their claims about a less-than-ideal death penalty in a realist notion of the inevitability of human error. Ideally, everything would go perfectly, but the reality is different. Error may occur at several steps in the execution process: while mixing drugs, while setting the IV, or while monitoring the inmate for signs of distress (Barron et al. 12–19). The petitioners ask the Court to see execution as inevitably plagued by the problems that human involvement brings. The petitioners' version of harm transforms lethal injection's deliberate obscurity into its own kind of certainty. Rather than reading a lack of visible harm as evidence that everything is fine, the petitioners suggest that pain *must* exist behind the veneer of calm that the paralytic drug creates, because human error is inevitable. The absence of visible pain becomes the certainty of invisible pain—perhaps not every time, but frequently enough to matter.

This version of harm destabilizes the ocular epistemology of suffering and contests the law's emphasis on direct responsibility by asking the Court to evaluate execution as an ongoing social practice rather than focusing on specific incidents of "botched" executions. For the petitioners, the whole process is botched. More subtly, they also construct death row inmates as a vulnerable population who should not be subject to undue risk. This feature of their argument is in tension with dominant rhetoric around incarceration. As Michelle Brown explains, prisoners are often constructed as threats to be contained; this is especially true of death row prisoners (986). While the rhetoric of retribution over revenge encourages moderation, it does not typically suggest that prisoners *deserve* to suffer less. Rather, the community chooses to do "too little" to reinforce its members' moral superiority.

The petitioners' argument for optimization hews more closely to the ocular epistemology and shared standards for punishment. To make medical optimization seem possible, the petitioners reinvest in a modernist understanding of pain as observable within the body and controllable through medical intervention. They argue that more training and better monitoring technology could reduce the risk of unnoticed improper anesthesia. Responding to a request for details from Justice Ruth Bader Ginsburg during the oral arguments, Donald B. Verrilli, arguing for the petitioners, states that Kentucky should have "a physician, a nurse or anyone trained by them adequately in this process" monitor the inmate's anesthetic depth during the execution process (Oral Argument, *Baze*). The emergency medical technician who observes the execution from a separate room would need additional training to meet this standard. The petitioners also argue for monitoring technology that would be typical in surgical procedures. Verrilli explains that the state "would use the available equipment, EKG and blood pressure cuff which is the standard practice used for monitoring for unconsciousness, but in addition, as the expert testimony in the case established, you have to have . . . close visual observation by the trained person" (Oral Argument, *Baze*). The petitioners assert that the warden and deputy warden do not have adequate training to monitor anesthetic depth, so their presence does not constitute an appropriate safeguard against unconstitutional pain and suffering.

The petitioners' push for increased medicalization also constructs death row inmates in interesting and potentially contradictory ways. The prisoner's body is treated as a source of data that prison officials can access to better understand the prisoner's experience. This could be read as dehumanizing, as the prisoner's account is not only impossible, but unnecessary. Additionally, however, the adoption of observation technologies used in surgery pushes lethal injection closer to medicine. This optimized version of the death penalty suggests that the state owes more care to condemned inmates, even as it kills them.

As the petitioners describe it, Kentucky's lethal injection protocol is neither inherently cruel nor an uncivilized relic. Instead, it is an ongoing social practice with inherent complexities and risks that human efforts can mitigate. The petitioners thus use the dissociation of appearance and reality and ideal and real as a generative space from which corrections can begin. As the next section shows, however, the appropriateness of the petitioners' suggested modifications is far from settled. The state and the Court construct the state's obligations differently, remapping and sometimes disregarding the dissociations that structure the petitioners' argument.

Adequate as Ideal

While the petitioners' version of execution is complex and dangerously entangled with imperfect human action, the respondents' version is straightforward. Representing the state, Roy T. Englert Jr. argues that additional training and technology are unnecessary because any distress that the inmate experiences would be legible to a layperson. He explains, "In the executions that have gone wrong the main problem is an IV goes into tissue instead of the vein. If that happens . . . the inmate would be awake and screaming. The warden and the deputy warden know how to tell the difference between someone whose eyes have closed and who seems to have gone to sleep and someone who is awake and screaming" (Oral Argument, *Baze*). The state rejects the idea that the condemned person might experience pain hidden by the use of a paralytic drug. Instead, the prisoner's body is readily legible through a vernacular ocular epistemology. There is no separation of appearance and reality, so anyone who can see the prisoner should be able to tell when something has gone wrong.

Justice Antonin Scalia addresses the state's commonsense understanding of pain in execution in an exchange with Verrilli. Challenging the argument that Kentucky must incorporate technology to monitor unconsciousness, Scalia notes that the respondents "assert that to know whether the person is unconscious or not, all it takes is a slap in the face and shaking the person" (Oral Argument, *Baze*). Of course, the state does not employ those methods—there is only what Verrilli describes as "visual observation by an untrained warden and an untrained deputy warden who had testified in this case that they don't know what to look for to determine whether somebody is conscious or unconscious." But the images the state provides—the slap in the face, the screaming after IV infiltration—suggest a readily legible body. The alleged obviousness of any problems combined with the work involved in Kentucky's actual protocol construct Kentucky as an overachiever, already doing more than is necessary to ensure a painless execution. The Court reinforces this claim by noting that Kentucky is using a method "believed to be the most humane available" and has safeguards in place to reduce risk (US Supreme Court, *Baze* 23).

This line of argument constructs lethal injection as unnecessarily humane, rather than unnecessarily cruel. To impose further restrictions, especially procedural changes based on medical practice, is positioned as not just unnecessary, but problematic. For example, in response to Verrilli's description of the additional procedures the petitioners deem necessary for the three-drug protocol, Scalia says, "Mr. Verrilli, this is an execution, not surgery. The other side contends that you need to monitor the depth of the unconsciousness. When you expect to bring the person back and do not want harm to the person" (Oral Argument, *Baze*). The plurality opinion concurs, noting that the "supplementary procedures" that the petitioners recommend are "drawn from a different context," and the petitioners have not shown that they are necessary (US Supreme Court, *Baze* 21). Even Justices Ginsburg and David Souter's dissent reinforces the boundary between punishment and medicine, noting that "no one is advocating the wholesale incorporation of medical standards into the Eighth Amendment" (US Supreme Court, *Baze*, Ginsburg fn. 3, pp. 6–7). In advising a change to the lethal injection protocol, Ginsburg emphasizes the ease with which Kentucky could incorporate these standards, distinguishing this minor upgrade from a more significant and problematic overhaul.

The respondents' argument and the Court's conclusions both echo and complicate the dissociation of real and ideal. Part of this argument is concerned with what the state can "realistically" accomplish, as opposed to the version of execution that might exist with unlimited time, resources, and commitment. It seems, however, that some suffering is not something that stakeholders *must* accept, but rather a part of even the ideal version of lethal injection. Mishaps are fine, even if they result in suffering. Asking for more is risky not just because it could make executions more challenging, but because it disrupts their cultural logic by pushing lethal injection too close to medicine.

Importantly, while the Court's opinion rejects the petitioners' calls for a medically optimized execution, it does not reject all optimization. Per the assumptions of evolving standards of decency, the Court suggests that states will improve their methods, even if they are not required to do so. The opinion concludes with the note that while the Court has never invalidated a state's chosen method of execution, "society has nonetheless moved to more humane methods of carrying out capital punishment" (*Baze* 23–24). It goes on: "Our approval of a particular method in the past has not precluded legislatures from taking the steps they deem appropriate, in light of new developments, to ensure humane capital punishment. There is no reason to suppose that today's decision will be any different" (24). Optimization should (and, the Court suggests, will) happen, but only on "society's" timeline. Within this logic, Kentucky is doing as well as can be expected, according to shared values around lethal injection and the community's expectations for what constitutes "humane" execution.

The conflict in *Baze,* then, is less about revealing hidden pain than about competing understandings of how much anyone must know, care, or do about that pain. In trying to create a more achievable "ideal," the petitioners are faced with different legal and cultural understandings of what execution needs to be. It is through these differing standards that Kentucky's protocol can become both adequate *and* ideal.

GLOSSIP V. GROSS: WEIGHING THE OPTIONS
Introduction and Background

Like the petitioners in *Baze,* the petitioners in *Glossip* attempt to reveal the hidden cruelty of lethal injection, but their approach has some important differences. Rather than suggesting a diffuse model of harm based on inevitable error, the petitioners attach pain to a weapon: midazolam, the first drug in Oklahoma's lethal injection protocol. They argue that midazolam cannot provide adequate anesthesia and will thus result in a cruel execution. In the oral arguments and the Court's opinion, however, the petitioners' claims of cruelty conflict with understandings of lethal injection as already "ideal" when compared with older methods of execution. Like the respondents in *Baze,* these respondents rely on a commonsense argument: Lethal injection is the best option, so there is no need to do better.

Oklahoma began using midazolam rather than sodium thiopental as the first drug in its three-drug protocol in response to a material exigence. In 2009, pharmaceutical manufacturer Hospira moved production of sodium thiopental to Italy. Italian authorities allowed the drug's production only on the condition that it would no longer be used in executions. In 2011, Hospira announced that it would stop producing the drug because, as a spokesman noted, "We determined we could not prevent the drug from being diverted for use in capital punishment" (Stein). This decision resulted in a shortage of sodium thiopental. In May of 2016, Pfizer, after acquiring Hospira, announced that none of its drugs could be used in lethal injections, thereby further reducing the amount of available execution drugs. In response to the drug's limited availability, states with the death penalty delayed executions, sometimes indefinitely, or struggled to find alternative drugs to use in their lethal injection protocols.

Oklahoma had used midazolam before *Glossip,* including in the 2014 botched execution of Clayton Lockett. Accounts show multiple problems with Lockett's execution, including some of the problems about which petitioners in *Baze* were concerned. Before his execution, Lockett had cut himself, allegedly to make setting an IV line more difficult. The paramedic tasked with setting the IV line arrived to find equipment different from what she was used to and had to ask a doctor for help. The doctor, who believed he was there only to verify death, finally established an IV line in Lockett's femoral artery. Because Lockett was covered with a sheet up to his chest, the execution team could not see that the IV had dislodged. When Lockett woke up after the injection of the paralytic drug, there was confusion and panic; ultimately, the team decided to stop the execution, having run out of both drugs and locations for IV lines, but Lockett died anyway, about one and a half hours after the paramedic had first attempted to set the IV (Stern).

Oklahoma revised its execution protocol after Lockett's execution, focusing on minimizing the risk of error in the injection process, but they retained midazolam as one option for the first drug in a three-drug sequence. Oklahoma death row inmates filed a civil action for deprivation of rights, arguing that the new drug would not render them insensate and thus could result in a painful execution. They filed a motion for a preliminary injunction that would prevent them, at least for the time, from being executed with this drug. The District Court denied their motion, holding that "the prisoners failed to identify a known and available alternative method of execution that presented a substantially less severe risk of pain" and "failed to establish a likelihood of showing that the use of midazolam created a demonstrated risk of severe pain" (US Supreme Court, *Glossip,* Syllabus 1). The Tenth Circuit Court and the US Supreme Court ultimately agreed, and the injunction was denied.

Revealing Pain

To argue that lethal injection is cruel, the petitioners in *Glossip* construct midazolam as a weapon. To show how midazolam could cause suffering in lethal injection, the petitioners explain the drug's pharmacological class, how it differs from sodium thiopental, and its interactions in the body. The petitioners cannot provide visual evidence with an immediate, visceral impact; instead, they must describe the problematic interactions of a complex ecology of components. Midazolam is also an unusual weapon in that it does not directly harm, but rather *allows* condemned inmates to suffer with the injection of the second and third drugs. Its cruelty thus fits uneasily among existing examples of cruel punishment, like burning at the stake or crucifixion (US Supreme Court, *Wilkerson* 136).

Using information from the Food and Drug Administration (FDA), medical practice, and expert witness testimony, the petitioners argue that midazolam is pharmacologically inappropriate for execution anesthesia, particularly given the risk of pain from the second two drugs. In their petition to the Court, they note that midazolam is not an analgesic, which means that it has no pain-relieving properties (Sands et al. 7; citation omitted). Pain-relieving could be important, the petitioners argue, because midazolam is also "not approved by the FDA for use as general anesthesia and is never used as the sole anesthetic for painful surgical procedures" (i). If midazolam cannot create the "deep, coma-like unconsciousness" that petitioners argue it should, then analgesic properties could help the state hedge its bets. They also argue that the state's use of a "massive dose" (500 milligrams) of midazolam cannot overcome these pharmacological deficits because the drug's effectiveness plateaus at a certain (but unknown) dose (9). Contrasting their case with *Baze*, the petitioners state that while sodium thiopental was not inherently risky, "with midazolam, there is no dose that can reliably maintain unconsciousness at the surgical plane of anesthesia, and increasing the dose cannot overcome the risk. Simply put, even the *proper* administration of midazolam results in an inhumane execution" (21). This argument attempts to transform lethal injection from "humane" to "inhumane" rather than dwelling in the liminal space of risk.

The evidence that the petitioners can provide is limited, however, by the fact that lethal injection is itself a liminal space: both medical and nonmedical, with policed but selectively permeable boundaries. While the petitioners can point to pharmacological research, they cannot determine exactly where a ceiling effect would occur, because no one would ever receive such a high dose of midazolam for therapeutic purposes. The lack of research on high doses of midazolam becomes a problem in the oral argument, in which Robin Konrad, representing the petitioners, argues that the lower courts made factual errors in finding that the drug did not have a ceiling effect:

ALITO: Did you introduce any evidence to show the dosage at which the ceiling effect would occur?

KONRAD: We had testimony from our expert who—who indicated that it could be calculated, but it was not calculated. But, Justice Alito, that doesn't matter because what matters is that we know that the drug has a ceiling effect, and that is what matters.

ALITO: Well, what if the ceiling effect is 1,000 milligrams?

KONRAD: There is no evidence in the record to support that. And in fact—

ALITO: No. I'm just saying is there any evidence to show that it is any amount below 500?

KONRAD: It doesn't matter. It doesn't—

ALITO: Of course it matters.

Justice Samuel Alito's questions suggest issues of practice and certainty. The petitioners cannot point to a person who certainly experienced the ceiling effect; their key examples, Joseph Wood and Clayton Lockett, both had other complications in their executions (Sands et al. 4, 9). The ceiling effect also does not lend itself to this kind of potentially more persuasive demonstration, in part because it does not work the way that Alito's questions suggest that it does. If midazolam can never produce anesthesia, a person who received it would be sub-anesthetized regardless of the dose. The ceiling effect is important to the petitioners' argument as a counter to the idea that the state could overcome midazolam's pharmacological limits by giving the person being executed a massive (and likely lethal) dose.

Like the petitioners in *Baze*, the petitioners in *Glossip* try to dissociate appearance and reality and reveal hidden pain. Here, though, lethal injection's quasi-medical nature causes different problems. As the petitioners reinvest in a modernist understanding of pain as measurable and located in the body, the Court asks for more concrete details: When does it happen in the body? To whom has it happened? Because there is no execution-specific research, those questions are impossible to answer. Lethal injection retains the "civilized" sheen of medicalization without being subject to the same careful evaluation.

Alternatives

While the petitioners provide medical evidence to support their claim that midazolam cannot produce adequate anesthesia, the argument often returns to lethal injection's relative appropriateness. There is a recurring suggestion that lethal injection's obvious superiority to older methods outweighs potential flaws in Oklahoma's protocol. The challenge of finding execution drugs, not an issue in *Baze,* underlies this part of the debate. The petitioners refuse to provide an alternative to Oklahoma's lethal injection protocol, and at this time, Oklahoma did not have the drugs to return to an older drug combination. To avoid suspending executions, the state would have to find a way to secure preferred drugs or revert to an older method of execution. Here, political "realism" becomes a problem for the petitioners. Because an "ideal" protocol may be impossible, some of the justices suggest that a flawed but extant protocol is the only option.

In the oral argument, the justices ask about what will happen if the Court holds that Oklahoma cannot use its chosen method of execution. Justice Ginsburg asks whether a firing squad, presented as a possible alternative to lethal injection, would cause unconstitutional pain. Konrad responds that "we don't know how, if the State chose to carry out an execution by firing squad, whether, in fact, it would cause—rise to the level of unconstitutional pain and suffering under the Eighth Amendment." Justice John Roberts pushes Konrad on this point:

ROBERTS: Well, you don't know. Do you have a guess? I mean, is there a reason that the States moved progressively to what I understand to be more humane methods of execution? Hanging, firing squad, electric chair, death—you know, gas chamber?

KONRAD: Yes.

ROBERTS: And—and you're not suggesting that those other methods are preferable to the method in this case, are you?

KONRAD: I'm not suggesting that, Mr. Chief Justice, but the reason why States moved to more humane methods is, as we learn more, and as we learn more about science, and develop, then, as a society, we move forward. We have evolving standards of decency.

ROBERTS: But you have no suggestion as to what—to what would be an acceptable alternative to what you propose right now for Oklahoma. . . .

. . .

KONRAD: The new statute provides that if the lethal injection protocol is found unconstitutional, or drugs are unavailable, then they can go to other methods.

ROBERTS: What other method?

KONRAD: They go to nitrogen gas, and then go to—

ROBERTS: And are you suggesting that that's okay with you?

KONRAD: I'm not—I don't know anything about that protocol. They have not—

ROBERTS: Well, what do you think? Do you have an instinct about whether or not the gas chamber is preferable to lethal injection or not?

Roberts repeatedly pushes Konrad for what he suggests is a commonsense answer: Of course lethal injection is more humane than older methods. Lethal injection is already optimized, particularly when compared with the alternatives. While Konrad cites evolving standards of decency, it seems as if this teleology works against the petitioners' argument. The narrative of evolving standards of decency suggests the United States is and always has been progressing, so newer methods will always be more humane than older ones. Within this logic, returning to older methods is counterintuitive and may make the death penalty unusable.

Alito emphasizes the importance of maintaining a functional death penalty in the Court's opinion. The opinion reiterates the claim in *Baze* that because the death penalty is constitutional, "there must be a [constitutional] means of carrying it out" (US Supreme Court, *Glossip* 4; citation omitted). The petitioners' argument fails in part because it does not provide an alternative to Oklahoma's existing protocol. The Court's reiteration of this reasoning has a strangely fatalistic tone:

> And because some risk of pain is inherent in any method of execution, we have held that the Constitution does not require the avoidance of all risk of pain. After all, while most humans wish to die a painless death, many do not have that good fortune. Holding that the Eighth Amendment demands the elimination of essentially all risk of pain would effectively outlaw the death penalty altogether. (US Supreme Court, *Glossip* 4; citation omitted)

This part of the opinion naturalizes the death penalty and its cruelty. While similar to the *Francis* Court's logic of cruel punishment, this excerpt has an important distinction. As I noted above, the *Francis* Court presents Francis's failed execution as a random occurrence for which no one is responsible, similar to a fire in a cellblock. The Court's analogy erases the structural culpability that would apply in both cases. In describing a painless death as "good fortune," the *Glossip* Court similarly erases structural responsibility while also flattening the distinctions between execution and more common ways of dying. While, as the Court notes, many people are not lucky enough to die a peaceful death, the majority of those people are dying in radically different circumstances. Someone who dies painfully in an execution is presented as the same as someone who dies in a car crash or after a terrible illness. The resulting image is one of a world in which little can be done about anyone's death, even the deaths that the state controls directly. The risk of pain is not specific to execution; it is a condition of terrible, uncontrollable life itself. Execution—including occasional cruel execution—becomes part of the natural order of things.

While the petitioners attempt a different dissociation of appearance and reality, the overall function of lethal injection as it appears in *Glossip* is similar to the version that emerges in *Baze*. Like *Baze*, *Glossip* ultimately centers on conflicts between optimized and "good enough" versions of the death penalty. Ultimately, too, the version that emerges from the debate has elements of both: It is optimized, but only relative to other methods of execution, with a resistance to incorporating procedures that would challenge dominant values or the relationship between the prisoner and the state. More than *Baze*, *Glossip* highlights lethal injection's place as the endpoint of "evolving standards of decency" and the rhetorical challenges that placement presents.

CONCLUSION

I have tried to show that lethal injection is neither a useless update of a once-functional public ritual nor the straightforward equivalent of older methods, dressed up in civilized clothing. It is not an ostensibly nonviolent practice that can be easily revealed as problematically violent. Instead, a dual status as violent and nonviolent helps to sustain lethal injection as a cultural practice. The law allows for some suffering, and the Court's opinions discussed above indicate that lethal injection does not have to be purged of all markers of violence. Some violence may even be desirable, as protocols that move too close to care—for example, additional medical monitoring—complicate the state/ prisoner relationship. These legal and cultural constructions of lethal injection have important implications for anti–death penalty rhetoric. If lethal injection's apparent contradictions are the source of its strength, then arguments that try to reveal them through dissociation are likely to fail.

While executions are rare, focusing on the challenges and limits of materializing cruelty in deliberately unspectacular punishment has broader implications. Making suffering "visible" is already a fraught process in which an observer determines whether another person's pain merits response.[11] I have tried to argue that the dissociation on which this move in death penalty rhetoric relies assumes discrete philosophical pairs that are not consistent in the law or the dominant punitive culture. Awareness of this issue can also inform arguments against more common forms of punishment. While executions have declined, incarceration rates remain high, and arguments that expose incarceration or solitary confinement as "violent" may encounter problems

---

11. See Hesford.

similar to those that anti–death penalty arguments face.[12] A structural and cultural devaluation of prisoners' experiences sustains these punishments, and countering that devaluation likely requires different kinds of engagement.

Since I began work on *Baze v. Rees* and *Glossip v. Gross,* legal action against the death penalty has continued. *Arthur v. Dunn* (2017), a case specifically concerned with the requirements established in *Glossip,* is the most closely connected to the arguments in this chapter. Alabama death row inmate Thomas Douglas Arthur filed a petition for a writ of certiorari with the US Supreme Court in 2016, arguing that Alabama's lethal injection protocol posed a substantial risk of pain that could be avoided with an alternative method: the firing squad (Han et al.). The Supreme Court issued Arthur a stay of execution to review the petition but declined to hear the case.

Justice Sonia Sotomayor's lengthy dissent on this denial addresses the legal intractability of cruel punishment. Joined by Justice Stephen Breyer, Sotomayor argued that Arthur had met the "macabre challenge" of *Glossip* by providing what the *Glossip* petitioners did not: an alternative method of execution (1). Sotomayor notes that while the firing squad may seem "regressive," there is evidence that it provides a relatively painless death (17). Perhaps most importantly, Sotomayor's dissent pushes against a judicial history that seems stacked against Eighth Amendment contests. Quoting the Court's statement that it "has never invalidated a State's chosen procedure for carrying out a sentence of death as the infliction of cruel and unusual punishment," Sotomayor writes, "We should not be proud of this history. Nor should we rely on it to excuse our current inaction" (17; citation omitted). While the Court has been disinclined to see punishments as cruel and unusual, Sotomayor suggests that there is room for change.

Given the challenges of obtaining execution drugs and the public distaste for older methods, however, it is possible that the death penalty will disappear without federal judicial intervention. While the US Supreme Court has been the site of many death penalty contests, the history of these cases suggests that the law is inadequate to reshape an ecology of violence that positions lethal injection as relatively humane. Instead, the shift away from execution may come from logistical disruptions that interfere with its constitutive message. In addition to amplifying the horrors of botched executions, recent media coverage of the death penalty frequently focuses on states' struggles to get supplies: for example, Arkansas's plan to execute eight men in ten days before

---

12. In 2014, the United States had the "highest prison population rate in the world, 716 per 100,000 of the national population" (Walmsley).

the state's supply of potassium chloride expired and Nevada's and Nebraska's proposed use of fentanyl, a notoriously deadly opioid, in their lethal injection protocols (Haag and Fausset; Siemaszko). While the death penalty may not always seem cruel, then, these stories make lethal injection seem haphazard and unprofessional rather than streamlined and, relative to the other options, optimized. A scramble to execute may disrupt lethal injection's constitutive function more effectively than the revelation of terrible but invisible cruelty.

CHAPTER 3

Spectacular Violence, Mundane Resistance

ON APRIL 28, 2004, *60 Minutes II* broadcast photos of torture at Abu Ghraib prison in Iraq, most of which were taken in October 2003. Abu Ghraib held detainees captured during the early years of the United States' "War on Terror." The now-famous images show military police (MPs) torturing the detainees they were charged with guarding, often while posing for the camera. While Amnesty International released a report critiquing US treatment of detainees in 2003, the photographs had a more immediate public impact.[1] President George W. Bush publicly disavowed the MPs' actions, stating that they did not "reflect the nature of the American people" (Rhem). He also apologized, somewhat perplexingly, to the King of Jordan (Puar, *Terrorist Assemblages* 83). Congress held hearings on prisoner abuse. Brigadier General Janis L. Karpinski, in charge of Abu Ghraib at the time of the abuse, was suspended from her command of the 800th Military Police Brigade ("Chronology of Abu Ghraib"). Several MPs were court-martialed. Perhaps most importantly, the photographs started a conversation about torture in the War on Terror, draw-

---

1. Some government officials had more information. A soldier reported abuse at Abu Ghraib in January 13, 2004, and Major General Antonio M. Taguba's investigative report on those accusations was available to some government officials nearly two months before *60 Minutes II* broadcast the torture photographs. Congress was not briefed on the Taguba Report until April 28, 2004, the day the photographs were broadcast ("Chronology of Abu Ghraib").

ing attention to the military and CIA's use of "enhanced interrogation techniques" in prisons like Abu Ghraib and in secret "black sites."

While many in the United States had a strong reaction to the images from Abu Ghraib, the photographs' release did not have the structural impact or legal consequences that many horrified observers expected. As Karen J. Greenberg writes, many assumed that "the [interrogation] programs would be terminated, the perpetrators would be punished, Americans would lament the error, and chalk it all up—ruefully—to the misbehavior unleashed by the shock and fears of 9/11." Of course, that is not what happened. No upper-level government or military officials were prosecuted for their actions in connection to Abu Ghraib. While the Justice Department investigated the CIA's torture program, no one was charged, and the last two cases were dismissed in 2012 (K. J. Greenberg). The failure to prosecute was so glaring that the head of the American Civil Liberties Union (ACLU) suggested pardoning George W. Bush, Dick Cheney, and others involved in CIA and military torture programs "because it may be the only way to establish, once and for all, that torture is illegal" (Romero). Romero's op-ed, published shortly after the release of the executive summary of the Senate Select Committee on Intelligence's report on CIA torture, suggests despondence at the fact that evidence of torture did not lead to criminal charges. No such charges would be forthcoming, despite the Torture Report's detailed accounts of CIA misconduct. Less than two years later, the United States elected an openly pro-torture candidate to the presidency.[2]

Much of the conversation about torture in the War on Terror has focused on the photographs from Abu Ghraib and the absence of substantive change in their wake. While perhaps not surprising, the gap between expected and actual change after Abu Ghraib was dramatic. Writing about a month after the photographs were first broadcast, Susan Sontag speculated that horrific photographs would continue to emerge and circulate, threatening the United States' imperial projects and damaging its reputation abroad. She wrote that "the pictures aren't going to go away" and described the proliferation of visual evidence of torture as "unstoppable" ("Regarding the Torture"). When it became clear that the effects of this evidence *were* stoppable, other scholars addressed

---

2. Donald Trump was explicitly pro-torture during his presidential campaign, claiming that "torture works" and that detainees "deserve it," regardless of its effectiveness (Jacobs). Several Trump nominees and appointees (as of August 2017) also have connections to Bush-era torture: Steven Bradbury, who wrote legal memos authorizing CIA torture; Christopher Wray, who failed to prosecute torturers while he was the Justice Department; and Gina Haspel, deputy director of the CIA, formerly in charge of a "black site" prison (M. Benjamin and Harveston).

how and why the photographs had so little material impact. In this way, the Abu Ghraib photographs came to exemplify what is desirable and undesirable about photographs of atrocity. While they may shock some viewers, their effects do not last, and the images cannot produce justice for the victims they depict. Like so many other instances of violence made visible, the story of Abu Ghraib, and of an anti-torture moment in the United States, becomes one of failure.

This understanding of the aftermath of Abu Ghraib raises questions about which responses are perceptible in conversations about violent spectacle and where we might find new options to address the ecology from which carceral violence emerges, along with the violence itself. As Wendy Hesford notes, many responses to the torture at Abu Ghraib participate in an inherently limited narrative in which the United States, traumatized by 9/11, traumatizes others and is subsequently retraumatized by those misdeeds (69–70). This narrative centers the United States as victim, obscuring both the complex processes that facilitate violence and responses that do not simply force viewers to reencounter a traumatic spectacle. It is also, importantly, a narrative that centers shock and surprise. The audience member's trauma is a rupture between what she thought she knew about the United States and the alternative vision with which she is presented. There is little room for torture's familiarity except as a repeating trauma, nor is there room for gradual engagement with state violence.

This chapter examines texts that model a post-shock response and encourage a different form and pace of audience interaction. I focus on two sets of texts, both connected to the ACLU's anti-torture work: *Salim v. Mitchell,* a lawsuit filed by former detainees against two psychologists who developed the CIA's "enhanced interrogation" program, and *Did You Kiss the Dead Body?,* a collection of modified autopsy reports created by artist Rajkamal Kahlon. For both works, dwelling is a part of process and product. *Salim* and *DYKTDB?* represent years-long efforts to transform underexamined archives into legible narratives of violence. Their public-facing final forms offer insight into torture as cultural and structural (as well as direct) violence. Because they foreground accumulation and dwelling as valid and even necessary responses to violent spectacle, these works suggest a gradual audience engagement that avoids some of the pitfalls critiqued in commentary on Abu Ghraib.

In examining these texts, I draw attention to how critique that dwells within and near problematic structures can address violent spectacle. I follow Wendy Hesford in using a modified version of spectacle to describe the rhetoric around torture at Abu Ghraib. While Guy Debord's definition of spectacle emphasized hierarchical oppression, Hesford describes the "human rights spectacle as a rhetorical phenomenon through which differently empowered social constituencies negotiate the authority of representation" (17). Spectacles need not be entirely visual, but they are flashpoints around and through which groups define relational identity (16).

This chapter examines the constitutive force of sites that do similar relational work, but more slowly and with less fanfare than the events that we typically recognize as *spectacle*. In "Ecological, Pedagogical, Public Rhetoric," Nathaniel A. Rivers and Ryan P. Weber argue for increased attention to the ways in which rhetorics that may seem insufficiently radical can still participate in social change. Using the Montgomery bus boycott as an example, they address the data gathering, meetings, and public education that preceded Rosa Parks's refusal to give up her seat for a white passenger (198). While less well-known than the "rhetorical fireworks" of prominent figures in the civil rights movement, these mundane actions worked alongside more noticeable acts to create change. Suzanne Bordelon builds on this idea by focusing on the work of "muted rhetors," or rhetors silenced within dominant discourses (335). Citing Jacqueline Bacon, Bordelon explains that while rhetors may be forced to work in mundane spaces, mundaneness can be a virtue. In these largely unmonitored spaces, rhetors may find greater—if still constrained— opportunities for expression and persuasion (335). When highly visible and revolutionary action is not accessible, these overlooked everyday spaces offer an alternative. While these texts emerge from institutional contexts, their critique-from-within makes apparent the critic's inevitable embeddedness in ecologies of violence. A response that engages with and occupies mundane spaces can address violence as the rule rather than the exception and reject the shock that too often structures dominant narratives.

While violent spectacle merits a rapid, substantive response, it does not often receive it, and exploring how responses unfold over time can extend scholarly understanding of a violent spectacle's public life. First, I will discuss how the torture at Abu Ghraib has shaped the conversation about carceral violence in the War on Terror and how a different kairos of response could offer other opportunities for critique. I will then address how both *Salim* and *Did You Kiss the Dead Body?* critique structural and cultural violence by composing with and against the grain of damaging institutional rhetorics. Each of these texts intersects with comparatively "mundane" rhetorics to show the violence within and create a more accessible public space for engaging that violence. I will conclude by reflecting on what these texts communicate about vernacular resistance and "making do" in response to intractable violence.

INTERPRETING ABU GHRAIB

A focus on the photographs from Abu Ghraib has shaped scholarship on torture in the War on Terror. This focus has important effects because while the torture at Abu Ghraib emerges from a shared culture of violence, it alone cannot represent the internal diversity of the United States' torture programs. The CIA, the Defense Intelligence Agency (DIA), and the US Armed Forces all approved the use of coercive interrogation techniques during the War on Terror, including (at various times) waterboarding, stress positions, the "insult slap," and the use of "controlled fear" (American Civil Liberties Union, "About"; White). While the CIA's torture program was exceedingly well documented at the institutional level, making it easier to directly connect interrogator actions in black sites to higher-level personnel, the MPs at Abu Ghraib were regulated differently. Rather than being issued a playbook for their torture, Abu Ghraib MPs were given instructions to "soften up" detainees for interrogation and allowed some creativity in their torture techniques (Zernike). The torturers' "documentation" of torture was apparently for fun, rather than an explicit part of the institutional process. This version of torture—authorized, improvised, and enjoyed—raises different questions than the clinical violence of the CIA program. Scholars and other commentators had to work to establish that the direct violence of Abu Ghraib was connected to less-visible structural and cultural violence. Understanding the torture, its evident normalcy, and its relation to quotidian institutional and media practices then became a key focus of scholarly attention.

Focusing on Abu Ghraib has also involved a focus on the images of torture and the questions of responsibility that their portrayal of joyous torturers raises. Scholarly responses to Abu Ghraib counter the Bush Administration's attempts to other the torturers and reinforce a narrative of individual responsibility. George W. Bush repeatedly described the torturers and their actions as un-American. In a news conference with King Abdullah II of Jordan, Bush insisted that the torture at Abu Ghraib did not represent "the true nature and heart of America" ("President's News Conference"). In a speech a few weeks later, he separated the "good America" from the torture at Abu Ghraib, describing the torture as "disgraceful conduct by a few American troops who dishonored our country and disregarded our values" (Milbank). US secretary of defense Donald Rumsfeld expressed similar sentiments, stating that the conduct at Abu Ghraib was "un-American" and "inconsistent with the values of our nation" ("Rumsfeld Apologizes"). The "bad apples" narrative also appeared in comments from senators: for example, Norm Coleman's statement that the torture at Abu Ghraib was "pretty disgusting, not what you'd expect from Americans" (qtd. in Hodge). This narrative allows speakers to condemn the torture (albeit without using the word "torture") while resisting implications for national identity. Despite evidence of torture, the United States could continue to claim an identity as a human rights leader.

This pattern, in which ostensible condemnation reinforces pro-torture tropes, was common in the rhetoric around torture in the War on Terror. As I noted above, Hesford identifies a dominant narrative in which the United States is the victim of torture, continually shocked and retraumatized by the horrors of Abu Ghraib. Similarly, Jasbir Puar notes that often-repeated Orientalist rhetoric made it seem as if the torture victims were responsible for their own trauma. Torturers devised their tortures based on an Orientalist understanding of "Muslim culture," in which "sexuality is repressed, but perversity is just bubbling beneath the surface" (Puar, *Terrorist Assemblages* 83). Even anti-torture rhetoric often reiterated the claim that forced nudity and sexual acts were especially harmful to Muslims because of their "culture." This rhetoric, represented in much of the public discourse around Abu Ghraib, suggests that victims are affected by sexual torture *because* they come from a repressive and homophobic culture; the victims are thus equally, if not more, responsible for their trauma than the torturers (Puar 91). This line of argument reinforces a contrast between the "backwards" victims and the supposedly freethinking and sexually liberated United States. The reiteration of an othered Muslim culture also erases diversity among Muslims and the existence of Muslim citizens and residents of the United States. Speakers could thus express disgust and disapproval while still maintaining the Orientalist logic that facilitated torture in the War on Terror.

A dominant emphasis on legal retribution—punishing those who tortured or authorized torture through the law—also reinforces torture's founding logic. Michelle Brown explains that post–Abu Ghraib narratives traced responsibility either to the torturers themselves (the "individual responsibility" narrative) or to the higher-ups who authorized the torture (the "just following orders" narrative) (979). While different, both narratives place problematic emphasis on what the law can name, focusing on entities who could be brought to justice within a retributive frame. There is much outside of this frame—for example, racism and imperialism—that the law cannot directly address. Emphasizing retribution in response to Abu Ghraib is especially troubling, because a culture of retribution fueled the War on Terror and the torture at Abu Ghraib. Brown links the treatment of prisoners at Abu Ghraib to problematic shifts in domestic attitudes about punishment. A retributive approach to punishment brings with it an "oppositional, binary, and dehumanizing logic" in which prisoners present a constant threat to both prison staff and the outside world (Michelle Brown 981). Penal shifts toward supermax prisons and police militarization exemplify this world view. Prisoners are enemies to be subdued and contained; to humanize them is to risk lives. The war in Iraq was already constructed as retribution for the attacks of September 11, 2001,[3] and prisoners in Abu Ghraib were assumed linked, however obliquely, to terrorism.[4] As in many US prisons, detainees at Abu Ghraib were treated as violent threats that could only be manipulated and contained. A logic of "criminals" as monstrous others carries over from domestic penal culture and facilitates mistreatment.

While the responses to Abu Ghraib often reinforced problematic values, commentators also valued the images of torture for making direct, structural, and cultural violence visible. As a counter to the Bush administration's distancing rhetoric, Susan Sontag famously argued that "the photographs are us"—that is, integral to US identity and stemming from US structures and shared beliefs ("Regarding the Torture"). Sontag explained that the photographs were "representative" because "the nature of the policies prosecuted by this administration and the hierarchies deployed to carry them out made [torture] likely." In other words, structural violence enabled direct violence. Responding to the photographs and Sontag, Judith Butler suggests that the photographs' simultaneous representativeness and mobility can raise questions about shared norms and which lives are grievable (78). Because they enact oppressive cultural logics, the photographs from Abu Ghraib can expose dominant frames of representability. Butler writes:

> As a visual interpretation, the photograph can only be conducted within certain kinds of lines and so within certain kinds of frames—unless, of course, the mandatory frame becomes a part of the story; unless there is a way to photograph the frame itself. At that point, the photograph that yields its frame to interpretation thereby opens up to critical scrutiny the restrictions on interpreting reality. (71–72)

Because they are mobile, the Abu Ghraib photographs can offer insight into the cultural and structural violence that facilitated their creation. There are

---

3. Wendy Hesford notes that guards interviewed for the documentary *Ghosts of Abu Ghraib* also used retributive logics to justify their actions (78).

4. Of course, this connection was specious. For more detail on the rhetorical strategies that the Bush administration used to link Saddam Hussein and the 9/11 attacks, see Chang and Mehan.

limits to what the photograph can do; it cannot "restore integrity to the body it registers," the bodies that are shown in torment (78). But through circulation, Butler suggests that images "[become] the public condition under which we feel outrage and construct political views to incorporate and articulate that outrage" (78). By allowing viewers to interpret the interpretation, the images from Abu Ghraib can help viewers see a frame that is already present in their lives. If the images are shocking, then, it is not because they are new, but because they are familiar.

This potential of the images from Abu Ghraib, combined with an often unsatisfying and problematic public response, raises questions about what to do with this familiarity, particularly once feelings of shock fade. Those are questions that the scholarship focused solely on the origins and immediate aftermath of Abu Ghraib has fewer opportunities to answer. By taking a longer view and looking to the texts that proliferated once the mainstream conversation about Abu Ghraib was over, scholars can see what other spectator positions and critiques are possible and expand our understanding of the public discourse around torture.

POST-SHOCK AND CYNICAL DWELLING

The texts I discuss below engage mundane rhetorics to both model and construct different spectator orientations than the dominant rhetoric around Abu Ghraib suggested. The audience space that develops in the aftermath of shock is both affectively and temporally distinct. In "Re-Seeing Abu Ghraib: Cynical Rhetoric as Civic Engagement," Laura Sparks argues for a reevaluation of cynicism as a public stance, focusing in particular on cynical rhetorical production. For Sparks, cynical rhetorical production is provocative and thus "interactive"; it is designed to disrupt shared values and norms of civil discourse. In mapping a space of post–Abu Ghraib response, Sparks's assertion that cynicism evinces a kind of entanglement is especially helpful. Sparks argues that cynical rhetorical production acknowledges the impossibility of existing in a society without being shaped by its problematic norms. In this way, a cynical response collapses the space between viewer and violence. As Sparks explains, "Rather than positioning us above the fray, a cynical approach calls attention to our implication in the value system that creates and sustains torture." Unlike the dominant rhetoric that Hesford critiques, in which the shock of US publics transforms the United States into a victim, a cynical rhetoric assumes complicity.

While complicity sounds negative, accepting entanglement with problematic norms as a given can also create space for substantive response. When deliberately adopted, cynicism offers a flexible affective orientation toward violence: not immune to shock, but also not reducible to it. This version of cynicism differs from the prophylactic anxiety of "premediation." While premediation creates "an almost constant, low level fear or anxiety" that is supposed to protect audiences against the shock of violence, cynicism need not preclude strong feelings about violence (Grusin 2). As many of the responses to Abu Ghraib suggest, it is possible to feel horror and revulsion in regard to unsurprising violence; it is also possible to be shocked and know that you shouldn't be. A cynical stance, however, can leave space for responses other than shock and horror. While the ocular epistemology of suffering offers one option for response, shock, and visual studies scholars have offered a second, apathy, a cynical observer may have conflicting responses or different feelings at different times.

A cynical orientation toward representations of torture also suggests a potentially productive temporality of response. While Sparks does not address this potential feature of cynicism, in the circumstances that she describes, cynicism is the result of hard-learned lessons: People are terrible, and change is hard. A moment of hope in the wake of Abu Ghraib becomes, in retrospect, a moment of unwarranted idealism. It is a different kairos of response than what the ocular epistemology encourages. Cynicism operates from and through world-weariness, suggesting persistence in a perpetual aftermath. In this way, a cynical stance is connected to the affordances of mundane rhetorics. A muted rhetor may need to seize whatever opportunities are available to her to create change, no matter how incremental. Cynicism's acknowledgment of entanglement does not have to be a resignation; instead, it can be a site for "making do" and gradually carving out space for structural and cultural change. The mundane rhetorics that result lack the "rhetorical fireworks" of more overtly revolutionary responses but may still be well equipped to address the grind of cultural and structural violence (Sparks 188).

I use the idea of cynical response as a starting point from which to consider post-shock responses to torture. By "post-shock," I do not mean to suggest that everyone who responds to or encounters texts related to torture after Abu Ghraib is immune to shock. Instead, I use "post-shock" to mark shock's diminishing returns as a rhetorical resource in public discourse on torture. While many people undoubtedly remain invested in fighting interrogational torture, both within and outside of the War on Terror, at the time of my writing, it is no longer a flashpoint within national debates about foreign policy or incarceration. That does not mean, however, that torture is not still affecting; its afterlife is simply different than we might have hoped. Those conditions lead to questions: What is that afterlife? What feelings and responses circulate when the initial outrage is gone? What sort of spectator or third-party relationships become available in the wake of a jolt of violence? As Sparks indicates, cynicism is only one option. How might we describe engagement that continues beyond or develops after shock and that exceeds the boundaries of spectacular texts?

Audiences occupying this post-shock temporality may choose to stay engaged by dwelling with violence and its representations. To some degree, viewers are always dwelling with images. As Chris Carter points out, "Even split-second emotional responses to images have discursive histories, bespeaking cultural habits of reception that precede the visual-rhetorical encounter while conditioning its brevity" (128). What feels instant is, in fact, the result of a longer process of coexistence with both images and the social norms that dictate their reception. A deliberate engagement with and extension of this discursive history can allow viewers to see how opportunities for response change over time, moving beyond the "shock-apathy" trajectory that discussions of visible violence sometimes assume. Rather than succumbing to "image fatigue" and thereby abandoning their responsibility to look, viewers could dwell and search for other ways to engage within the space they share with violence.[5]

To address these issues, Ariella Azoulay proposes that audiences should "stop looking at the photograph and instead start watching it." She goes on:

> The verb "to watch" is usually used for regarding phenomena or moving pictures. It entails dimensions of time and movement that need to be reinscribed in the interpretation of the still photographic image. When and where the subject of the photograph is a person who has suffered some form of injury, a viewing of the photograph that reconstructs the photographic situation and allows a reading of the injury inflicted on others becomes a civic skill, not an exercise in aesthetic appreciation. (14)

For Azoulay, this relationship between subject, photographer, and viewer offers a model for citizenship in which the governed are obligated to each other through their shared status, rather than according to the fleeting moment of seeming intersubjectivity that a photograph can suggest (24). Watching, being watched, and watching oneself in this reflexive way are reframed as structural

---

5. Azoulay writes that in describing a kind of "image fatigue," Roland Barthes, Jean Baudrillard, and Susan Sontag "loudly proclaimed that viewers' eyes had grown unseeing, proceeding to unburden themselves of the responsibility to hold onto the elementary gesture of looking" (11).

conditions of public life. Watching the photograph, Azoulay's argument suggests, is also a way of being with others.

I adapt Azoulay's notion of "watching" into "dwelling" to emphasize multimodal engagement from within the "shared space" of structural and cultural violence. While *Salim* and *DYKTDB?* do not address the Abu Ghraib photographs directly, they are a part of the extended fallout from that revelation of torture and, thus, part of an overlapping rhetorical ecology. I argue that attending to aftermath—in this case, the uncovering of more documents and the transformation of those documents into various forms of actionable evidence—is a way of dwelling with the images and the torture they represent. The process I describe is similar to "slow looking," "a thoughtful and conscientious method of interacting with visual representations of human violence" (Fleckenstein et al. 13). By switching to a spatial metaphor, I hope to retain the temporality of both "watching" and "slow looking" while foregrounding entanglement. Dwelling with violence and its representations requires acknowledging that you are already in and with it, and finding ways, however small, to reckon with those conditions.

Salim v. Mitchell and *Did You Kiss the Dead Body?* encourage and benefit from a cynical, dwelling response in different ways. Both exist in a post-shock landscape and make use of torture-related texts that received less public attention than the photographs from Abu Ghraib. *Salim* composes along the grain of retributive rhetoric to create an actionable version of torture. The argument carves out room for cultural and structural violence and creates a space for muted rhetors to share their experiences in a way that the photographs from Abu Ghraib do not. While *Salim,* as a civil case, requests a retributive exchange, its discussion of responsibility also exceeds the limits of the law, distorting the frame in which it is embedded. *DYKTDB?* composes along the grain of medical rhetoric, literalizing and extending its assumptions to show their damaging consequences and emphasize cultural violence. In reproducing a culture of violence in visual form, the images place torture within a broader cultural logic that includes, but is not limited to, an objectifying medical gaze.

SALIM V. MITCHELL

Introduction

In 2015, the ACLU filed suit against James Elmer Mitchell and John "Bruce" Jessen, "two psychologists contracted by the CIA to design, implement, and oversee the agency's post-9/11 torture program" (American Civil Liberties Union, "*Salim v. Mitchell*—Lawsuit"). Mitchell and Jessen adapted their experience with Survival, Evasion, Resistance, and Escape (SERE) training to design interrogation techniques that they claimed would be effective, even on detainees who were trained to resist interrogation (L. R. Baker et al. 12–15). Plaintiffs Suleiman Abdullah Salim, Mohamed Ahmed Ben Soud, and Gul Rahman were subjected to "enhanced interrogation techniques" (EITs) while in custody at Bagram Air Force Base (Salim) and a secret CIA site referred to in the documentation as COBALT (Ben Soud, Rahman). Salim and Ben Soud were released without charges; Rahman died of hypothermia while in custody and is represented in the suit by Obaid Ullah (L. R. Baker et al. 4–6). The suit alleges that as architects of the torture program, Mitchell and Jessen are responsible for the suffering that plaintiffs experienced during and since their imprisonment. The initial complaint lists charges of torture; cruel, inhuman, and degrading treatment (CIDT); nonconsensual human experimentation; and war crimes (Baker et al. 3). The parties settled in August 2017. While the terms of that settlement are not public, all parties agreed to sign a document "in which the psychologists said that they had advised the CIA and that the plaintiffs had suffered abuses, but that they were not responsible" (Fink).

Salim v. Mitchell is an example of a vernacular response that employs and encourages dwelling with torture, its origins, and its effects. While its rhetoric and the resulting decisions are important for past and future torture victims, the case's necessary focus on details important to a relatively small discourse community makes it less accessible as public argument about torture than the images from Abu Ghraib. The features that make it "mundane," however, are also essential to its critique. The plaintiffs, muted by dominant discourse (including a lack of will to prosecute), use the available resources to seek some measure of justice. The case's entanglement in problematic rhetorics of retribution makes it uniquely suited to address the structural violence that inheres in institutional frameworks and encourage a slower, considered response to torture. While the focus of *Salim* is on individual liability, its arguments work through the constraints of law to highlight how institutional and scientific cultures of violence can facilitate harm. Through publicly available legal documents and vernacular descriptions on the ACLU's website, the plaintiffs encourage an engagement with torture that is both horrified and cynical.

Salim's form as a civil case facilitates its critique of structural violence, because it is both connected to and apart from the retributive carceral rhetoric that Brown describes. While some actions (like torture) are justiciable in both criminal and civil courts, civil proceedings have some key differences that make them particularly useful to muted rhetors. Civil actions can subvert problematic systems from within by allowing people who have been systemically and culturally marked as disposable to get public acknowledgment of and compensation for their injury. While criminal cases must be initiated by the state or federal government, private individuals can bring civil suits, so civil suits are not dependent on the decisions of elected or appointed prosecutors.[6] Some cases, like *Salim,* also compensate for the absence or failure of criminal prosecution. The standard of evidence that the plaintiffs in a civil suit must meet is also lower. While criminal cases require the prosecutors to prove "beyond a reasonable doubt" that the defendant is guilty, civil cases require only that the plaintiffs prove that their allegations are "more likely true than not true" ("Preponderance"). For this reason, a case that was not successful in criminal court may succeed in civil court.

While civil cases are separate from the carceral system, they are not free of the retributive logic that structured many responses to Abu Ghraib. Civil courts cannot sentence defendants to incarceration; they can only require compensatory and, if deemed appropriate, punitive damages. Even without incarceration, however, there is a retributive exchange: the defendants' money for the harm they caused the plaintiff. As Sarah Lochlann Jain notes, in personal injury suits, the plaintiff's "physical body serves as the collateral for the 'justness' of that culture such that certain practices—child labor, dumping toxic waste—become morally reprehensible" (6). Money cannot un-injure the person; in *Salim,* it cannot heal victims of torture. Instead, the civil verdict is a bandage on a damaged system in the form of retributive compensation and, perhaps, public condemnation. By bandaging, however, a civil suit can show that the system is broken and, over time, effect change.

Salim also performs and facilitates a post-shock response in its recuperation of overlooked sources. Especially early in the case, the plaintiffs in *Salim v. Mitchell* rely heavily on evidence from the executive summary of the Senate Select Committee on Intelligence (SSCI) Study on CIA Detention and Interrogation Program, commonly referred to as the "Torture Report." The executive summary is the only publicly available portion of report, which is over 6,700 pages in its full form (Feinstein). The SSCI began investigating the CIA's destruction of interrogation video tapes in 2007, and the study that would become the Torture Report began in 2009 (Feinstein). The executive summary, released to the public in December 2014, lists twenty findings, all of which describe CIA misconduct. Among other things, the

---

6. While it seems as if elected prosecutors would be more accountable to and representative of the populations they serve, the reality is more complex. Elected prosecutors often run unopposed and can "amass and wield enormous amounts of power" (Lantigua-Williams). As of 2014, all but four states had at least some elected prosecutors. According to the same study, 95% of elected prosecutors are white and 83% are male; only 1% are women of color (Kelly).

SSCI found that the CIA's techniques were "brutal" and that the agency misrepresented their effectiveness and "avoided or impeded congressional oversight" of their program (SSCI 3, 2, 5). The report also describes how individual detainees were tortured and includes details of Gul Rahman's death (63 n. 314; 102 n. 596).

Despite this potentially revelatory content about the scope and careful planning of CIA torture, the Torture Report executive summary received minimal public attention compared to the photographs from Abu Ghraib.[7] The coverage that did exist disproportionately emphasized the report's more shocking portions: specifically, the use of medically unnecessary "rectal feeding" and "rectal rehydration" (SSCI 4).[8] While the Torture Report itself required slower parsing—even the executive summary is 528 pages long—this coverage reinforces the narrative of shock and trauma that dominates post–Abu Ghraib rhetoric. For this reason, *Salim*'s transformation of the Torture Report data is significant. Neither the legal arguments nor the public-facing website of *Salim* emphasizes shock in the same way. Instead, they show torture as both tool and process, a transformative and structuring force that pervaded the CIA's prisons and black sites.

Cultural and Institutional Responsibility

The plaintiffs in *Salim* critique structural violence by highlighting how the defendants' version of torture moved through detainment facilities, affecting even prisoners that the defendants did not personally torture. The legal structure in which they argue makes it impossible for the plaintiffs to fully address this ecology of structural, cultural, and direct violence; in particular, the plaintiffs cannot emphasize the CIA's responsibility, since the institution is not (and cannot be) the target of the case. In composing along the grain of civil law, however, the plaintiffs also show its limits. The CIA's involvement is always present, but at the periphery, notably outside of what law can touch.

The defendants in *Salim* create an ecology of responsibility that excludes them. They construct their torture techniques as a tool that they deployed but could not control. After the defendants' argument that they were pro-

---

7. A search for "Abu Ghraib" in the *New York Times* returns 328 results from May 2004, shortly after the photographs were made public in late April. A search of the same database for coverage of the SSCI's report in December 2014 and January 2015 returns 52 results. While the coverage was still substantial, these numbers suggest that the Torture Report was not an all-consuming media event.

8. See, for example, Yuhas; Schilling; P. Caldwell et al.; Hayes Brown.

tected from prosecution through their close association with the government failed, Miller and Jessen deflected responsibility onto the CIA, constructing themselves less as "architects" (as the CIA described them) than as technicians who maintained but did not direct the preexisting machinery of torture (Fink and Risen). A representative segment of this argument appears in a court document from June 12, 2017. Here, the defendants argue that they only provided the "raw materials" out of which the CIA created its torture program (Tompkins et al. 17). They note that the techniques they recommended were drawn from SERE training and were thus not "original"; instead, they offered techniques that "had been used . . . for fifty years" (9). In a striking rhetorical move, the defendants compare themselves to Joachim Drosihn, a technician who was acquitted of criminal charges stemming from his employer's work with the Nazis because he could not "influence" the use of the gas he helped to provide (qtd. in Tompkins et al. 20). The defendants argue that they were helpless to influence the CIA's use of their torture techniques and therefore cannot be held responsible for torture. In this version of events, the defendants are awash in a preexisting culture of violence that would proceed in the same manner regardless of their participation. Their actions, they argue, were both minor and essentially meaningless.

The plaintiffs describe the violence in CIA black sites as similarly widespread and accepted but construct the defendants as agents within this ecology whose actions reverberate beyond their allegedly limited intentions. The plaintiffs' initial complaint addresses the defendants' participation in direct and structural violence. While the complaint contains accounts of each plaintiff's torture, it begins, like this version of the CIA's torture program, with Abu Zubaydah, an allegedly "high-value" detainee (L. R. Baker et al. 16). While Abu Zubaydah was responsive to the FBI's noncoercive interrogation techniques and had been seriously injured during his capture, the CIA chose to subject him to the newly developed "enhanced interrogation" program (16–17).[9] The torture had two phases: Phase I, in which torturers applied ostensibly nonviolent techniques to psychologically traumatize Abu Zubaydah, and Phase II, the "aggressive phase," in which torturers used more direct violence (18–20). During Phase I, Abu Zubaydah was kept in a brightly lit cell, naked and shackled to a chair. He was deprived of sleep and of food beyond minimal sustenance and "constantly bombarded with either loud rock music or discordant noise" (18–19). When these methods failed to produce useful intelligence, Mitchell recommended that Abu Zubaydah be held in complete isolation, in

---

9. Before being transferred to a CIA black site, Abu Zubaydah was hospitalized "for serious gunshot wounds to his thigh, groin, and stomach sustained during his capture" (L. R. Baker et al. 16).

part to give the CIA team time to discern their next steps. Abu Zubaydah was held in solitary confinement without being questioned for forty-seven days (19–20). For Phase II, Mitchell recommended that Abu Zubaydah be subjected to a regimen of more "aggressive" techniques, devised by Mitchell and Jessen (20). The CIA interrogation team proposed twelve techniques recommended by the defendants, and ultimately received approval for all but one (mock burial) (21). In addition to maintaining the abusive conditions established in Phase I, interrogators in Phase II slammed Abu Zubaydah against the wall, forced him into two small boxes (one coffin-sized, one smaller), and water-boarded him "83 times in August 2002 alone" (23–24). Abu Zubaydah's torture stopped in late August 2002, and the defendants told the CIA that the torture had been successful because they were now sure that he did not possess any actionable intelligence (25).

The extended description of Abu Zubaydah's torture, drawn from the SSCI's Torture Report, establishes torture as a repeated protocol that entered CIA black sites through Mitchell and Jessen. While the defendants were directly involved in Abu Zubaydah's torture, the detailed account in the complaint also links the defendants to torture that they did not directly commit or supervise. The complaint divides the torture of Suleiman Abdullah Salim, Mohamed Ahmed Ben Soud, and Gul Rahman into "Phase I" and "Phase II" to show how the defendants' recommendations served as a template for ongoing violence. For example, during "Phase I" of Suleiman Abdullah Salim's detention, he was kept shackled, in total darkness, and subjected to "loud western pop-music sometimes interrupted by a mixture of cacophonous sounds like yowling and the clanging of bells" (L. R. Baker et al. 35). During "Phase II," Suleiman Abdullah Salim was subjected to repeated water tor-ture, slapped, forcibly shaven, deprived of food and sleep, and forced into one coffin-sized and one smaller box (Baker et al. 43–46). The plaintiffs do not explicitly address the overlap between Suleiman Abdullah Salim's and Abu Zubaydah's respective tortures. Instead, they show the torture as a part of a protocol that, even when the specifics differ, mirrors the torture that Mitch-ell and Jessen recommended for Abu Zubaydah. This structure, repeated for Mohamed Ahmed Ben Soud and Gul Rahman, places the plaintiffs' suffering in a repertoire developed by the defendants.

Showing torture as the application of this template helps the plaintiffs con-test the defendants' assertion that they were not responsible for how their techniques were used after they recommended them to the CIA. In later docu-ments, the plaintiffs argue that the defendants remained involved with the torture at all stages. They note,

It was Defendants who decided that the interrogation program should be 'psychologically based' and 'instill fear and despair.' . . . It was Defendants who came up with the specific abuses that would be systematically inflicted on prisoners. . . . And it was Defendants who told the CIA that their program would be safe and effective, who implemented it, tested it, evaluated it, and pronounced their design a success. (Tompkins et al. 16–17; citations omitted)

More importantly, however, the plaintiffs suggest that regardless of their level of involvement with any particular application of torture, the defendants remain responsible for the torture they designed. The plaintiffs argue that the tools that Mitchell and Jessen provided to the CIA did not have many possible uses, of which torture was only one; rather, they were methods of torture, designed for torturing people. For that reason, it does not matter that Mitchell and Jessen only intended their torture to be used on "high-value" detainees. The plaintiffs argue, "Just as a defendant who supplies a weapon intended for shooting gang members is responsible when an innocent bystander is hit, Defendants' claim that they wished to assist in the torture of a specific type of CIA prisoner does not negate their liability for others subjected to the CIA program" (Tompkins et al. 31; citation omitted). The plaintiffs argue that the defendants' narrow notions of responsibility do not accurately describe the influence and persistence of their methods.

These arguments construct torture as both tool and actor, a semi-living force that proliferates through direct encouragement (from Mitchell and Jessen), perceived utility (also fueled, in part, by Mitchell and Jessen), and ease of application. The plaintiffs' and defendants' discussion of agency has a clear legal purpose: the defendants diminish their own responsibility by blaming the CIA and constructing torture as preexisting and inevitable, and the plaintiffs tie torture to the defendants by constructing it as fundamentally unacceptable and predictably mobile. In both cases, torture exceeds the defendants' grasps. In the plaintiffs' argument, however, Mitchell and Jessen are responsible for the full range of torture's application. By introducing methods of torture, they become responsible for its proliferation, even when they did not specifically order or participate in the torture of individual victims. While still within a retributive frame, this version of responsibility shifts a little beyond the "just following orders" defense that Brown critiques. The defendants do not need to directly order torture to be held responsible; instead, they need only to have created conditions for torture.

To better map this ecology of violence, the plaintiffs include detailed accounts of their torture, including techniques that the defendants did not specifically recommend. That these experiences of violence are present in the legal account of the plaintiffs' torture suggests a more expansive notion of responsibility, as well as an acknowledgment of pain beyond what the law can address. For example, the initial complaint recounts abuse that Suleiman Abdullah Salim suffered before arriving at the CIA black site where he was tortured. The complaint also describes how Suleiman Abdullah Salim was given injections that made him feel drunk and experience memory loss, a technique not listed among the defendants' documented recommendations (L. R. Baker et al. 47–48). By including this information, the plaintiffs emphasize how the recommended techniques reinforced a culture of violence, rather than reducing the plaintiffs' stories to torture that corresponds directly to the defendants' techniques. The plaintiffs note, too, that the defendants acknowledged the possibility of "abusive drift": that is, that permitting violence in one context facilitates violence elsewhere (Chiang et al. 33). The harm the defendants caused, then, is not reducible to their techniques or even the plaintiffs' experiences. Instead, they are potentially responsible—if not necessarily legally liable—for all violence that emerges from the culture they promoted.

Salim's version of torture is both attached to Mitchell and Jessen and in excess of their actions. While the plaintiffs cannot address the CIA's liability, their attention to responsibility beyond direct application of torture highlights the structural conditions that facilitate violence. It is in this present absence that *Salim*'s limits are also among its virtues as a response to violent spectacle. The impossibility of addressing the CIA does not hide the CIA's responsibility, and it is clear in the plaintiffs' narratives that there is plenty of blame to go around. Thus, while we can read *Salim* as retributive, it also shows the inherent inadequacy of the retributive exchange. There is only so much that *Salim* can do within the structure of civil law. Through its inclusion of elements that cannot be legally addressed, however, *Salim* shows the seams of its own narrative and offers space to imagine a more radical approach.

We can read *Salim*'s construction of torture, then, as productively distinct from both the images at Abu Ghraib and much of the media coverage of the Torture Report. As I described above, scholars discussing Abu Ghraib often lamented the challenges of showing these events as examples of cultural and structural violence rather than just the acts of a few "bad apples." As Michelle Brown wrote, even the narratives that attached responsibility to higher-level officials were largely reliant on a retributive mechanism that reinforces a violent boundary between "criminals" and "noncriminals" (979). While the arguments in *Salim* are still focused on personal liability for violence, the plaintiffs' version of how this torture came to be mixes structural and cultural violence in with direct violence. Torture, in this narrative, is not as simple as "person hurts person" or even "person orders other person to hurt a third person." Instead, torture emerges from and contributes to an ecology of harm.

DID YOU KISS THE DEAD BODY?

Introduction

In form and content, *DYKTDB?* critiques the mundane rhetorics that underlie carceral violence in the War on Terror and offers a model for how we might dwell with violent spectacle. While there have been many artistic responses to torture in the War on Terror (and particularly the torture at Abu Ghraib), this project addresses how *historical* structural and cultural violence undergird torture, thereby providing an answer to the causal question that appears in much of the Abu Ghraib commentary.[10] Like *Salim, DYKTDB?* is a part of the ACLU's body of anti-torture work and a modification of an existing archive: autopsy reports that the ACLU made public through Freedom of Information Act requests. These reports are now searchable online in the ACLU's Torture Database, and I used the database to find the reports that Kahlon used when I could not find them reproduced elsewhere in her work. Operating from outside and explicitly against a legal framework, *DYKTDB?* works differently than *Salim*. Kahlon adds images to autopsy reports, but also complicates the typical function of both images and the reports themselves. Neither the reports nor the images can function clearly as "evidence." The medical gaze of the reports, Kahlon explains, obscures more than it reveals, and the images do not represent the torture described within the reports, frustrating the expectation that images will serve as transparent windows into past events. Instead of serving as direct evidence of crime, these images emphasize other forms of responsibility: specifically, a racist and objectifying medical gaze that "turns the dead body into a corpse" (Kahlon, "Did You" 338).

As Kahlon explains, *Did You Kiss the Dead Body?* began with dwelling. In an essay on her work in *Comparative Studies of South Asia, Africa, and the Middle East,* Kahlon recounts the project's evolution, beginning with her first encounter with the autopsy reports:

> I originally became aware of the documents in 2004, when they were released to the public. I printed out several of the autopsy reports and kept them in various studios over the years, tucked into the back of a sketchbook.

---

10. Examples include Forkscrew Graphic's "iRaq" poster, which reimagines a famous Abu Ghraib image in the form of an iPod advertisement, and Fernando Botero's paintings of Abu Ghraib prisoners being tortured ("Forkscrew-Graphics"; Smith).

Periodically I would take them out, read the details of the dispersion of hair or bruises on the deceased body, or of how the remains arrived in a diaper or naked in a body bag. The documents hit me with a wave of nausea and repulsion. I could only look for a minute or two and would have to put the reports away. After several years of this process, I finally began to work with the reports in 2009. ("Did You" 337)

Kahlon describes a process of dwelling with the images that involves repeated affective jolts and a kind of ambient persuasion. The autopsy reports were never as present in US public consciousness as the Abu Ghraib photographs, perhaps in part because there were no images. Kahlon describes them as similarly affecting, however, and rather than recoiling from them or reckoning with them immediately, she dwells with them, keeping them in her workspace for years. While Kahlon was not actively working with the documents, they remained affecting from the periphery. Kahlon describes this dwelling as part of her "process." Only after dwelling with the documents could she produce *Did You Kiss the Dead Body?*

The images Kahlon created with these autopsy reports are varied but share an aesthetic. At the time of my writing, the drawings are available online at didyoukissthedeadbody.com. Here, they are grouped, but they do not have titles; published elsewhere, they are named according to the autopsy report they modify. The autopsy reports are marbled, a technique that Kahlon describes as important because of its origin in Turkey and Iran. The reports also include drawings of bodies and body parts "sourced from Renaissance and Victorian-era anatomical illustrations" (Kahlon, "Did You" 340). The marbling, in red and pink, suggests a microscopic view of blood cells. Some bodies are shown partially "open" or flayed: for example, an image of a face and neck with visible musculature, or an image in which a person's chest and gut are open to show the organs within, as if in an autopsy. Many bodies are shown in pieces: a head and neck, a torso, a hand, a mouth. Some of these anatomical illustrations also show signs of torture. It looks as if a person is being autopsied, but the person's hands are bound with rope; a mostly flayed person sits against the wall as in a stress position; a face in profile with arteries and veins visible through the skin also has a collar and leash around the neck. Some images also show hands interacting with bodies in nonviolent (checking a pulse) and violent (holding scissors near a penis) ways. While the autopsy reports are not always legible beneath the marbling and illustration, the introduction of these elements of violence into the anatomical drawings links the drawings to torture.

Representative Images

The images that Kahlon adds to the autopsy reports critique the cultural violence that inheres in the medical gaze and invite audience members to dwell
with torture. I discuss one image from each of the three untitled groups on
the website. The first image is also reproduced in Kahlon's essay on *Did You
Kiss the Dead Body?* and is designated there as "Autopsy No.: ME04–38, pp.
1–11: the teeth appear natural and in good condition." The text of the autopsy
report redacts the name and "internment sequence number" of the deceased.
It does contain a date of birth (November 15, 1978) and of death (January 16,
2004), indicating that the deceased was twenty-five years old when he died of
"myocarditis," or inflammation of the heart, in Abu Ghraib prison. For "Circumstances of Death," the report states, "Collapsed while performing morning
prayers." The death is ruled "natural" (Kahlon, "Did You" 346).

Added to this autopsy report is an image of a person positioned as if lying
on a table for an autopsy, but with no visible table. The person is nude, and
the abdomen has been opened, with two large, triangular flaps of skin on
either side. No organs are visible; instead, there is what seems to be abdomi-
nal muscle, as well as the bottoms of the pectoral muscles. The marbling in
the background echoes the shapes on the inside of the body. The person's
neck is in a noose, and a hand comes from the right side of the image to hold
the frayed end of the rope. Only the hand and arm of the person holding the
noose is visible. The main figure's position does not look like that of a hanging
person—the neck is not bent or broken, and the flaps of skin hang as if the
figure is lying horizontally rather than hanging vertically—so it seems as if the
noose is both touching and not touching the body. The body is positioned at
the intersection of two planes—the horizontal plane of the examination table
and the vertical plane of the noose—without being fully in either. The image's
composition thus suggests a dual violence of torture and its erasure within
medical discourse.

This image critiques the clinical gaze by bringing it into the same space
with more overt violence. The violence may not be representative of what happened to the deceased prisoner; he *may* have been subject to a mock execution, but this page of the report does not indicate that kind of trauma. The
illustration does not exactly indicate trauma, either: The noose does not visibly affect the body, and the only visible wounds are from the autopsy. As with
the detailed accounts of torture and abuse in *Salim,* however, this representation of violence suggests a broader culture of harm that cannot be listed as a
cause of death. The image creates tension with the autopsy report's brief story

of a "natural" death for which no one is responsible. What caused this person's heart to become inflamed? What wear, physical and psychological, did this person suffer before death, and what were the effects of that wear? The image suggests that a clinical gaze violently obscures more complex narratives of life and death.

In another example, an image is added to the first page of an autopsy report for an acknowledged homicide on December 3, 2002. While the autopsy report does not provide a name, the ACLU notes on the document indicate that the victim was Mullah Habibullah. In "Circumstances of Death," the report describes how the twenty-seven- or twenty-eight-year-old man "was found unresponsive, restrained in his cell" and was "dead on arrival" when moved to Bagram Airfield (Autopsy Report: Mullah Habibullah). Unlike the autopsy report discussed above, this one provides detailed information about injuries. The deceased person died of a pulmonary embolism caused by blunt force trauma. The report notes "multiple blunt force injuries" on the head and neck, torso, and extremities. The bottom of the page notes the cause of death as homicide.

While this autopsy report directly represents violence, the image that Kahlon has added does not. Instead, it has a figure in profile, fully fleshed, with a slight smile. The figure's head is a phrenology map, indicating which parts of the head were supposedly connected to personal characteristics like morality, perception, and domesticity. While the image above visually maps the link between medical and carceral violence as they play out on a body, this image suggests that connection through the history of phrenology. Phrenology, a theory of "character analysis" based on the idea that examination of the skull would allow insight into the brain, was popular in Britain in the nineteenth century (Bank 388–89). Phenology was originally conceived as a method for understanding individual psychology, but it quickly came to serve as a tool for naturalizing racial oppression. As Andrew Bank explains, "The leading proponents of the new discipline almost uniformly adapted their science of the brain to issues of racial differentiation," so phrenology could be used to justify slavery and other forms of imperial violence (389). Phrenology was also used to designate prisoners as inherently deviant (390). Both phrenology creator Franz Gall and prominent British practitioner George Combe researched prisoner physiology, and Combe recommended using physiological data to inform penal decisions (390).

Juxtaposing the long-debunked science of phrenology with the autopsy report draws attention to how even ostensibly "neutral" contemporary medical rhetorics reproduce inequality. Like the post–Abu Ghraib rhetoric in which Muslim torture victims were blamed for their own trauma, phrenology made victims of violence the source of that violence. Phrenology practitioners justified slavery and other forms of oppression through "scientific" claims about the natural aptitudes of oppressed peoples (Bank 389). This narrative of slavery allowed slavers to construct themselves as liberal and even merciful, just as narratives of sexual torture at Abu Ghraib could reinforce the idea that the United States was sexually liberated and thus "more advanced" than the countries from which its torture victims came. While contemporary audiences are likely to recognize phrenology as a pseudo-science used to justify abuse, the objectifying gaze of current medical rhetoric may be less apparent. By drawing them together, Kahlon raises questions about the medical rhetorics that informed not just the autopsy but the imprisonment that preceded it.

Like the second image, the third connects a violent and racist medical history to the torture and the contemporary medical gaze. While Kahlon modifies a later page in the report, I searched the ACLU's Torture Database to find the full report and get more information about the death that the report documents. The report has the name redacted, but the database indicates that it is the autopsy of Abbas Alwan Fadil, who died in Abu Ghraib prison on May 19, 2004. For "Circumstances of Death," the autopsy report states, "This male died while in U. S. custody at Abu Ghraib prison. There is a verbal report only of pain." The cause of death is listed as "peritonitis of undetermined etiology," and the manner of death is listed as "natural" (Autopsy Report: Abbas Alwan Fadil). These details are not present on the page that Kahlon modifies. Instead, that page lists the results of internal and microscopic examinations of various bodily systems, including the genitourinary system and the gastrointestinal tract. The page thus provides a survey of systems that would presumably lead to a conclusion, but the conclusion itself, listed at the beginning of the report, is absent. Additionally, most of the text is obscured by the image that Kahlon adds. When I searched for this report in the ACLU's database, I identified it through the placement of the term "genitourinary," one of the only words I could see on the modified report.

The image that obscures the system survey results is of a pelvis and uterus. The coxal bone is present around the uterus, which contains a well-developed fetus. The fetus looks large in relation to other elements of the image and its head is pointing downward, suggesting that it is near birth. A hand and sleeved forearm are visible reaching into the uterus; black spots radiating outward from the hand suggest blood. The pelvis and uterus are framed with a decorative oval. The pelvis is twisted somewhat within the frame, not mirroring the oval perfectly, and the arm reaching into the uterus comes from outside of the frame.

While the image does not directly represent Abbas Alwan Fadil's cause of death, it hints at unrepresented tortures during and beyond the War on Terror. The image suggests violent rupture; the hand that goes into the uterus breaks the decorative frame around the pelvis and is surrounded by what looks like blood spatter. This invasive movement framed as medical suggests two parallel referents. Like the image discussed above, this image seems to reference a violent and racist history of medical practice: in this case, gynecology.[11] Additionally, the violent rupture of a body with a uterus suggests the largely ignored torture of women detained in the War on Terror. While unreleased images from Abu Ghraib evidently show rape and other forms of sexual abuse inflicted on female prisoners, the public conversation remained focused on the torture of the male prisoners visible in the initially circulated photographs (Harding). The action portrayed in the image may be framed as for the patient's benefit or for the benefit of the fetus. The anatomical illustration combined with this action, however, renders this person an object. The absence of any features beyond the pelvis suggest objectification as well. The person is transformed into body parts.

The title of the project juxtaposes medicine's alienating gaze with the suggestion of intimacy. The title, *Did You Kiss the Dead Body?*, comes from Harold Pinter's 1997 poem, "Death (Births and Deaths Registration Act 1953)," which Pinter read as part of his Nobel Prize lecture in 2005. In his lecture, Pinter criticized the war in Iraq and US foreign policy, noting that in the second half of the twentieth century, the United States supported right-wing groups that terrorized and murdered people in their respective countries. He stated,

> Hundreds of thousands of deaths took place throughout these countries. Did they take place? And are they in all cases attributable to U. S. foreign policy? The answer is yes they did take place and they are attributable to American foreign policy. But you wouldn't know it.
>
> It never happened. Nothing ever happened. Even while it was happening it wasn't happening.

Pinter's poem, especially when juxtaposed with his speech and Kahlon's images, shows the objectifying force and structural violence of government intervention. Pinter's poem lists questions about a corpse that become gradually more intimate, ending with "did you kiss the dead body." The questions sound as if they would appear on a form that one would fill out when leaving a body at the morgue. The kissing question could, perhaps, be medically

---

11. The "father of modern gynecology," J. Marion Sims, honed his expertise by performing experimental procedures on enslaved Black women (S. Brown).

relevant—even in 1953, long before the advent of DNA testing, a kiss could leave traces behind that a medical examiner would notice. Its placement in the poem, however, brings the intimate act of kissing a loved one good-bye into a harsher, institutional space. To kiss the dead body of a loved one is to remember the body as *someone*: a person you loved. The autopsy's reduction of the body into component parts from which answers to a mystery can be derived is obviously different. Kahlon's images ask us to reflect on that intersection of intimacy and objectification.

The autopsy reports tell limited stories and, these images suggest, stories that are problematically entangled with an objectifying medical gaze. *Did You Kiss the Dead Body?* represents that entanglement by highlighting both the medicalization of violence and the violence of medicine. This visualized entanglement complicates the evidentiary logic of the images from Abu Ghraib. The images are not immediately legible; viewers may need to dwell with them, as Kahlon dwelled with the autopsy reports, to understand them. This project thus asks viewers to consider and respond more gradually. *DYKTDB?* shows violence unfolding on a longer temporal scale, and it offers space for a similarly drawn-out response. The cultures of violence that the images illustrate cannot be remedied quickly.

CONCLUSION

These texts each offer models of response that complicate typical rhetorics of violent spectacle. Neither text constructs the United States as the victim of torture, as many post–Abu Ghraib rhetorics did. Instead, both texts draw attention to the cultural and structural sources of the violence at Abu Ghraib and, in doing so, highlight the need for a discourse of violence that is not centered on trauma or retribution. The audience for *Salim* and *DYKTDB?* already knows about torture, so the information that they provide is not revelatory in the same way that the Abu Ghraib photographs were for some audiences. Instead, the spectator that these texts invite is always already living with violence, and the texts themselves provide insight into how that dwelling can be made productive.

In this way, *Salim* and *DYKTDB?* suggest that working from within violent rhetorical ecologies, while not necessarily ideal, offers insight that detachment and shock do not. *Salim*'s internal critique cannot fully reckon with structural and cultural violence, but it can show both the limits of the existing system and, through those limits, possibilities for more radical reform. A substantive response to the limits of *Salim* would require rethinking both the structural options for redress available to victims of violence and the cultural rhetoric of retribution and compensation. Kahlon's attention to the entangled objectifying rhetorics of punishment and medicine suggests a similar need for structural and cultural reform. How might communities create spaces for healing, variously defined, that do not rely on an objectifying gaze? How might distant audiences understand harm without transforming the body into an object of analysis? Finally, in keeping with this chapter's focus on underexamined responses, where are these transformations happening now, and what structural features affect their public prominence?[12]

Through their overlapping institutional contexts, *Salim* and *Did You Kiss the Dead Body?* also raise questions about the possibilities and limits of institutional antiviolence work. While neither text is reducible to its connection to the ACLU, this shared institutional affiliation suggests that we can read them as complementary. As a civil suit in response to a civil rights violation, *Salim* is more consistent with the ACLU's typical work. Kahlon's project, however, suggests the need for more varied approaches to "justice." *Did You Kiss the Dead Body?* specifically constructs the "evidence" of forensic and medical documents as inadequate to address the fullness of suffering. The images do not offer a clear path to justice; instead, they dwell in a space of unjust objectification. By including this work under their institutional umbrella, the ACLU indicates the limits of its own projects and, perhaps, provides a site for institutional growth. As Kahlon's project comments on the other work that the ACLU does, it invites modifications to that work or, perhaps more accurately, the cultures and institutions in which that work must operate. It would seem that the changes that *Did You Kiss the Dead Body?* demands are beyond what a single institution can do. Including this message as part of the ACLU's work, however, allows us to imagine working beyond typical paths in ways that complement the ACLU's incremental progress within structures of violence.

I have argued that scholarship and vernacular discourse around violent spectacle creates limited options for spectator engagement and that looking beyond the immediate aftermath to slower, mundane responses can expand scholarly understanding of the rhetoric of violence. The next chapter continues this work by examining how critical memorial rhetorics create space for public mourning. Like *Salim*, these memorial practices foreground experiences of pain that are rarely welcome in dominant public discourse. Like *DYKTDB?*, they refuse closure in favor of extended critique.

---

12. See Kaba for information on transformative justice and related community-based initiatives.

CHAPTER 4

Loss and Critical Memorialization

SINCE 2005, a group has gathered annually in Monroe, Georgia, to mourn the victims of the Moore's Ford lynching (Owen and Ehrenhaus 72).[1] On July 14, 1946, Roger Malcolm, a Black man, stabbed Barney Hester, a white farmer who was rumored to have had sex with Malcolm's partner, Dorothy Dorsey Malcolm.[2] On July 25, Loy Harrison, a white farmer, bonded Malcolm out of jail. Harrison told Malcolm that they would go to Harrison's farm so that Malcolm could work off his bond, a common arrangement at the time. When he picked Malcolm up, Harrison had with him Dorothy, Dorothy's brother George, and George's partner Mae Murray (Wexler 57). On the way to the farm, approximately twenty men stopped the car and demanded first Roger,

---

1. Portions of this chapter were published as "Loss and Lived Memory at the Moore's Ford Lynching Reenactment" in *Advances in the History of Rhetoric*. Copyright American Society for the History of Rhetoric (ASHR), https://ashr.org/. Reprinted by permission of Taylor and Francis Ltd. (tandfonline.com) on behalf of the American Society for the History of Rhetoric (ASHR).

Research for this chapter was supported in part by a Lightsey Fellowship from Clemson University's College of Architecture, Arts, and Humanities.

2. There were rumors about the exact nature of Dorothy's alleged relationship with Barney. Laura Wexler notes that while some community members thought Dorothy was sexually promiscuous, others suspected that Barney and/or his brother were forcing or coercing Dorothy into sex (11–12).

then George. When one of the women in the car cursed a member of the mob by name, the men also removed both women from the car (Wexler 62). The mob put a noose around Roger Malcolm's neck, dragged the group down an embankment, and shot them. Their bodies were found shortly after near the Moore's Ford Bridge (Childers 577).

While there is no recurring formal memorial for Charles Brooks Jr., his family's grief is documented in the archives of the Texas After Violence Project (TAVP). On December 7, 1982, the state of Texas executed Brooks, referred to by family and community members as "Charlie."[3] It was the state's first execution since *Gregg v. Georgia* lifted the de facto moratorium imposed by the US Supreme Court in *Furman v. Georgia* (1972). It was also the first execution of an African American since the moratorium was lifted and the first ever execution by lethal injection. Per Brooks's apparent request, his sons and ex-wife did not witness his execution. Surprised that Brooks was going to be executed after several stays, the family drove to the Huntsville Unit and, after being denied entry to the witness area, watched the clock tick down to midnight and saw the witnesses file out, signaling that the execution was complete (D. Brooks, Interview 1; Easley).

While these two incidents are different in important ways, I bring them together to address the intersections of memorial rhetorics and ongoing structural violence. Until recently, lynching was largely excluded from dominant memorial rhetorics; the loss that the families of executed people experience still is.[4] I examine the atypical memorial rhetoric around a lynching and an execution to trace how they create public space for typically obscured grief. As memory studies scholars have explained, physical and digital memorials are rich sites for examining how community values and identities are reinforced. Memorials serve as "archives of public affect," the construction or performance of which often involves contentious arguments about shared values and appropriate sentiment (Doss 13, 2). Memorials establish how community members should feel about a past event or whether they should feel anything at all, since some events do not meet the criteria for public memorialization. While all memory requires selection, dominant forms of memorialization are particularly ill-suited to engage with ongoing, widespread, and culturally sanctioned violence. Memorials are often discrete "memory places," imbued

---

3. Charlie Brooks Jr. converted to Islam in prison and changed his name to Shareef Ahmad Abdul-Rahim (Easley). I refer to him as Charlie Brooks Jr. in this chapter because the sources I discuss all use that name.

4. The first national lynching memorial, the National Memorial for Peace and Justice in Montgomery, Alabama, opened in April 2018.

with authority in part through their connection to artifacts, that position visitors as tourists with only circumscribed access to the past (Blair et al. 26). Memorials can segregate violence, giving visitors the sense that they are not a part of it. Additionally, as a memory aid, a memorial assumes that forgetting is possible and even permissible. When individuals are ready to remember, the memorial will be there. In this way, traditional memorials can give the incorrect impression that the violence they represent is both over and equally forgettable for all audiences. They do not typically represent violence as part of a persistent ecology with pervasive, ongoing effects.

The respective memorial rhetorics around the Moore's Ford lynching and the execution of Charlie Brooks Jr. adopt strategies of critical memorialization to address ongoing, widespread, and culturally sanctioned violence. By "critical memorialization," I mean memorial tactics that critique dominant narratives of the events they memorialize as well as norms of memorialization. The memorials I discuss push back against both the violence they document and the absence of adequate public space for mourning and reckoning, insisting that the violence and mourning are perpetual and expansive. In so doing, they create new affective ecologies, distinct from but marked by the oppressive ecologies from which they emerged. While most of the memorial rhetoric around lynching takes the form of photographs taken by lynch mobs, the Moore's Ford Movement's annual memorial is a day-long event that includes a gathering at an African Baptist Church, visits to the victims' grave sites, and a reenactment of the lynching and events leading up to it. The memorial is a recurring presence, re-marking Monroe, Georgia, and the surrounding area as spaces of violence. The other text examined in this chapter memorializes a kind of loss for which there is even less public space for mourning. The Texas After Violence Project's oral history interviews with Charlie Brooks Jr.'s family serve as an important counter to the severely limited narratives of execution that exist in corrections documents and dominant public rhetoric.[5] By critiquing dominant narratives and making space for loss and mourning, both sets of memorial rhetorics offer distinct modes of belonging that facilitate survival and antiviolence action.

Bringing a lynching and a state-run execution together as events that merit mourning feels risky, because lynchers adapted the rituals and rhetoric of state-run execution to construct lynching as "legitimate" violence (Wood 23–24). As I discussed in chapter 1, antilynching activists had to demonstrate

---

5. Other interviews in the archive serve this purpose as well, but not all are focused on mourning. I discuss the overall impact of the archive below.

that lynching was *not* a necessary punishment for a crime (as lynchers alleged) but, instead, a terrorist performance of white supremacist violence. Similarly, historical and current applications of the death penalty make it clear that state-run execution is not the *necessary* result of the executed person's actions.[6] While Roger Malcolm and Charlie Brooks Jr. committed crimes, those crimes did not cause their deaths or the deaths of Roger Malcolm's family members. Their deaths serve a larger cultural logic: respectively, white supremacy and a version of "retribution" often inflected with white supremacy. This is not to dismiss the value of refuting lynchers' lies about their motivations or in exonerating lynching victims and executed persons. In considering memorial rhetoric, however, it is worth considering which victims are typically shown as worthy of memorialization, and I examine these two texts together in part to that end. Beginning with the premise that no one *must* die in these ways creates more possibilities for mourning and response.

I am also wary of my position in relation to these memorial practices, and that wariness informs my research methodology. I am removed, in several senses, from these sites of mourning. I am white, and the violence I am discussing primarily affects people of color. While I attended the Moore's Ford Memorial for two years, I did not participate in its organization. I have never been affected by the carceral system, and my involvement with the Texas After Violence Project was years ago and minimal. I am aware of the risk of being a tourist to other people's grief, and I have tried to work against that in both gathering evidence and writing this chapter. Rather than positioning myself as the primary authority on these memorial practices, I try to situate each in relation to existing memorial practices and other rhetoric around lynching and execution. I selected these responses to violence because they stand out within these larger bodies of rhetoric. I also use the words of organizers and other involved speakers whenever possible while still treating the performances and interviews as texts with meaning beyond what their creators intended. However, my position still affects my account. I have only lived in the South; its problems (including but not limited to white supremacy) are my problems. Dwelling with these memorial texts felt like a way to continue reckoning with the violence that shapes the spaces and institutions around me, and it was an experience that I found profoundly affecting. My hope is that in

---

6. Whether someone is sentenced to death is dependent on a variety of factors, including the location of the crime, skill of counsel, and race of the victim (American Civil Liberties Union, "Race"). Brooks and his accomplice, Woody Loudres, were tried separately on the same charges because prosecutors could not determine which one of them had shot David Gregory. While both were initially sentenced to death, Loudres's sentence was reduced to forty years after a successful appeal (Reinhold).

attending carefully to these memorial rhetorics and the words and actions of the people involved, I can avoid falling into the complacency that they critique and highlight options for remembrance and resistance that few have had the opportunity to discuss.

First, I will review existing scholarship in memory studies to define strategies of critical memorialization. Memorialization is a powerful form of public rhetoric, but the affective ecologies that memorials produce often obscure the day-to-day work of mourning and survival. I will then discuss how both the Moore's Ford Memorial and the TAVP interviews adapt the affordances of memorial rhetoric to critique structural and cultural violence and suggest new ways of being in a community. I will conclude by briefly exploring the significance of memorial work as a means of responding to violent ecologies.

CRITICAL MEMORIAL PRACTICES

I use the term "critical memorialization" to describe the use of memorial techniques (official, vernacular, or a combination) to create or expose oppositional or alternative affective ecologies. Memorials as affective sites (permanent or ephemeral) constitute communities through a constitution of the past. Unsurprisingly, memorial sites and rituals have often reinforced versions of history that are easily digestible for privileged audiences (Haskins, "Between" 402–3). While memorialization is often oppressive, however, the constitutive power of memorial rhetoric also offers an opportunity. The Moore's Ford and TAVP memorials adapt tropes of dominant memorialization to circulate feelings that are otherwise obscured. The memorial's oppositional strategies also strain at the limits of memorialization, suggesting the need for new ways to address pervasive violence.

My definition of critical memorialization is drawn in part from the texts I discuss, each of which differs significantly from dominant memorial rhetorics. The Moore's Ford Memorial is more obviously a "memorial" in traditional terms. It is an annual event, which I attended in 2015 and 2016. According to my research, it is the only event of its kind, and it remains one of very few lynching memorials of any kind in the United States. It lasts most of a day, beginning in the African Baptist Church in Monroe, Georgia, and ending near the site of the lynching in Walton County. It contains several performed scenes, including the reenactment of the lynching, as well as singing, prayer, personal testimony from community members, and visits to the victims' graves. While more than seventy years have passed since the lynching, organizers Hattie Lawson and Cassandra Green believe that there are Walton County residents who have information about the perpetrators (Ford). By keeping the atrocity in the public eye, the Moore's Ford Movement hopes to inspire community members to share any information they may have about who committed the crime.

The Texas After Violence Project is a nonprofit organization dedicated to documenting the experiences of those affected by the death penalty (and, more recently, the carceral system). The organization conducts oral history interviews with a variety of people connected to the death penalty: activists, corrections officers, attorneys, families and friends of victims, and families and friends of the executed. These interviews are recorded, transcribed, and preserved via the Human Rights Documentation Initiative (HRDI) at the University of Texas. The interviews are publicly available via the HRDI site. Like the Moore's Ford Memorial, these TAVP interviews document the past to affect the present. The project's website explains, "Our mission is to conduct holistic research and build an archive of stories and other records that serve as resources for community dialogue and public policy. We hope these resources will help prevent future violence and promote restorative, nonviolent responses when violence occurs" (*Texas After Violence*).

Both the Moore's Ford Memorial and the TAVP interviews deploy the power of memorialization to critical ends. Rhetoricians have long cited commemorative practices as powerful sites of epideictic rhetoric (Haskins, *Popular Memories* 9–12). While, as I noted in chapter 1, epideictic rhetoric was traditionally devalued as "empty show," more recent rhetorical scholarship positions it as essential for establishing the "basic codes of value and belief by which a society or culture lives" (Haskins, *Popular Memories* 9; Walker 9). Memorials communicate the "right" way to feel about the event they memorialize and, in doing so, make claims about "how to *be* in a community" (Hartelius and Asenas 369). Monuments to Confederate leaders, for example, reinforce an understanding of Southerners as white, male, and hopelessly devoted to their region. These memorials typically elide that devotion to the "Lost Cause" is inextricable from chattel slavery, but the white supremacist message is clear in both the existence of the memorials and their strategic placement (Parks). It is this epideictic function, Haskins suggests, that may lead marginalized rhetors to see dominant memorial forms (for example, historical plays, statues, and museums) as resources for transformative claims about citizenship (Haskins, *Popular Memories* 12). By adapting these forms, rhetors can offer alternative modes of being in community while still harnessing the rhetorical force of a memorial object or performance.

The adaptability of memorial forms informs my choice to focus on critical memorial *practices* rather than critical memorials. Rhetors may use different memorial forms—for example, a live performance or an archival interview—to critique dominant narratives to similar effect. Additionally, the categorization of memorial "types" elides the complexity of many contemporary memorials. Memory studies scholars once emphasized the contrast between "official" memory, typically based in archives and emphasizing straightforward narrative, and "vernacular" memory, based in community practice and assuming ephemeral forms. This division corresponds to another: the division between "archival" and "lived" memory, or what Diane Taylor calls "the archive and the repertoire." Archival memory, long the dominant form for official public representation of history, relies on objects (like the tools of ancient people) and places (like battlegrounds or museums) as tools for accessing the past. These objects and places emerge as and remain significant based on existing understandings of authority and authenticity. For that reason, the objects that archivists gathered "were typically products of intellectual and artistic elites rather than illiterate artisans and performers" (Haskins, "Between" 402), and the memory places that visitors deem credible appear to them as neutral windows into the past (Ott, Blair, Dickenson 26–27). Vernacular or lived memory, on the other hand, owes its persistence to transmission from one generation to another, often through ephemeral forms like performance. Haskins notes that vernacular memory practices often have a substantially different logic than archival memory practices, emphasizing "non-hierarchical, sometimes subversive symbolism and . . . egalitarian interaction and participation" ("Between" 403). They are grounded in community responsibility and, necessarily, loss and transformation. As Taylor describes, performances "are, in a sense, always in situ: intelligible in the framework of the immediate environment and issues surrounding them" (3). While a performance may carry the past with it, the meaning of those past events may change over time, even if the performance does not.

Contemporary memorial practices collapse these distinctions, often drawing on both archival and ephemeral resources to create an interactive and open-ended version of the past. For example, the Vietnam Veterans Memorial in Washington, DC, designed by Maya Lin, is a permanent memorial that invites participation and, in its reflective surface, visually connects past and present (Haskins, "Between" 404). The Moore's Ford Memorial and the Texas After Violence Project archives similarly complicate these divisions. Neither could be called "official" in the word's traditional memory studies sense, as they are neither top-down representations from the state nor the dominant narratives of their respective losses. Instead, they mix archival and lived methods, constructing memorials that are both attached to spaces and objects and produced through community experience. While the Moore's Ford Memorial is a performance, it relies on static memory places (the site of the lynching, grave sites, the courthouse) as prostheses for accessing the past. The memorial is also recorded and posted online, creating an archive of the event available even to those who did not attend. While the TAVP interviews are part of an archive, their oral history format documents ephemeral lived experience. The interviewers and the archive treat all of the stories that interview subjects share as true and relevant, rather than pushing for a singular version of what it means to be affected by the death penalty. Neither memorial text is reducible to one form or the other; rather, each makes use of different facets of archival and lived memory to critique dominant narratives of violence.

Similarly, the form in use does not necessarily indicate whether a memorial will be critical of dominant narratives. A more "vernacular" form does not ensure that the memorial in question will disrupt existing structures of power. As McDonald and Smith note, videos produced and circulated by soldiers from the Iraq War may be "vernacular," but that alone does not make them critical. While their form, source, and participatory options are more democratic than a state-constructed memorial statue, the videos also reinforce many of the problematic values (racism, toxic masculinity) that fuel war. Even relatively traditional static memorials may not provide the same kind of evidence or experience that we might associate with "official" memory—for example, if they include atypical subjects, are structured in an unusual manner, or refuse closure. For example, the Civil Rights Memorial in Montgomery, Alabama, is placed in a well-trafficked space so that passersby have to choose to confront or ignore it. Even as a static object, it performs the disruptive practices of peaceful protest that activists used during the civil rights movement (Blair and Michel 40). The memorial resists a touristic rhetoric that encourages separation of spectator and history.

In examining the Moore's Ford Memorial and the TAVP interviews, I focus on three characteristics of critical memorialization: contesting dominant narratives, making space for grief, and constructing alternative communities. These characteristics are not exhaustive; there are other ways in which memorial practices can be critical. These features, however, mark the memorials as radical when compared to the violent rhetorical ecologies from which they emerge and dominant practices of memorialization. I begin by discussing how the Moore's Ford Memorial adapts lynching's violent spectacle to create a new ecology of grief and survival. The Moore's Ford Memorial's movement through a mostly rural Southern space marks the landscape with lynching's violence and the community's mourning. I will then discuss the TAVP interviews with the family of Charlie Brooks Jr. These interviews are inherently radical in that they provide public space for an executed person's family members to discuss their grief. Additionally, the family's discussion of their experiences with the carceral system offers critiques of structural and cultural violence far beyond what typical narratives of executions offer.

MOORE'S FORD: REMAKING LYNCHING'S SPECTACLE
Placing Moore's Ford in Context

Unlike state-run execution, Southern spectacle lynching has a well-established public archive. As I noted in chapter 1, lynchers often photographed their victims, sometimes posing next to them as if they were hunting trophies (Wood 75). The most prominent lynching archive is composed of these photographs taken by lynchers, recontextualized in books and exhibits to highlight the horrors of such routine violence.[7] While a contemporary audience is likely to view these images differently than the audience that produced them, the story they can tell, particularly about Black resilience and mourning, is limited. These photographs reproduce the Black body as an object of the gaze and a source of feeling and information. It is this evidentiary function that made lynching photographs essential for antilynching activism, but their continued prevalence means that many are still viewing lynching primarily (and literally) from perpetrators' points of view (Mitchell 6). That insight into white supremacy is shocking for some, but the photographs may retraumatize viewers already haunted by white brutality (Wolters 418). In addition to these concerns, lynching photographs elide a great deal about how communities experienced and responded to lynching (Mitchell 4). While lynching photographs can highlight some of the horrors of mob violence, they do not show the victim's life beyond the frame, nor the family's and community's mourning. To do so would make these photographs useless for their original function: spreading and celebrating white supremacy.

Turn-of-the century lynching dramas, perhaps the closest historical analog to the Moore's Ford Memorial, offer a different but under-discussed lynching archive. In her landmark study, *Living with Lynching: African American Lynching Plays, Performance, and Citizenship, 1890–1930*, Koritha Mitchell explains the affirmative work of these plays. Lynching dramas did not typically dramatize the lynching itself. Instead, they showed African American families at home, persevering and succeeding in a hostile world (2). In showing these everyday practices of survival, lynching dramas functioned as "a continuation of African Americans' self-affirmation" (4). The plays resisted

---

7. For a prominent example of this archive, see Allen.

white supremacy, but that was not their only task (7–8). They thus value different kinds of evidence (evidence of African American love and resilience in family life) and, unlike lynching photographs, make a clear statement about how African Americans can survive. These short plays were widely published and set in African American homes, so families and friends could easily stage small-scale performances (14). These performances reinforced the Black home and family as sites of strength in the face of white supremacists eager to tear them down.

While, unlike lynching plays, the Moore's Ford Memorial *does* dramatize a lynching, it also refuses to reduce lynching's impact to direct bodily harm. Instead, it refutes lynchers' narratives of crime and punishment by emphasizing the structural origins of direct violence. The memorial situates the lynching in the broader context of white supremacist rhetoric and voter suppression to decenter an initial act of violence—Malcolm stabbing Hester—as a cause. Rather than reproducing the lynchers' narrative, the Moore's Ford Movement echoes the rhetorical framing that emerged shortly after the lynching and made it a prominent example of ongoing racial violence in the South. By including white supremacist activities that preceded the lynching and the civil rights movement that followed it, the memorial shows the lynching as part of a larger history of racial violence and Black resistance.

While less well-known today, the Moore's Ford lynching received national news coverage in 1946 and was one of two events that shaped President Harry Truman's decision to create the President's Committee on Civil Rights (Childers 572). Specific qualities of the Moore's Ford lynching and its subsequent rhetorical framing helped it to become a "focusing incident" in national conversations about civil rights (574). Racial violence was common in 1946, but a "mass lynching," as the murders were described in the news, was unusual (579). Framing the murders as a lynching also positioned them as "a violation of the rule of law," enabling people to think of it as "a direct affront to the nation's democratic foundations" (Childers 583, 584). News and editorial coverage of the lynching also tied it to larger problems with white supremacist rhetoric in the South, specifically the rhetoric of gubernatorial candidate Eugene Talmadge. Talmadge, who won the gubernatorial primary just days before the lynching, had "campaigned openly on a white supremacist platform" (584). At least one commentator, Eustace Gay, stated that Talmadge was "as culpable [for the murders] as if he had taken actual part in them" (qtd. in Childers 584; note omitted). This narrative created a synecdoche in which the lynchings and Talmadge became emblematic of the racial hatred in Georgia and the South overall (586).

The reenactment portion of the memorial reproduces features of this framing and, in doing so, disrupts narratives that isolate the suffering Black body as an object of the gaze and a totalizing source of information. Two additions to the basic narrative connect the Moore's Ford lynching to the white supremacist rhetoric that preceded it and the civil rights movement that followed. In 2015, the reenactment portion of the memorial included the following scenes: two opening monologues, Malcolm fighting with Dorothy and assaulting Hester, a re-creation of one of Talmadge's "stump" speeches, Loy Harrison picking up Malcolm from jail, a white mob removing the couples from the car, the lynching itself, and two post-lynching scenes. Talmadge's scene, which occurs immediately before Loy Harrison arrives to bail Malcolm out of jail, links the lynching both to Talmadge as an individual and to white supremacist efforts to disenfranchise people of color. The scene took place at the courthouse in Monroe, formerly the jail where Malcolm was held. The actor playing Talmadge walked to the front of the courthouse from a side parking lot, trailed by enthusiastic supporters in period dress. He gave a brief speech emphasizing the importance of white supremacy in Georgia, and his audience applauded. During the speech, the memorial attendees were across the street, separate from the scene. Organizers emphasized that for realism, the audience would need to stay back. Only the crew recording the reenactment could get closer.

The inclusion of Talmadge's speech destabilizes narratives of crime and punishment by positioning lynching as part of a broader campaign of oppression. Significantly, the scenes at the courthouse are the most publicly visible of the reenactment. It would be hard to accidentally encounter the reenactment of the lynching itself because of its rural setting, but passersby seemed to notice the group of people in old-fashioned clothing waving Confederate flags in downtown Monroe. The Moore's Ford Movement's Facebook page, one of few online resources for information about the organization and the reenactment, also emphasizes this connection between political power and racial violence. A post by former state representative Tyrone Brooks, chair of the Moore's Ford Movement, describes the lynching as a "Voting Rights Massacre," situating it in relation to other acts of violence that occurred after the election in Georgia on July 17, 1946. The inclusion of voting rights in both this performative element and the surrounding rhetoric suggests that the political context for the lynching is vitally important. Lynching, as this framing shows, was not just an act of personal hatred, but also a means to achieving white supremacist political goals.

Another addition appears at the end of the reenactment and links the Moore's Ford lynching to the civil rights movement that followed it. During the 2015 reenactment, the actors playing the victims were lying in the grass, having already been shot by the lynch mob, and a man dressed in white emerged from the woods behind them and sang "A Change Is Gonna Come." Sam Cooke recorded that song in 1964, more than fifteen years after the Moore's Ford lynching, and it became an anthem for the civil rights movement (NPR Staff). It is a song of pain and hope, and its inclusion in the reenactment links the lynching to the activist movement that would come to prominence shortly after. It also adds a note of hope after the reenactment's most harrowing portion, suggesting that while this crime remains unsolved and racial violence still proliferates, change is still a possibility.

The reenactment's narrative structure also disrupts causality. Performers staged the first part of the reenactment, in which Roger Malcolm stabs Barney Hester, in the African Baptist Church. This decision, organizers noted, was partially logistical; the actual location of the stabbing, Hester Farm, was a relatively long drive for a short scene. Regardless of reason, the result of this choice was that rather than moving directly from Malcolm stabbing Hester to Malcolm's removal from jail and subsequent death, the reenactment moved from violence to mourning to violence. After this first portion of the reenactment, attendees left the church to visit the grave sites of Mae Murray Dorsey, Roger Malcolm, and Dorothy Dorsey Malcolm and George Dorsey. It was not until after that journey that attendees saw the next portion of the reenactment. This choice also moved the stabbing from the hostile territory of "Hesterville" to a space of community and forgiveness. As I will discuss below, mourning is an essential part of the Moore's Ford Memorial, and this choice of context suggests acceptance of Malcolm as a victim despite his violent act.

These narrative choices emphasize the historical importance of the Moore's Ford lynching as both an example of continuing racial violence and a catalyst for action against it. The version of the lynching that it provides, then, is distinct from the useful but still limited narratives of lynching photographs. By situating the reenactment of the lynching among references to other historical practices and events, the organizers indicate that lynching was about more than the suffering bodies of its victims. Instead, that suffering was part of a larger campaign of violence, as well as the various campaigns of resistance that Black communities waged against it. The lynching's direct violence is embedded in a white supremacist ecology. This context contributes to the reenactment's broader memorial function. As Owen and Ehrenhaus explain, the memorial functions "metonymically, to reference all race lynching since emancipation" (88). By evoking the structural and cultural violence and resistance that preceded and followed the lynching, the memorial allows viewers to reckon with past and continuing violence through the lens of Moore's Ford.

Expanding the Site of Violence and Mourning

The Moore's Ford Memorial's use of place constructs a tension between lived and archival memory. The memorial is attentive to place but refuses to take on a single memory place as adequate, instead remaking large swaths of territory as sites of mourning. The temporary importance granted these otherwise unmarked or minimally marked spaces keeps the duty of remembrance in the community and highlights the gap between what happened and what remains. The memorial's movement and expansiveness also suggests that loss cannot be contained and instead permeates and defines the surrounding area.

While memory places are typically static, movement is a key feature of the Moore's Ford Memorial. Both the 2015 and 2016 events involved a significant amount of time spent in a motorcade, particularly compared with the time spent watching performances or talking at the motorcade's various destinations. In 2015, attendees spent the morning in the church, singing songs, listening to various speakers, and seeing the first portion of the reenactment. Attendees then returned to their cars and traveled in a motorcade to five additional locations: three grave sites, the former jail in Monroe, and the approximate site of the murders. This journey took us out of Monroe and into the surrounding county. Upon arriving at the last site, attendees parked their cars on a distant side road so as not to impede the reenactment, which includes the lynch mob stopping the car carrying Malcolm and his companions. Attendees watched that portion of the reenactment while standing on the side of the road, then moved into an adjacent field to watch the reenactment of the murders.

Unsurprisingly, the spaces to which the motorcade travels bear few or no references to the Moore's Ford lynching. Even the lynching's historical marker, like many of its kind, is a significant distance (2.4 miles) from the site of the murders, and the rural space gives no other indication of what happened there. The other sites are without markers that would distinguish them as "historical" in the way of a memory place; rather, they appear as ongoing sites of everyday life. The grave of Mae Murray Dorsey, the first that the motorcade visits, is in a small wooded area adjacent to a parking lot. One of the organizers mentioned that other graves in the area had been paved over. It would be easy for a passerby to miss that there are graves there at all, and no information is provided about Dorsey's connection to the lynching.[8] The grave sites of Roger Malcolm and George Dorsey and Dorothy Dorsey Malcolm (the latter

---

8. While there is no historical marker at the site, the inscription on Mae Murray Dorsey's tombstone alludes to her violent death: "May your suffering be redeemed in brotherly love."

two buried together), while in more visible and well-tended graveyards, are otherwise ordinary spaces of mourning, and the courthouse, while located in a historic downtown, does not advertise that the man who would deliver Roger Malcolm to his death picked him up from that location. There is no evidence of exceptional attention paid to any of these spaces, other than the temporary presence of memorial attendees.

Placing this performance in these otherwise unmarked spaces highlights the dual nature of lynching as both spectacular and quotidian. While some lynchings attracted crowds of thousands or tens of thousands, many, like the Moore's Ford lynching, were smaller affairs. Even large lynchings, while marked in various ways as "special occasions," were deeply ordinary. The South lagged behind the North in outlawing public executions, so many Southerners had seen someone hang as part of official state proceedings (Wood 24). The idea that families might enjoy a picnic while watching someone die was not yet unusual. Additionally, the total lack of political will to prosecute lynching offenders meant that nothing in a community had to change after a lynching. As I described in chapter 1, lynching reiterated existing ideas about race and gender in the South to maintain a white supremacist status quo in a post-Reconstruction era. Each lynching committed with impunity constituted brutal violence as a normal part of Southern life.

The remapping of these spaces through persistent movement also creates an expanded site of mourning and responsibility. While the reenactment attaches value to the site of the lynching itself, the sites of kidnapping, burial, and contemporary community engagement are all significant as well. Apart from typical grave markers, these are almost all unmarked sites; someone stumbling upon these graveyards or other spaces would be unlikely to find information about the Moore's Ford lynching. Through this repeated reconstruction of space, the reenactment suggests a palimpsestic version of the area in which seemingly innocuous spaces hold traces of violence and grief. The result is a narrative of mourning and causation that goes beyond both the site of the murders and the murders themselves. There is more to mourning this loss and addressing this injustice, the reenactment suggests, than a single memory place could hold.

The loss is neither separate nor static, as it would be if confined to a museum or formally designated memorial site. Unlike lynching photographs, the memorial brings audience members into the space of loss while also suggesting that this loss cannot be reined in. The loss pops up, perhaps as a partial memory of seeing people gathered in an overgrown graveyard or through stories community members tell each other as they walk by the former jail. The reenactment's use of space suggests a community forever entangled with loss, but to varying degrees and in different and sometimes unpredictable ways. Just as lynching forged a white supremacist identity, the memorial builds a shared identity through what was left behind, including material traces and persistent mourning.

Trauma, Survival, and Care

The Moore's Ford Memorial uses a variation of lynching's epideictic form to create an oppositional community. While lynchers solidified white supremacy by constructing themselves as the masters of racial violence, the community of the Moore's Ford Memorial is defined in part by vulnerability. The foregrounding of violence and mourning suggests that to be in this community means to be subject to violence and to try to survive in spite of it. Several features of the memorial highlight appropriate modes of community membership. Portions of the performance foreground resistance in spite of risks and the toll that ongoing resistance can take on community members. In placing these experiences of violence and mourning in a regional context, the memorial also shows the degree to which Black experience has been excluded from "Southernness," in part (but not exclusively) through the circulation of lynching as a definitive Southern ritual.

The memorial's first two performances illustrate ways of being in a community continually besieged by violence. The reenactment begins with two monologues by actors placed within the church pews rather than backstage with the other actors. The first actor was an older woman, walking with a cane. She delivered her monologue while walking slowly from the back row to the front of the church and back. This character was not identified as a historical figure but rather embodied a communal pain and desire for justice. Her speech emphasized the ongoing pain that the community experiences and the need for someone to come forward with the truth. It included the refrain, picked up by the audience, "No justice, no peace." The second actor, an older man, did represent a historical figure: Lamar Howard, a young man beaten for testifying about the lynching before a grand jury. The actor portraying Howard did not, as the first actor did, return to the back of the church. After recounting the horrors of the beating he experienced, Howard instead sunk into a pew at the front of the church, as if he could walk no further.

These additions foreground the impact of violence on the community and suggest that being in the community means feeling pain and demanding justice in spite of it. Both of these opening monologues suggest that violence and resistance are wearying. The first speaker's refrain of "No justice, no peace," however, indicates that community members must continue to move forward in spite of exhaustion and danger. Connecting this weariness to members of an older generation—and positioning those speakers first—underlines respect for prior generations' struggles and a need for younger community members to continue their work. If resistance is exhausting, then no one can be expected to carry its burden forever. In this way, the opening monologues suggest that community members are bound to each other. It is a claim that the memorial's overall project reiterates. In seeking justice for the victims of the Moore's Ford Memorial, even decades after the fact, the Moore's Ford Movement carries on the resistant acts of earlier generations.

A portion of the lynching scene also highlights the risks and importance of resistance. As Childers notes, the only account of the lynching itself is from Loy Harrison, and there are reasons to distrust his claims.[9] The reenactment retains a key detail from Harrison's account, however: the claim that the lynch mob was only initially planning to kill Roger Malcolm and decided to murder both couples after Dorothy recognized a member of the mob (Owen and Ehrenhaus 76). Given that lynchers typically framed their murders as punishment for a crime, it is possible that Harrison added that detail to give a better impression of the mob as "civilized" men.[10] In the context of the reenactment, however, the moment of recognition represents Dorothy as brave in the face of near-certain death. Her willingness to name perpetrators of violence also contributes to the memorial's argument to the surrounding community. If Dorothy was prepared to name names, even when she was in mortal danger, then community members with information about the lynching should be willing to share what they know.

Perhaps most important for its social justice mission, an ethic of care inheres in the structure and performance of the memorial, suggesting that being in the community involves a balance of trauma and collective recovery. The beginning in the church, in which many community members and organizers share their knowledge of and experience with the Moore's Ford lynching, anchors the memorial in a shared experience of listening. Owen and Ehrenhaus describe the speeches in the 2008 memorial in detail, noting that many speakers discussed trauma associated with the lynching. Ariel Young Sullivan, daughter of the funeral director who prepared the victims' bodies, described how their mutilation and the lack of justice affected her father, explaining that "justice for the Malcolms and the Dorseys [was] my father's

---

9. See Childers 577–78.

10. For more on the rhetoric of masculinity, civilization, and defenses of lynching, see chapter 1.

dream" (qtd. in Owen and Ehrenhaus 81). In addition to speeches about the lynching's effects, the 2015 memorial featured performances from community members, including two self-identified veterans who performed a Christian rap and a child whose mother introduced her before she sang. Making room for these performances, which were not directly related to the Moore's Ford lynching, indicates the importance of varied community response. After the reenactment, attendees gather to talk and share a meal. Bookending the event in this way acknowledges the potential trauma of watching violence reenacted and the need for self-care in social justice work.

The memorial's performance both creates and reinforces a community that is not limited to the memorial's duration. While the memorial uses a reenactment of violence as an anchor to bring community members together, it also complicates a straightforward narrative of victimization. The memorial emphasizes the affective horror of the lynching and the ongoing vulnerability to violence that Black Americans face; attendees "experience the past viscerally through the liminal space that performance opens" (Ehrenhaus and Owen 86). Through its emphasis on resistance and care, however, it also suggests a way forward that photographic representations of lynching's horrors do not. A lynching photograph provides evidence of violence, against which the viewer is (presumably) supposed to act. The Moore's Ford Memorial constitutes that community in action, bringing them together to witness, mourn, and imagine a different future. Particularly in its annual repetition, the memorial argues for and constitutes a community that is persistent and resistant, despite occupying a space that is defined by violence.

THE TAVP ARCHIVES AND THE IMPACT OF CARCERAL VIOLENCE

Ecologies of Crime and Punishment

The Texas Department of Criminal Justice (TDCJ) offers what we might consider an "official" narrative of Charlie Brooks Jr.'s alleged crime. The "summary of incident" states:

> Brooks went to a car lot under the pretense of wanting to test drive a car. A mechanic accompanied him on the drive. Brooks stopped to pick up a co-defendant. The mechanic was put in the trunk of the car. Brooks and his co-defendant went to a motel. The mechanic was brought out of the trunk and taken into a motel room. The mechanic was bound with coat hangers,

gagged with adhesive tape, and shot in the head, causing his death. Brooks and the co-defendant fled the scene. ("Offender Information")

The narrative here is minimal. There is no room for context, and motive is not mentioned. As the passive voice in this narrative indicates, prosecutors never determined whether it was Brooks or his accomplice, Woody Loudres, who shot the victim (Reinhold). An article about Brooks's execution in the *New York Times* offers more detail. The article describes the lethal injection process, witness responses, and Brooks's last words. It concludes with a brief profile of Brooks, noting that he was "generally considered bright and personable," came from a "comparatively well-off family in Fort Worth," and "married his high-school sweetheart and fathered two sons, now in college" (Reinhold). While it includes more detail than the TDCJ site, the article still leaves gaps in the story. Beyond a brief recounting of the crime, it does not provide a narrative of how this "bright and personable" individual came to be on death row.

Public narratives of execution tend to be sparse, more along the lines of the "offender information" than even the slightly expanded context that *New York Times* offers.[11] Most people in the United States never have direct contact with the death penalty. Instead, they encounter it through retentionist and abolitionist rhetoric, stories of egregious crimes and botched executions, and popular culture representations. These representations are often anchored in a retributive logic. Public defenses of the death penalty rely heavily on the condemned person's responsibility for her actions and the community's responsibility to punish her (Sarat, *When the State* 210). This narrative allows for a "relatively precise moral calculus" in which a jury weighs the severity of a crime (and thus the "evil" of the perpetrator) and chooses a proportional punishment. This version of punishment does not accommodate structural and cultural factors that contribute to violence and that may affect sentencing (214). Instead, punishment is rendered simple: A bad person commits a crime, and a responsible community punishes that person. As I discussed in chapter 2, abolitionist rhetoric does not always contest this framework. By emphasizing "cruel and unusual" punishment and the exoneration of the innocent, even anti–death penalty rhetors can suggest that a clean retributive exchange is possible. These critiques raise questions about specific applications but leave a violent rhetorical ecology intact.

Interviews with Charlie Brooks Jr.'s family expand the narrative around the death penalty by situating Brooks's crime, conviction, and execution in

---

11. National coverage for an execution is unusual. It is likely that Brooks's execution received an article in the *New York Times* because Brooks was the first person to be executed by lethal injection.

relation to racism, drugs, and the limits of the legal system. The TAVP archive includes interviews with Joyce Easley, Brooks's ex-wife and friend, and their two sons, Keith and Derrek Brooks. While the family members seem to believe that Brooks committed at least one crime, their discussion of the circumstances of his trial indicates that his guilt or innocence was largely irrelevant. Instead, the interviews suggest that personal prejudice and structural violence contributed to Brooks's conviction. Keith and Derrek, for example, both mention the possibility of prejudice on the jury. Keith states that Fort Worth was segregated until 1974, just two years before Brooks's trial. He explains that "the bitterness of desegregation was still fresh in those who didn't agree with it, which probably was a majority of those on that panel too—On the jury" (K. Brooks, Interview 1). Similarly, Derrek expresses concern that Brooks might have had an all-white jury, noting that all-white juries were common in Dallas and Fort Worth at the time. He states, "I think an all White jury is biased. I think an all White jury sees a Black person and says 'Guilty.' They don't give a damn. If he isn't guilty of that, he's guilty of something" (D. Brooks, Interview 2). Derrek notes that he is not sure if Brooks had an all-white jury, but that he would "bet a hundred million dollars" that Brooks did (D. Brooks, Interview 2). His expression of near-certainty constructs racism as a key part of the judicial process and a likely explanation for why Brooks was sentenced to death.

Other portions of the interviews describe how racism is more subtly entrenched in standards of evidence. Describing the outcome of Brooks's trial, Derrek explains,

> One of the flaws was eyewitness testimony because they're saying—and I'm sorry to say this—but a lot of people feel like Black people look alike. So if you have eyewitness testimony, you got five Black guys, "Oh it was him" or "Maybe it was him" or "Probably could have been him." They don't know. (D. Brooks, Interview 2)

Joyce makes a similar claim, noting that "all races, all whites look alike and all blacks, and all that. But how would you identify a person if you did not know that person, and it is just for a second or two, or maybe thirty minutes" (Easley). In these statements, racism is both malicious and structural. In Derrek's account, misrecognition sounds variously accidental and resigned: "Oh it was him," "Maybe it was him," and "Probably could have been him." Derrek's statement that "a lot of people feel like Black people look alike" also suggests that misrecognition is a choice motivated by personal racial prejudice. Joyce's critique is more structural, with racist misrecognition as a specific manifestation of a larger problem. Joyce indicates that identifying an unfamiliar person is always challenging, and that problem is worse when the person is of a different race. For that reason, eyewitness testimony is inherently flawed, particularly in cases that involve a witness and a defendant of different races.

The family's articulation of possible racism in Brooks's trial and in the legal system complicates the "moral calculus" of capital punishment, as well as the supposed victory of post-*Furman* reforms. Since Brooks was the first person executed in Texas after *Gregg v. Georgia* reestablished the death penalty, it would ostensibly follow that his sentencing would be free of the racial bias that tainted pre-*Furman* capital cases. In *Furman v. Georgia*, the US Supreme Court found that Georgia and Texas lacked clear criteria for death eligibility and were thus administering the death penalty in a cruel and unusual manner. As Justice Potter Stewart explained in his concurring opinion, "These death sentences are cruel and unusual in the same way that being struck by lightning is cruel and unusual," because many people were sentenced to death for crimes for which others received life in prison. Stewart goes on to say that if there is any basis for why some individuals receive death sentences and others do not, "it is the constitutionally impermissible basis of race" (US Supreme Court, *Furman*). Post-*Furman* reforms clarified the criteria by which individuals could be sentenced to death, but the potential for racial discrimination remained. The racism that Joyce and Derrek describe is entangled with what counts as "evidence" and is thus harder to address through minor procedural changes.

Along with the racism in the legal system, the family also describes how drugs transformed their community and Brooks himself. Both Joyce and Derrek identify an external origin for the drug problem in their community. Derrek explains that drugs were not always present in his neighborhood and suggests that their sudden availability may have been strategic: "So we feel like, we can't say who, but you know, upper, upper powers that be, would flood the Black and Mexican neighborhoods, you know, to keep the people down, to keep them from progress, from moving forward" (D. Brooks, Interview 1). Joyce describes the transformation in similar terms but locates its origins in the Vietnam War:

> And I think it started mainly from the Vietnam War. When those guys came back and they had been in the opium patches and the trees were already growing with the stuff on it. And so they just was told to smoke it, because it would calm you, which it did.
>
> But it became something that, apparently made them feel at ease in your mind. So who don't want to feel ease at the mind? So you go, but then it

started being homemade, chemically made. And it ruined a lot of people, good people, very, very good people.

While Derrek describes intentional and direct harm through drug distribution, the structural violence that Joyce describes is subtle but no less harmful. In each case, individuals harm communities of color by encouraging drug use and making drugs available. While Joyce does not attribute intent as explicitly in her narrative, linking the heroin epidemic to the Vietnam War could be read as an indictment of structural violence. Without the Vietnam War, this narrative implies, soldiers would not have had access to or need for opium.

Like the family's discussions of racism, their emphasis on the structural violence of a heroin epidemic broadens the narrative of Brooks's crime and execution and disrupts the moral calculus of the death penalty. There are layers of culpability in the family's narrative. If Brooks is not solely responsible for his alleged crime, then executing him cannot constitute adequate retribution, but the other sites of responsibility—the Vietnam War, segregation, personal and structural racism—are much harder to incorporate into a retributive criminal proceeding. The family's testimony suggests that the process could be improved with policy changes: for example, ensuring representative jury demographics and rejecting eyewitness testimony. But procedural changes would not address all of the issues they raise. Different procedures for criminal trials would not erase the trauma of the Vietnam War, disproportionately inflicted upon the poor and people of color, nor would it remove drugs from Black neighborhoods. As I discussed in chapter 3, a retributive system is simply not equipped to handle these forms of violence; they are outside of what the law can name. In this context, then, the additional details about Brooks's addiction mark both loss and the law's inadequacy in addressing structural violence.

Execution in Everyday Life

The TAVP interviews with Brooks's family members also remake the space of violence by showing how an execution affected people beyond the victim, perpetrator, and victim's family. The interviews show a landscape of execution effects instead of the few key scenes (crime, sentencing, execution) dictated by a crime-and-punishment narrative. The moments discussed below expand those scenes to show members of Brooks's family experiencing Brooks's crime, imprisonment, and execution from the periphery. These scenes introduce new places—a home, a college campus—to a narrative that does not usually include places of everyday life, particularly as they are occupied by families of executed persons. As the interview subjects indicate, capital punishment's effects extend beyond prison walls to structure quotidian experiences.

The family's descriptions of events that happened before the execution show life variously affected by Brooks's incarceration and offer glimpses of action outside the frame of retributive narratives. One such incident, which appears in both Derrek's and Keith's respective interviews, shows how family life was disrupted by Brooks's arrest. The following excerpt is from Derrek, answering the interviewer's question about when he first knew his father was in jail:

> I specifically remember me and Keith and my grandmother, Big Momma, we were there and it was his [Charlie Brooks Jr.'s] birthday. And I remember that morning him asking her, "Momma, I need some money." And she said, "I don't have none," and she told us, "I'm gonna give your dad some money, but it's gonna be in the evening, when he comes back; we're gonna surprise him with a birthday cake and give him the money." And I remember, he never came back. I think I was told that he committed some crime—robbery or something—and got caught, and I remember it being 8, 9, 10 o'clock at night and we're thinking he's gonna show up any minute. Cake's right there, we're there, we're excited, and he never came home. And he just never came home. (K. Brooks, Interview 2)

Through its hints of possible alternative history, this story marks a loss. The image of Brooks's mother and sons waiting for him could have resolved differently, and, as Derrek notes, the family expected that it would. When Brooks does not return, the alternate version of the family's evening becomes impossible, but its loss lingers. Keith explains that the cake itself lingered as well. While Brooks never returned home, Brooks's mother put the cake in the freezer, where it remained until her death (K. Brooks, Interview 2).

Like the story of the cake, which places the family apart from but still affected by the crime, the family members' accounts of the execution show how they experienced a violent loss from the periphery. Here, it is especially clear that there is little space for family of the executed in narratives and practices of execution. Joyce, Derrek, and Keith describe being excluded from most of the process leading up to Brooks's death. Derrek explains that since Brooks had been given several stays of execution, "on the final execution date, our family was thinking, 'No, you know, they're not gonna execute him, because we've been through this, time and again.'" When Joyce, Derrek, and Keith drove to the Huntsville Unit where Brooks was being executed, they were told that Brooks did not want his sons to see his execution, so they waited in a room near the witness chamber. Derrek describes how they knew the execution was over:

> So, we were in the room and the time went by, at 12:05 or so we knew it had happened. They had did it and all the witnesses came out and they all had sad faces. Some of them couldn't look at us in our face; they were looking down. And we were just upset. . . . Keith threw a chair. (D. Brooks, Interview 3)

Joyce describes the experience of learning about and then attending the execution similarly. She explains, "I'm thinking, we're talking on the phone and all. They're going to get a stay, they're going to get a stay. And then I saw on TV, that he's fixing to go to death—they're fixing to kill him." She goes on:

> So we went down there and true enough it happened. . . . We all looked at our watches. But like I said, the lights dimmed kind of like. And I said, not to them, I said, "Well, it must be over." By this time he [Keith] kicked a chair, he threw a chair, or something. And this officer says, "It's alright ya'll, it's going to be alright." People were very sympathetic. They were very, very sympathetic. (Easley)

As the end of Joyce's narrative indicates, the family members do not describe deliberate cruelty, but rather a structural exclusion. Some of this exclusion is Brooks's apparent choice, as the corrections officer stated that Brooks did not want his sons to see his execution. The indeterminate space to which they are relegated, however, exemplifies the lack of public space, even in a carceral context, for execution's extensive impact.[12] The family members are affected, but they are not witnesses, so their relationship to the scene of execution is undefined. This structural exclusion is enhanced by the fact that there is no clear external sign that the execution has taken place; while Joyce interprets the lights dimming as that sign, no one tells the family members what to watch for. They are ushered out of the prison shortly after the execution, before the victim's family emerges from the witness area (K. Brooks, Interview 3).

---

12. Other family members were allowed to witness the execution. Brooks's girlfriend, Vanessa Sapp, witnessed his execution, and Keith stated that he thought his cousin Geno was present as well, but in a different room than the victim's family (K. Brooks, Interview 3).

Discussing the aftermath of the execution, the family highlights the challenges of mourning an executed loved one. Both Keith and Derrek were in college when Brooks was executed, and Derrek missed class to return home. Derrek recounts explaining his absences to his professor:

> I remember coming back and my teacher goes, "Uh, Mr. Brooks, where you been?" And I said, "Well, my dad was executed by the state of Texas." And she just looked at me, and—cause it was on the news—but I don't know if they knew that it was me. But then when they heard it they was like "Oh my god, I'm so sorry. You know, that was your dad, we didn't know that was your dad, I'm so sorry." How do you comfort a person? You just say "I'm sorry" and we just . . . class as usual, books as usual, and life just went on. Just went on. (D. Brooks, Interview 1)

Derrek's story shows the lack of public space for addressing the grief that can affect the families of executed persons. As Derrek's question, "How do you comfort a person?," suggests, there is no script for this kind of loss, particularly within the scenes of Derrek's upwardly mobile life. While it is often challenging to comfort someone who is mourning, Derrek's story suggests that the professor was surprised and, while kind, could not possibly understand his circumstances.

Keith also describes the struggle of discussing Brooks's execution. When the interviewer, Rebecca Lorins, asks Keith if he talks to his daughter about what happened to Brooks, he describes a complicated situation. He notes that Texas high schools teach about Brooks, since he was the first person executed by lethal injection. He goes on:

> But just for the last twelve years there's not been a need or opportunity to tell my daughter. But because I knew this was about to come out, I talked to her about it. I let her read some articles about it, and I could see just the stress and the sadness that came over her, to realize that this happened to her father's father. Let alone her own grandfather, was executed. (K. Brooks, Interview 3)

The narrative of Brooks's death thus appears as an intergenerational trauma with no easy resolution. The story, when Keith has to tell it, does not fit easily into their lives. Keith notes that this story is not one that his daughter can tell her friends, so in telling her, he has "given her this dark chamber that you'll probably repress, or try to repress. You won't go to school saying, 'Guess what happened to my dad's dad!'" (K. Brooks, Interview 3). There is, again, no public space for this story, so, according to Keith, repression is one of few available tactics for coping with these events.

The scenes the family members describe move the impact of execution from crime scene, court room, and execution chamber to quotidian spaces that are largely absent from dominant death penalty narratives. In this way, their descriptions of grief and persistence constitute an act of critical memorialization. While execution is supposed to be a discrete exchange between the state and the family of the condemned, their stories show that it spills over, affecting people and spaces outside of immediate carceral contexts. Violence continues to structure their lives, in part because there is no or minimal public space to acknowledge its continued effects, even as those effects are also everywhere. While the Texas After Violence Project provides a space for these stories, the stories themselves suggest the inadequacy of a single oral history interview to resolve problems of structural exclusion. The family's narratives highlight the need for alternate modes of public belonging that the TAVP, as a relatively isolated archive, cannot fully address.

Competing Modes of Survival

While the Moore's Ford Memorial creates a community through its performance, the TAVP archive operates differently. Like the Moore's Ford Memorial, the TAVP archive indicates that "being in a community" means persisting despite the long-term effects of violence. The stories in the archive are united by those effects, and people with varied experiences and connections to carceral violence are grouped together, with their stories on equal footing. The community that the TAVP archive constructs is thus piecemeal, mostly involuntary, and internally diverse in terms of structural and personal relationships to violence. A visitor to this archive can pull together a version of a community based on any combination of these narratives, and the public assertion of such a community is itself a resistant act. However, the structural separation of viewer and speaker, as well as the distance among the speakers in the archive, limits the community that the archive can create. The interviews suggest, but do not enact, a resistant community.

While the interviews with Brooks's family members focus on their experiences of Brooks's life and death, the interview subjects also raise questions about whether attachment to the past is desirable or useful. While Keith's interview often describes structural violence, the way forward with which he concludes mixes individual and structural action. When asked about final thoughts for the interview, Keith suggests a coping strategy:

Children of executed people will experience devastation in their life, they will, they will make bad choices because there's going to be a lot of emotions with it and there's just not a lot of venues, healthy venues, to express that emotion.

There are a lot of unhealthy venues that you can express the rage and the anger, you have with the government that you feel has defrauded you. But there are not a lot of positive ways to do it, except that you turn it into a negative—turn a negative into a positive. The fact that you doubt me means that I'm going to try harder. (K. Brooks, Interview 3)

Keith argues that rather than dwelling on "the government that you feel has defrauded you," children of executed people should work harder to demonstrate that they do not deserve to be othered. Earlier parts of his interview, in which he describes careful reflection on the Bible as a strategy for coping with his experiences, also suggest personal responsibility for healing.[13] Importantly, however, Keith also indicates that eliminating the death penalty would reduce violence. He describes the death penalty's violence as contagious, stating, "I just think that the mindset of killing people regardless of innocence or not will be disseminated from the government unto local people, to the point now that we have people killing innocent people. I think there would be less incidences of that if we didn't, if we were not killing people. We wouldn't have so many people killing people" (K. Brooks, Interview 3). These two solutions—moving forward as an individual and eliminating the death penalty as a community—coexist, indicating multiple strategies for progress.

Derrek's investment in exoneration aligns him with mainstream abolitionist rhetoric, but also makes him an outlier within his family. Derrek notes that his family members tell him to "leave it alone," but that he believes that his father did not shoot David Gregory and is exploring resources to get a DNA test that could posthumously exonerate him (D. Brooks, Interview 1). Keith dismisses this idea. Speaking to the interviewer, he says:

See, Derrek is mad. I don't know if you know—He wants some money, or a lawsuit, or somebody to do something about this. Some DNA. I say, "What you gonna DNA, Derrek?" Something to try to right that wrong. But my father didn't put that in my heart. He gave me the idea to let that go and then let it be your encouragement to do better. People are going to doubt you and they do. But now I'm so far gone past that. (K. Brooks, Interview 3)

---

13. Joyce similarly cites God as key to her sons' survival (Easley).

The resistance to exoneration in the interviews, despite consistent abolitionist stances among the interviewees and relatively consistent sympathy for Brooks, suggests possible conflicts between the strategies of anti–death penalty activists and the needs of people more directly affected by execution. At another point in the interview, describing how schools teach Brooks's case, Keith notes that "it actually hurts when they push that he was innocent so much" because that forces the family to dwell in the unfairness of the execution in addition to coping with the loss of a family member (K. Brooks, Interview 3). For Derrek, Brooks's possible innocence is actionable, because exoneration could offer closure. For Keith, posthumous exoneration cannot "right that wrong" of execution. Instead, the exoneration process keeps Brooks's execution in their lives in potentially problematic and retraumatizing ways.

The family's internally diverse perspective on survival strategies is a microcosm of the larger archive's diversity. Because the archive contains stories from families and friends of victims and the executed, as well as activists, journalists, lawyers, and law enforcement, the ways in which interview subjects are affected by violence and their preferred ways forward vary. As the dissonance between Keith's and Derrek's interviews shows, these differences cannot always cohere. One speaker's preferred solution to carceral violence may be actively damaging to someone else. For this reason, the archive cannot cohere into a single narrative or an obvious path forward. Instead, it asks the visitor to the archive, a person who may or may not have been affected by violence, to imagine these experiences of violence as connected and thus to see the death penalty as a problem with unexpected effects. This format cannot connect the victims to one another, nor the viewer to the victims beyond the problematic lens of sympathy. While the Moore's Ford Memorial builds a community in the moment, the TAVP archive suggests a community that is still in progress, the next steps for which remain unclear.

CONCLUSION

The memorial rhetorics of the Moore's Ford Memorial and the Texas After Violence Project offer insight into the rhetorical opportunities of critical memorialization. As memory studies scholars have indicated, the rush to memorialize can be problematic, especially when memorialization offers a seemingly complete version of past events. A possible alternative, practiced in both these memorials, involves foregrounding loss *as loss*: slippery, ephemeral, always present but impossible to grasp. As David L. Eng and David Kazanjian explain, loss can be generative, particularly if we ask not "what is lost?" but "what remains?" (2). Focusing on what remains assumes that loss can never be known otherwise; it is impossible to recuperate what is lost, so survivors can only sort through what was left behind. This focus also suggests that the past is never over and, instead, that its trauma inheres in contemporary material traces. In refusing to resolve loss, the Moore's Ford and TAVP memorials reject an oversimplified relationship between past and present. Instead, they highlight the gap between what could have been and what is, as well as the gap between what happened and what contemporary communities can access. Incompleteness is a key feature, rather than a deficit, of both memorials. The limits of access help the memorials convey loss as loss, rather than as something to be recovered or remedied.

Dwelling in loss makes these memorials part of a larger pattern of memorial work that refuses to "get over" traumatic events. Public rhetoric and dominant memorial practices often construct past violence against marginalized people as irrelevant to the present, even as similar violent events are privileged as instructive. Slavery in the United States, for example, receives comparatively little attention as a national tragedy with continued reverberations; unlike the Holocaust or the 9/11 terror attacks, there is not a public mandate to "never forget" the horrors of slavery. Instead, the mandate is usually the opposite. Marginalized people with legitimate complaints are often characterized as "oversensitive" to current oppression or inappropriately angry about past violence.[14] Refusing to "get over" past and present direct, structural, and cultural violence thus becomes a resistant act. Describing oversensitivity as an asset, Sara Ahmed argues that "oversensitive" people are "sensitive to that which is not over" ("Against Students"). When applied to memorial contexts, this affective commitment resists the common memorial impulse to situate violence and grief in that past, particularly when those examples of violence and grief disrupt dominant identity constructions. Acknowledgment of lynching as a form of state-endorsed and community-run terrorism with an ongoing impact disrupts narratives of a post-racial United States. The Moore's Ford Memorial asks community members, including whites, to see the community as marked by violence and hatred. Similarly, the Easley/Brooks family's mourning complicates execution's constitutive function. Instead of constituting a righteous community purged of evil, Charlie Brooks Jr.'s execution and the long legal process that preceded it constitutes a new group of victims. These memorials acknowledge and make space for people affected by violence to be affected, even years later. The result is a version of loss that is familiar without being

---

14. As Danielle Fuentes Morgan notes, entreaties to "get over" slavery often appear in defenses of Confederate memorials.

comfortable. The continued presence of pain and the gap between what was lost and what remains make comfort impossible and, these memorials suggest, potentially undesirable.

Critical memorialization is an important tactic for addressing violent rhetorical ecologies. Designating a memory place (for example, a battlefield) to memorialize lives lost to violence suggests that violence can be reducible to a single event or series of events. As I have discussed in prior chapters and as these memorials demonstrate, reckoning with violence requires engagement with its operation in direct, structural, and cultural forms. This point of view also supports the memorials' implicit claims that the violence they document is not over. While the particular violence of state-run execution is falling out of favor, its retributive logic and "tough on crime" ethos remain in the form of mass incarceration and the advent of "supermax" prisons.[15] While not identical to Southern spectacle lynching, the legal-to-semi-legal murders of Black men, women, and children for minor offenses continue in the form of police violence. Claims that affected populations should "get over" older forms of violence are a form of cultural violence that sustain these practices. By addressing cultural, structural, and direct violence as persistent sources of pain and loss, the Moore's Ford and TAVP memorials expose the inhospitable climates of violent rhetorical ecologies and demonstrate ways of surviving in spite of them.

---

15. Supermax prisons are "prisons-within-prison systems" in which solitary confinement and lockdown protocols, typically reserved for crisis management, are standard operating procedure (Michelle Brown 986–87).

CONCLUSION

Working through
Rhetoric and Violence

CONVERSATIONS ABOUT rhetoric and violence often center on rhetoric's utility as an antiviolence tool. What, if anything, can rhetoric do to respond to violence? If the answer is "nothing," what are the consequences for the study of rhetoric? Discussing the United States' War on Terror, Cynthia Haynes explores this idea. She writes, "Because the economic and social disasters that it has caused cannot be undone with rhetoric, this is the first time I sense the powerlessness of rhetoric to effect such a mass change. This is the first time that rhetoric seems, to me, doomed" (134). This excerpt suggests that rhetoric's incapacity to fully address violence is also its death knell. However, Haynes does not argue that rhetoricians should abandon the study of rhetoric, even though rhetoric alone is an inadequate solution to widespread violence. Instead, citing Derrida, she rejects the focus on value, stating that rhetoric should take responsibility for itself rather than seeking "to absolve itself 'for' the world" (137). For rhetoric to remain useful and meaningful, rhetoric scholars must address without rationalizing its entanglement with violence. Haynes's argument suggests that the rhetoric/violence relationship is less a question of value than one of fact. Rhetoric and violence share an address (3). All rhetoric scholarship must account for this co-occupancy.

The concept of violent rhetorical ecology is one way of accounting for the co-occupancy of rhetoric and violence. Rather than asking what rhetoric can do about violence, the preceding chapters have focused on mapping what rhetoric and violence are already doing together. *Ecologies of Harm* has argued that the entanglement of violence and rhetoric produces and reproduces people, systems, and environments. In this way, an ecological focus posits the overlap of rhetoric and violence differently; rhetoric and violence do not just share a space, but rather *produce* a space, their combined force defining the available means of survival. The exact nature of these spaces will vary, but the structuring question of this approach can inform analysis of many ecologies of violence and rhetoric. By asking what rhetoric and violence are already doing, scholars can reject the formal trace of their separation and attend instead to their multimodal material force.

This conclusion addresses a final question: How can rhetoricians study rhetoric from within violent rhetorical ecologies? I have tried to show that rhetorical methods can highlight the constitutive force and cumulative effects of ostensibly nonviolent actions: for example, defending retributive notions of justice, arguing for a victim's "purity," or insisting on a false equivalence between neo-Nazis and nonviolent protesters.[1] Focusing on how practices of direct, structural, and cultural violence build and reinforce group identity is one way to make violence's multimodal force legible as rhetoric. Importantly, this approach also contests the cultural structures that separate "real" violence from the slow wear of debility. As I have described, planned forms of direct violence tend to be more intelligible as both violence and rhetoric, but violence's materiality extends beyond those events. *Ecologies of Harm* does not treat violence as exceptional. Instead, it examines how violence inheres in a variety of practices and how those practices intersect to create an oppressive rhetorical ecology.

Studying rhetoric from within a violent rhetorical ecology, then, requires acknowledgment of violence's pervasive force and a methodology designed to address it. The methodology of *Ecologies of Harm* derives from the violence I study. While direct violence seems straightforward—one person harms another—its rhetoric is slippery. Discussing the constitutive force of even a carefully orchestrated violent performance requires attention to the surrounding rhetoric. How did this person become a target? What is the significance of these particular violent rituals? How are participants in and victims of violence supposed to feel about this performance, and how do their public reactions compare to that mandate? I situate violence in/as a rhetorical ecology to account for this shifting and multifaceted context and its cumulative effects.

---

1. Donald Trump's assertion that "both sides" were to blame for violence at the Unite the Right rally in Charlottesville, Virginia, is an example of the cultural violence of false equivalence (Merica). See also Roberts-Miller, *Demagoguery*.

The context of violence, I argue, is also violence, and not merely because it leads to direct violence. Instead, I have tried to show that structural and cultural violence also harm their victims, even in the unlikely event that no direct violence befalls them. Violence's constitutive force is a significant part of this harm. In narrowing the space for public being, structural and cultural violence create circumstances in which targeted people are always perilously out of place.

This conclusion explores the implications of violent rhetorical ecologies for both the rhetorical study of violence and rhetoric more broadly. I argue that these ecologies, along with strategies for resisting and responding to them, complicate existing understandings of human/nonhuman boundaries, valid rhetorical response, and rhetorical failure. In this way, the conclusion frames my initial question, "How can rhetoricians study rhetoric within a violent rhetorical ecology?," as an opportunity. Given violence's pervasiveness, there may be no way to study rhetoric *outside* a violent rhetorical ecology. Rather than resisting the entanglement of rhetoric and violence, then, rhetoricians must consider what an acknowledgment of ongoing violence can bring to rhetoric as a discipline.

HUMANS AND OBJECTS

To illustrate the implications of violent rhetorical ecologies on rhetoric scholarship, I return to Michael Brown's murder and its aftermath. Two iterations of Brown's body show how violence and resistance complicate the human/object divide. Darren Wilson shot Brown in the street shortly after noon on August 9, 2014. Brown's body remained in the street until at least 4:00 p.m., when police officers indicated that Brown's body could be taken to the morgue (Hunn and Bell). In the time that Brown remained in the street, his body served as a site of terror and anguish for neighborhood residents and Brown's family members. Before Brown's mother, Lesley McSpadden, had been allowed to identify the body, a girl showed her a photo she had taken and asked, "Isn't this your son?" (Hunn and Bell). Speculating as to why Brown's body remained in the street for so long, one Ferguson resident stated, "They shot a black man, and they left his body in the street to let you all know this could be you. . . . To set an example, that's how I see it" (qtd. in Hunn and Bell).

A second iteration of Brown's body is in the posture and refrain adopted by protesters after his death: "Hands up, don't shoot." Witnesses disagree on whether Brown had his hands up in a gesture of surrender when Wilson shot him. Regardless, the deliberately nonthreatening posture, framed in the language of the police, became an important facet of protests against police violence. As activist Binijuktya Sen explained, the "hands up" gesture "speaks to the concern that people, even when they submit themselves to police, they're still subjected to violence" (qtd. in Grinberg). When protesters adopt this position and refrain, they embody a version of Brown and the many other victims and potential victims of police violence. Brown's body in his last moments of life circulates here as an affective symbol, representing ongoing vulnerability and shared resolve.

Interdisciplinary scholarship on violence has long been concerned with how human beings become objects. It is a commonplace that violence, especially when it is organized and widespread, requires an othering logic. No one is automatically exposed to violence; instead, groups become targets of violence through structural and cultural processes.[2] A task of scholarship on violence, then, becomes determining how these processes work. Achille Mbembe, for example, asks what the state's "right to kill, to allow to live, or to expose to death . . . tell[s] us about the person who is thus put to death and about the enmity that sets that person against his or her murderer?" (12). Judith Butler's scholarship addresses similar concerns by examining how hegemonic frames construct some forms of life as "grievable." How does a human, deserving of life, become legible as dangerous or expendable? While the answer varies, the forms of violence discussed in this book suggest that the process often involves separation fueled by fear, hatred, or disgust. Before a person is lynched, executed, tortured, or shot in the street, she is a threat, an enemy, a source of potential contamination. In these processes, victims of violence are not necessarily made inhuman—they could be "bad" or "lesser" humans—but their reiteration as objects of negative feeling reinforces boundaries between self and other.[3]

Responding to violence also involves rhetorical processes that transform suffering people into objects of the gaze. The bodies of lynching, execution, and torture victims have all been used as evidence that the violence wrought upon them was unacceptable. As I will discuss below, Michael Brown's body has been treated this way as well. Even as it appears in antiviolence rhetoric, this formulation of body-as-evidence is problematic. Encountering the body as a map of possible legal or moral violations is not the same as encountering a victim of violence as a person. The ocular epistemology of human rights,

---

2. Mbembe links this process to modernity: "The perception of the existence of the Other as an attempt on my life, as a mortal threat or absolute danger whose biophysical elimination would strengthen my potential to life and security—this, I suggest, is one of the many imaginaries of sovereignty characteristic of both early and late modernity" (18).

3. See Ahmed, *Cultural Politics*.

of which this logic is part, allows viewers to maintain distance from the people they are viewing.[4] This is true even when viewers feel something for the viewed, as is often a precursor to (or substitute for) antiviolence action. The mechanics of empathy often depend on an erasure of personhood. Discussing the problem of empathy in narratives about enslaved people, Saidiya Hartman describes how John Rankin, a white author who wrote in detail about the horrors of slavery, conveys the suffering of enslaved people by writing himself into the scene. Rankin's antislavery writings detail a moment in which he imagines that he, his wife, and his daughter are enslaved and that his wife and daughter are subject to "the cruel lash" (qtd. in Hartman 18). This anecdote is likely meant to "humanize" enslaved people and awaken the moral will of a white audience comfortably distant from slavery (Hartman 18). But, as Hartman points out, this process only makes sense within (and thus reinforces) a system in which Black bodies are sites of inscription and exchange. Hartman writes that "the ease of Rankin's empathic identification is as much due to his good intentions and heartfelt opposition to slavery as to the fungibility of the captive body" (19). To present Black suffering as worthy of consideration, Rankin can and must replace it with his own, because the violent ecology in which he writes leaves no space for Black people to have their own experiences or perspectives.

In this way, the rhetoric of violence intersects with the promise and potential violence of posthumanism. While varied, posthumanist thought tends to decenter the human as a solitary agent, arguing instead for understandings of agency as distributed among human and nonhuman actors. As Casey Boyle explains, "The key for a posthumanist rhetoric . . . is an acknowledgment of a kind of *betweenness* among what was previously considered the human and nonhuman" (540). This mutability stems from a core relationality: Things (human and nonhuman) only come into being through interdependence. The idea that humans and nonhumans become perceptible as individuals only through their mutual imbrication supports claims for a flat ontology, in which humans are not privileged over nonhumans, but rather all things are understood as emerging together and constituting each other.[5] Rather than imagining fully formed humans entering a discrete scene, posthumanism requires thinking through the emergence of human and nonhuman actors, their relationships, and the ecologies that their continual interactions produce.

In addressing constitutive rhetoric and identity formation as a product of repeated, practiced violence, *Ecologies of Harm* intersects with a posthu-

---

4. See Hesford, especially chapter 1.

5. See Bogost.

man focus on how individuals emerge from and through rhetorical ecologies. I have, however, chosen to focus on human experience, in part because of how the variable boundaries of "the human" play out in violent practices. The violent ecologies I discuss constitute marginalized groups as less or other than human: as brutes, criminals, terrorists, and objects of an inquiring gaze. Given that domestic and international policies, as well as violence at all levels of society, suggest that the definition of "human" is still heavily contested, an ontology that puts humans and objects on the same level needs to acknowledge the degree to which this leveling already occurs, selectively, as a mechanism of oppression.[6] This acknowledgment does not require the reification of "human" as a useful term so much as attention to how people are already dwelling, often involuntarily, in this "betweenness," and what use they make of their liminal status.[7]

Several of the texts examined in *Ecologies of Harm* dwell in betweenness, alternating between presenting the body as an object of knowledge or empathy and obscuring it to avoid the unequal power relations that visibility can create. For example, Rajkamal Kahlon's *Did You Kiss the Dead Body?* critiques overlapping medical and carceral perspectives that present the body as a puzzle to be solved, unlocking either pathology (medicine) or truth (torture). While she represents bodies, she does so in a way that draws attention to their problematic framing and "opens up to critical scrutiny the restrictions on interpreting reality" (Butler 72). The Moore's Ford Memorial repurposes a white supremacist spectacle to create an antiracist community, thereby resisting both lynching's purpose and the physical separation that allows some viewers of lynching photographs to place its violence in the past. Both works mix critique of structural and cultural violence with construction of the body as a source of knowledge. This combination makes the violence of objectification and the nuances of betweenness more apparent.

The scenes from Michael Brown's death described above provide additional insight into the effects of an involuntarily betweenness produced by violence. Brown's body, left in the street, suggests dehumanization of both Brown and his loved ones. He remained in the street as an object of inquiry for the state, only to be released once the medical examiner had inspected him. His family was not allowed to see *or* not see him; his body was public, but, as

---

6. For more on the limits of posthumanism to address human rights issues, see Hesford.

7. While I am focusing on violence, these ideas are also applicable to technology-focused versions of posthumanism that threaten to create a false equivalence between early adopters of new technology and the disabled people who are simultaneously integrated with technology and excluded from dominant narratives around it. See Weise.

McSpadden reported, she was not permitted to officially identify it. Police actions privileged Brown's status as evidence over his continuing relationships to living people, and as a result, Brown's family and others near the incident had to dwell with his body as an object of terror and grief. His dual constitution as human (through his family) and object (through the state) continues the violence of his death.

When Brown's family members are forced to work with his body as object, they create a space for resistant interpretation, albeit one that is circumscribed by the oppressive medical logics that Kahlon critiques. Christina Sharpe describes Brown's family's choice to get a second autopsy, countering the state's interpretation of Brown's death, as an act of Black annotation (123). She writes, "They tried to come up with his body's harms as seen through their eyes in order to contest that body that was drawn by antiblackness" (124; figure omitted). Brown's autopsy made his body a site of contention, as experts attempted to reconstruct his death through his wounds. A gunshot wound on Brown's forearm was particularly controversial. Relying on the physical evidence alone, medical examiners differed in their opinions about where Brown's arms were when Wilson fired this shot. Based on a combination of crime scene and forensic evidence, medical examiners determined that he likely had his arms in front of him, but not above his shoulders, when he received the wound in question (Grinberg). This interpretation does not mean that Brown never raised his hands, but rather that his body, interpreted according to forensic standards, could not tell that story.[8] The private autopsy, which was conducted with limited access to the evidence police had gathered, differed from the state autopsy only in the finding that Brown was not shot at close range (Barajas). Regardless of what narrative resulted from the autopsy, however, Brown's family's insistence on interpretive rights is a significant resistant action. Through the private autopsy, Brown is still rendered an object, but one observed with a different eye. The family members do not escape the violent rhetorical ecology from which Wilson emerged to shoot Brown, but they also refuse to settle into it by grieving quietly from behind closed doors or performing public acts of forgiveness.[9] Instead, they use the available tools to tell their own story.

---

8. According to a CNN analyst and defense attorney, "What would conclusively give us hands up would be if he had a bullet wound in his palm" (Grinberg).

9. Lesley McSpadden, Michael Brown's mother, stated in 2015 that she would "never" forgive Darren Wilson (Whaley). This claim contrasts with those of the families of other victims of racial violence who have publicly forgiven the perpetrators, including Felicia Sanders, a survivor of the shooting at Mother Emanuel African Methodist Episcopal Church whose son, Tywanza Sanders, was killed in the shooting (Shapiro).

Protesters also interpreted and, ultimately, embodied Brown's body for resistant purposes. "Hands up, don't shoot" mobilizes Brown's body, functioning metonymically as a stand-in for all Black and Brown bodies, as a legible text that police deliberately misinterpret. Jasbir Puar describes the chant as "a compact sketch of the frozen black body, rendered immobile by systemic racism and the punishment doled out for not transcending it" (*Right to Maim* xxiii). The chant and pose replicate racist carceral practices that render the body as an object. Like "I can't breathe," a phrase used in protest after police killed Eric Garner in 2014, "Hands up, don't shoot" subverts precarity through a "coalitional gesture" (Pérez 82–83).[10] This engagement with objectification transforms police claims about incorrect communication, misunderstanding, and illegibility into an indictment. Standing still with hands raised, protesters present a stark silhouette; in large groups, the cumulative force of their legible bodies suggests that genuine misreading is impossible. Through this practice, protesters use their objectified bodies to reflect back the state's untenable claims.

These selective reiterations of the body as object reflect how unhelpful the category of "human" has been in preventing or addressing violence against marginalized people. Human is a narrow, exclusionary identity category, the nominal securing of which does not guarantee accompanying rights. Supposedly universal human rights still require institutional conferral; these inherent rights mean little if no one will recognize them (Hesford 37). Arguments that attempt to make the humanity of marginalized people legible for secure audiences reinforce the idea that humanity—or, at least, humanity deserving of respect or recognizable as precarious—is not self-evident. When the path to humanity involves remaking oneself as the object of a sympathetic gaze, then rejecting the category is a more radical way forward. Sharpe, for example, writes that she is "not interested in rescuing Black being(s) for the category of the 'Human,' misunderstood as 'Man,' or for the language of development. Both of those languages and the material conditions that they re/produce continue to produce our fast and slow deaths" (116). Instead, she is interested in ways of living and responding to "the terror visited on Black life" (116). People live and resist without having been conferred "humanity" by a white supremacist culture. Attention to the quotidian practices around and within violent rhetorical ecologies provides insight into these modes of persistence without reifying "the human" as an unproblematic default.[11]

---

10. Garner repeated, "I can't breathe" eleven times after police placed him a chokehold (A. J. Baker et al.).

11. For a detailed engagement with Blackness, subjectivity, and objecthood, see Moten.

Violence, then, raises particular questions for posthumanism, only some of which *Ecologies of Harm* has answered. Bodies, including Brown's, have material existence apart from how they are interpreted. But in cases of organized public violence, interpretation often means the difference between life and death and, thus, a significant transformation in the nature of that material existence. This violence is literally objectifying, and responses to Brown's death negotiate the ways in which Brown and other marginalized people are forced to exist in betweenness. In this way, intersections with the rhetoric of violence can help to expand posthumanism to address a common critique: that some new materialist approaches, including some iterations of posthumanism, are themselves a form of cultural violence. As Hesford et al. note, new materialist rhetorics "are not *new*," as indigenous people and people of color have long discussed "materiality's suasiveness and concomitant ethics of relationality" (5). When scholars position materialist frameworks as "new," they perform colonial cultural violence. Attending to the ways in which people are already dwelling in and working through "betweenness" can enrich rhetorical approaches to the intersections of human and object.

REGISTERING RESPONSE

Ecologies of Harm also raises questions about what it means to respond to violence, both in vernacular and scholarly senses. Violent situations often seem intractable because dominant strategies for contesting them actually reinforce their sustaining values. All of the chapters in *Ecologies of Harm* address this issue to some degree. Senator Robert Wagner's speech in chapter 1, in which he attempts to dissociate lynching from white Southern identity, and the anti–death penalty arguments in chapter 2, which incorrectly assume a shared need for painless execution, are both examples of how arguments can fail to disrupt the violent ecologies from which they emerge. There are similar examples related to the murders of unarmed Black people. Discussing public reactions to the murder of Trayvon Martin, Stephen Dillon and Allison Page note that even seemingly positive statements about Martin can reinforce "a methodology of social value where the law-abiding, good, normative citizen is recognized, protected, and incorporated against a disavowed, devalued, deviant non-normativity that is deserving of (social) death" (283). By treating some victims as exceptionally good, rhetors can suggest that victims who do not meet the same respectability criteria do not deserve safety or life.

Similarly, scholarly rhetoric often sustains problematic values by emphasizing the reactions of people geographically and emotionally detached from violence. As I noted above, vernacular antiviolence rhetoric often focuses on inspiring empathy in a distant spectator, thereby producing victims of violence as objects of the gaze. This rhetoric also has a structural impact on who emerges, in both vernacular and scholarly discourse, as an "audience" for violence. Much of the pivotal work on violence focuses on whether distant audiences care about violence and what it would take—if it is even possible—to make them care.[12] There is some logic to this approach in that a distant spectator may be better able to address violence because she is not immersed in it. A focus on detached audiences, however, elides the experiences of people affected by violence, as well as their responses, often produced within oppressive power structures. As I have noted, violence constitutes its victims as well as its perpetrators. Examining responses that emerge from within a violent rhetorical ecology foregrounds how people targeted for violence persist, rather than reiterating them as objects with whom distant audiences may or may not identify.

As the resistant arguments I have discussed indicate, resisting from within a violent rhetorical ecology often requires less visible, incremental challenges to structural and cultural violence. These strategies dismantle some of the values that structural violence reinforces but may gain the space to do so only by operating through existing oppressive systems. As I argued in chapter 3, less monitored rhetorical spaces, like institutional documents or civil lawsuits, provide opportunities for muted rhetors to critique dominant discourse (Bordelon 335). Chris Mays's work on rhetorical ecologies suggests that this kind of intervention, while not obviously revolutionary, may become transformative in aggregate. From an adapted systems theory perspective, Mays argues that "excess" within a rhetorical ecology fuels the ecology's constant self-sustaining flow, but can also, at any moment, accumulate the force to tip the system into transformation. Particularly from an outside perspective, this "excess" may not be readily perceptible as response until it becomes transformative, but its persistent circulation, even among a relatively small audience, does rhetorical work (see chapter 4).

In the wake of Michael Brown's death or any act of direct violence, it is worth examining the array of resistant responses, their relationships to each other, and their respective critiques (and sometimes reinforcement) of structural and cultural violence. The most widely circulated community responses

---

12. See Butler; Sontag, *Regarding the Pain*. For a critical approach to this framework, see Hesford.

to Brown's death were protests, first in Ferguson, then around the country. As I noted above, protestors used "Hands up, don't shoot" to show that no level of decorum or adherence to the rules would protect people of color from police violence. The lawsuit filed by Michael Brown's parents, Michael Brown Sr. and Lesley McSpadden, was less widely addressed but similarly critical of the structural and cultural violence of policing.[13] Brown Sr. and McSpadden's initial complaint against Wilson, former police chief Thomas Jackson, and the city of Ferguson uses evidence from the US Department of Justice's investigation of the Ferguson Police Department (FPD) to tie Wilson's actions to larger patterns of institutional racism. Importantly, the complaint avoids a reductive focus on personal responsibility without entirely eliding it. The plaintiffs note the department's racially biased use of "manner of walking" charges, indicating that racism was built into the structure of policing, complete with legal safeguards to provide plausible deniability (24). They also cite evidence of interpersonal racism, describing incidents in which officers used racial slurs, circulated racist emails, and harassed African Americans (25–27, 18). Additionally, the complaint highlights how Wilson's conduct indicated his own racism and personal responsibility for Brown's death. Citing Wilson's characterization of Brown as both sub- and superhuman, the complaint contests the "reasonableness" of Wilson's impressions, stating, "It is never objectively reasonable to perceive a human being as anything less than human" (10). The plaintiffs thus push the court to see Wilson's actions as connected but not reducible to the cultural violence embedded in the FPD.

Within a violent rhetorical ecology and in the wake of an inadequate institutional response to their son's death, the wrongful death lawsuit was one of few established avenues for acknowledgment of public wrongdoing. While it addresses some forms of cultural and structural violence, it also reinforces others. A civil suit forces Brown Sr. and McSpadden to quantify their grief, thereby setting up an inherently unequal and objectifying exchange: money for their son. This exchange is particularly troubling because the structural violence of capitalism contributes to racial and economic segregation and, thus, to police targeting neighborhoods where Black and Brown people live. Particularly when settled out of court, as this suit was, wrongful death suits also incorrectly suggest that loss can be healed with money. Within this logic, violence is permissible, provided that the victims are appropriately compen-

---

13. Within the text of the initial complaint, Lesley McSpadden's first name is spelled "Lezley." Because the majority of sources I have found refer to her as "Lesley," I have used that spelling.

sated.[14] Brown Sr. and McSpadden's particular use of the suit, however, resists these constraints. Brown Sr. and McSpadden do not quantify their grief or argue that Brown deserved life. Instead, they argue that Wilson deprived Brown of his right to life (2). Additionally, the "prayer for relief" that ends the initial complaint indicates that the individuals and institutions responsible cannot remedy the problem with money. In addition to compensation for their son's death, the plaintiffs request:

- An Order preliminarily and permanently enjoining the Defendant City's utilization of patrol techniques that demean, disregard, or underserve its African-American population; and
- An Order appointing a compliance monitor over the City of Ferguson's use of force practices and procedures for a period of five (5) years or until such time as the Court determines that the City of Ferguson has fully and effectually trained all of its police officers on the constitutional requirements of the use of deadly force. (43)

Like *Salim v. Mitchell,* discussed in chapter 3, *Brown v. City of Ferguson* shows the seams of civil law, even as the plaintiffs make use of it. Their request for long-term reforms helps to mitigate these limits. While the compensation they request for Brown's death is inherently inadequate to address their loss, structural and cultural change within the police department could prevent future losses.

Through its contextually constrained performance of structural critique, the lawsuit also invites broader structural critique from scholars of rhetoric and violence. I have argued that less visible forms of antiviolence discourse merit scholarly attention, particularly when they serve as sites of resistance from inside violent rhetorical ecologies. Rather than focusing on how or whether outsiders are reacting to distant violence, scholarship on violence should begin by assuming that people are responding to violence in their communities. The next step then becomes finding the responses, seeing what they do, and using them to better understand the cumulative conditions of a violent rhetorical ecology. This research process raises an additional question: Which options for response are available, to whom, and why? Asking this question allows for more detailed attention to antiviolence texts that fail to contest violence's structuring norms or that embed critique in problem-

---

14. Thanks to audience members at the 2018 Cultural Rhetorics Conference for pointing out this issue and discussing it with me.

atic frameworks. Through which structural and cultural forces does the civil suit become a compensatory strategy for families who have lost loved ones to police violence?[15] What rhetorical possibilities does this space offer, and how do narratives of violence and responsibility constructed there relate to the dominant narratives around this violent practice? Beginning with these questions can move scholars away from a focus on distant spectatorship and into the nuances of surviving violent rhetorical ecologies.

While I use Brown Sr. and McSpadden's lawsuit as an example, subtler modes of resistance and survival raise questions about the very mechanisms that many rhetoric scholars use to track response. Lauren Berlant offers one example. She argues that narratives of the self as deliberate and self-actualizing (or self-destructing) obscure forms of "ongoingness, getting by, and living on," including practices of "interruptive agency" that allow individuals to drift, however briefly, from their place within a structurally violent system (99–100). While Berlant is careful not to attribute cause or effect to the actions she describes, she suggests that lapses in self-care can be a response to a relentless wearying environment in which self-care is both required as part of the subject's ongoing self-improvement and structurally prohibited by the obligations of work and family (115–16). Within the field of rhetoric, scholarship on community survival strategies outlines other ways of making do and (unlike what Berlant describes) thriving in the face of structural violence. While this scholarship does not always address violence directly, it shows how individuals adapt to hostile environments: for example, by subverting capitalism's violence and cultural erasure through rasquache (Medina-López) or constructing rhizomatic communities that offer connection and support (Monberg). These projects show persistence and survival, but also practices of creativity and joy that are largely absent from discussions of direct violence (including this one). What methods of addressing rhetoric and violence would allow these practices to emerge, and how would this process shift the values embedded in that scholarship?

In studying rhetoric from within violent rhetorical ecologies, rhetoricians must address which responses were available, to whom, and why, as well as how existing responses strain those boundaries. *Brown v. City of Ferguson* and the critical memorial rhetorics discussed in chapter 4 provide examples of how rhetors can work both within and against existing structures of power, taking advantage of what is useful (a space for recognizing structural and cul-

---

15. The families of Freddie Gray and Sandra Bland also filed civil suits after losing their loved ones to police violence (Wenger and Puente; Hassan et al.).

tural violence and the epideictic force of memorial, respectively) in spite of less useful elements. Asking "Why these responses?" leads back to structural and cultural violence: of the carceral system, of "tough on crime" rhetoric, of dominant memorial practices that only document what they can valorize. Asking "Why *not* these responses?"—that is, why are these responses less visible, either to the researcher or to others—can also help rhetoricians address the cumulative effects of violent rhetorical ecologies and how scholarly practices may reinforce them.

RHETORICAL FAILURE

I will conclude by reflecting on a theme that appears throughout this book and conversations on rhetoric and violence: failure. As I noted in the introduction, violence was historically categorized as a failure of rhetoric. *Ecologies of Harm* has complicated this claim by showing how violence functions *as* multimodal constitutive rhetoric. The idea of violence as rhetorical failure is still relevant, however, because it persists in public discourse as a justification for direct violence. Building on the issues of response and objectification discussed above, I argue that an understanding of violent rhetorical ecologies can help scholars situate failure differently. Structural conditions affect whether nonviolent persuasion is available and to whom. Positioning violence as the failure of rhetoric, then, can obscure the ways in which communicative failure is a necessary feature of ongoing inequality.

To explore this idea, I turn to the less-than-ninety-second encounter between Darren Wilson and Michael Brown that resulted in Brown's death. Wilson was driving in his police cruiser when he saw Brown and Johnson. As recounted in Brown Sr. and McSpadden's lawsuit, Wilson told Brown and Johnson to "'get the [fuck]' out of the street or on the sidewalk" (4). Wilson started to drive away, then backed up in his car, blocking Brown and Johnson's path. Wilson fired his gun for the first time in the car. After Brown ran and Wilson pursued him, Wilson shot Brown several more times, killing him (6–7).

A common public framing, which includes Wilson's narrative of events, presents Brown's death as a result of his own ethos. According to politician Mike Huckabee, Brown might not have been killed "if he'd behaved like something other than a thug" (Jaffe). Wilson expressed even more stringent standards for Brown's behavior. Describing Brown's actions after he fled the car, Wilson stated, "It looked like he was almost bulking up to run through the shots, like it was making him mad that I'm shooting at him." It was only after Wilson fired the shots that killed Brown that, according to Wilson, "the demeanor on [Brown's] face went blank" and "the aggression was gone" (Sanburn). Huckabee's and Wilson's accounts both insist that if Brown had presented himself differently—perhaps by adopting a subservient ethos—then he wouldn't be dead. In this version of events, it is incumbent on Brown to present himself in a nonthreatening way and thus prevent his own death. He carries the burden of persuasion.

Huckabee's and Wilson's dehumanizing description of Brown evince the degree to which Brown's alleged communicative failure emerges from the violent structure of policing. This structural violence is clear in the lawsuit's account of Brown's death. The complaint notes that Wilson was immediately aggressive with Brown and Johnson, not issuing any commands or saying anything other than "'get the [fuck]' out of the street or on the sidewalk" (4). The lawsuit does not, however, suggest that things would have been different if Wilson had been nicer. Within the racist logic of policing in Ferguson, politeness to people of color is contraindicated, and the encounter between Brown and Johnson and Wilson was already an inherent performance of structural violence. In stopping Brown and Johnson, Wilson was enforcing statutes that the FPD used to target residents of color. These structural practices, as well as Wilson's later description of Brown as sub- and superhuman, suggest that the rhetorical "failure" began long before Wilson even saw Brown. The failure is that, within a dominant rhetorical ecology, Brown was never constructed as an interlocutor, but as a problem to be solved. Claims about his alleged criminality, his "thug" appearance or behavior, offer a false narrative of communicative possibility.

The rhetoric around Brown's death highlights how a common justification for violence—that the victim was not "getting the message"—functions constitutively. In vernacular rhetorics of violence, it is common to argue that violence sends a message to a recalcitrant other. Michele Emanatian and David Delaney identify "several hundred" uses of the metaphor in the rhetoric leading up to the 2003 invasion of Iraq: for example, "A U. S. triumph in Iraq would send a dramatic message. If we can defeat a terrorist regime in Iraq, it would be a defeat for terrorists globally" (298). Implicit in this logic is that "terrorists" can only understand violence, so the United States would be unwise to even attempt persuasion. Because this justification for violence relies on the appearance of stable identities, it must constitute them: "terrorists" as inherently violent and outside the realm of persuasion and the United States as reasonable, stable, and willing to use violence only when necessary. Like other forms of violence discussed in this book, claims of actual or imminent rhetorical failure constitute oppositional identities. In Brown's case, the "failure" was not that he did not *receive* a message, but that he failed to send the "correct" one through his quotidian comportment.[16] This impossible standard—that Brown become someone else as preemptive self-defense—constitutes Brown as permanently outside of the realm of respectful engagement.

In the context of rhetoric and violence, then, "rhetoric," understood as free and respectful debate, is a false promise that obscures structural and cultural oppression. The structure of racially biased policing did not leave room for a respectful interaction with Brown, just as lynching's dominant culture did not leave any room for "outsider" opinions (see chapter 1). In these conditions, the insistence that marginalized people must engage *anyway*—for example, by changing their appearance and affective performance and listening politely— is a form of cultural violence.[17] In the cultural moment in which I write, this violence takes a variety of forms, but frequently appears as an insistence that someone, usually a person of color or a white woman, must debate someone with abhorrent views or risk being labeled an enemy of free speech (Penny). These entreaties—for example, that then-political candidate Alexandria Ocasio-Cortez debate right-wing commentator Ben Shapiro—actively obscure the structural violence that allows some speakers seemingly endless opportunities to expound their views (Wright). As Sara Ahmed explains, "Whenever people keep being given a platform to say they have no platform, or whenever people speak endlessly about being silenced . . . you are witnessing a mechanism of power" ("You Are Oppressing"). This rhetoric can also construct the actual and potential victims of violence as its instigators: for example, in the recurrent argument that calling people Nazis (or racists or sexists) will transform them into Nazis (or racists or sexists).[18] The burden of listening and respecting is placed on those who, through structural and cultural violence, are typically silenced and disrespected.

Addressing rhetoric and violence, then, means considering in a more nuanced way where rhetoric has already failed, as well as where the promise of rhetoric as a means to avoid violence is itself violent. As my discussions of resistant rhetoric have suggested, this work also requires a reconsideration of success. Within a hostile rhetorical ecology, rhetors may be unlikely to receive audience adherence or inspire rapid social transformation, or they may do so only at the price of reinforcing problematic social values or addressing arguments that do not deserve a response. To succeed in one way often requires failing in another. In an era of ongoing violence, rhetoricians should address fraught successes, productive failures, and the role of rhetoric, still positioned as violence's other, in both. When I began work on this

---

16. This rhetoric has an obvious analog in the victim-blaming rhetoric of rape culture.

17. For discussion of the affective requirements placed on Black women, see Cooper.

18. For more on calling people Nazis in contemporary online discourse, see Ohlheiser.

project, I naïvely thought that, at the very least, some of the direct violence I was discussing would be irrelevant by the time I was done. Unfortunately, the opposite occurred, and modes of violence that I thought would fall out of favor (like torture) are once again treated as viable policy choices (see chapter 3). *Ecologies of Harm* has argued that rhetoric is not a savior; instead, it coexists with and as violence. That coexistence offers a starting place from which to work. Rhetoric's entanglement with violence gives rhetoric scholarship an opportunity—and, perhaps, a responsibility—to address the violent rhetorical ecologies in which all of us reside.

WORKS CITED

Ahmed, Sara. "Against Students." *The New Inquiry,* 29 June 2015, thenewinquiry.com/against -students/.

——. *The Cultural Politics of Emotion.* 2nd ed., Edinburgh UP, 2014.

——. "You Are Oppressing Us!" *feministkilljoys,* 15 Feb. 2015, feministkilljoys.com/2015/02/15/ you-are-oppressing-us/.

Allen, James. *Without Sanctuary: Lynching Photography in America.* Twin Palms, 2000.

American Civil Liberties Union. "About." *The Torture Database,* www.thetorturedatabase.org/ about.

——. "Race and the Death Penalty." *American Civil Liberties Union,* 2018, www.aclu.org/other/ race-and-death-penalty.

——. "*Salim v. Mitchell*—Lawsuit against Psychologists behind CIA Torture Program." *American Civil Liberties Union,* 17 Aug. 2017, www.aclu.org/cases/salim-v-mitchell-lawsuit -against-psychologists-behind-cia-torture-program.

"Another Lynching: Finds a Place in South Carolina's Long Calendar . . ." *Atlanta Constitution,* 11 May 1893, p. 1.

"Anti-Lynching Laws Urged by Council." *Atlanta Constitution,* 19 Feb. 1934, p. 7.

Associated Press. "Condemned Man's Mask Bursts into Flame during Execution." *New York Times,* 26 Mar. 1997, www.nytimes.com/1997/03/26/us/condemned-man-s-mask-bursts-into -flame-during-execution.html.

Autopsy Report: Abbas Alwan Fadil. *The Torture Database,* ACLU, 18 Apr. 2005, www. thetorturedatabase.org/files/foia_subsite/pdfs/DOD003619.pdf.

Autopsy Report: Mullah Habibullah. *The Torture Database,* ACLU, 18 Apr. 2005, www. thetorturedatabase.org/files/foia_subsite/pdfs/DOD003146.pdf.

Azoulay, Ariella. *The Civil Contract of Photography.* Zone, 2012.

Baker, A. J., et al. "Beyond the Chokehold: The Path to Eric Garner's Death." *New York Times,* 13 June 2015, www.nytimes.com/2015/06/14/nyregion/eric-garner-police-chokehold-staten -island.html.

Baker, La Rond, et al. "Complaint and Demand for Jury Trial." *Salim v. Mitchell,* United States District Court for the Eastern District of Washington, 2:15-CV-286-JLQ, 13 Oct. 2015. *American Civil Liberties Union,* www.aclu.org/legal-document/salim-v-mitchell-complaint.

Bank, Andrew. "Of 'Native Skulls' and 'Noble Caucasians': Phrenology in Colonial South Africa." *Journal of Southern African Studies*, vol. 22, no. 3, 1996, pp. 387–403. *Taylor & Francis*, www.jstor.org/stable/2637310.

Banner, Stuart. *The Death Penalty: An American History.* Harvard UP, 2003.

Barajas, Joshua. "What Does Michael Brown's Official Autopsy Report Actually Reveal?" *PBS*, 23 Oct. 2014, www.pbs.org/newshour/nation/michael-browns-official-autopsy-report-actually-reveal.

Barron, David M., et al. "Brief for Petitioners." *American Bar Association*, 5 Nov. 2007, www.americanbar.org/content/dam/aba/publishing/preview/publiced_preview_briefs_pdfs_07_08_07_5439_Petitioner.authcheckdam.pdf.

Bederman, Gail. *Manliness and Civilization: A Cultural History of Gender and Race in the United States, 1880–1917.* U of Chicago P, 1995.

Benjamin, Medea, and Kate Harveston. "The Torture-Friendly Trump Administration." *Huffington Post*, 20 July 2017, www.huffingtonpost.com/entry/the-torture-friendly-trump-administration_us_5970f6b2e4b0d72667b05f0d.

Benjamin, Walter. "A Critique of Violence." Translated by Edmund Jephcott, *Reflections: Essays, Aphorisms, Autobiographical Writing*, edited by Peter Demetz, Schocken, 1986, pp. 277–300.

Berlant, Lauren. *Cruel Optimism.* Duke UP, 2011.

Bessler, John D. *Cruel and Unusual: The American Death Penalty and the Founders' Eighth Amendment.* Northeastern UP, 2012.

Blair, Carole, et al. "Rhetoric/Memory/Place." *Places of Public Memory: The Rhetoric of Museums and Memorials*, edited by Greg Dickinson et al., U of Alabama P, 2010, pp. 1–54.

Blair, Carole, and Neil Michel. "Reproducing Civil Rights Tactics: The Rhetorical Performances of the Civil Rights Memorial." *Rhetoric Society Quarterly*, vol. 30, no. 2, 2000, pp. 31–55. *Taylor & Francis*, www.jstor.org.libproxy.clemson.edu/stable/3886159.

Bogost, Ian. *Alien Phenomenology, or What It's Like to Be a Thing.* U of Minnesota P, 2012.

Bohannon, John. "Scientists to Trump: Torture Doesn't Work." *Science*, 27 Jan. 2017, www.sciencemag.org/news/2017/01/scientists-trump-torture-doesn-t-work.

Bordelon, Suzanne. "Muted Rhetors and the Mundane: The Case of Ruth Mary Weeks, Rewey Belle Inglis, and W. Wilbur Hatfield." *College Composition and Communication*, vol. 64, no. 2, 2012, pp. 332–56. *JSTOR*, http://www.jstor.org/stable/43490755.

Boyle, Casey. "Writing and Rhetoric and/as Posthuman Practice." *College English*, vol. 78, no. 6, July 2016, pp. 532–54.

Bratta, Phil, and Malea Powell. "Introduction to the Special Issue: Entering the Cultural Rhetorics Conversation." *Enculturation*, no. 21, 20 Apr. 2016, enculturation.net/entering-the-cultural-rhetorics-conversations.

Brooks, Derrek. Interview with Rebecca Lorins (1). Texas After Violence Project, 6 Feb. 2013, *Human Rights Documentation Initiative*, av.lib.utexas.edu/index.php?title=TAVP:Derrek_Brooks_1.

———. Interview with Rebecca Lorins (2). Texas After Violence Project, 6 Feb. 2013, *Human Rights Documentation Initiative*, av.lib.utexas.edu/index.php?title=TAVP:Derrek_Brooks_2.

———. Interview with Rebecca Lorins (3). Texas After Violence Project, 6 Feb. 2013, *Human Rights Documentation Initiative*, av.lib.utexas.edu/index.php?title=TAVP:Derrek_Brooks_3.

Brooks, Keith. Interview with Rebecca Lorins (1). Texas After Violence Project, 6 Feb. 2013, *Human Rights Documentation Initiative*, av.lib.utexas.edu/index.php?title=TAVP:Keith_Brooks_1.

———. Interview with Rebecca Lorins (2). Texas After Violence Project, 6 Feb. 2013, *Human Rights Documentation Initiative*, av.lib.utexas.edu/index.php?title=TAVP:Keith_Brooks_2.

———. Interview with Rebecca Lorins (3). Texas After Violence Project, 6 Feb. 2013, *Human Rights Documentation Initiative*, av.lib.utexas.edu/index.php?title=TAVP:Keith_Brooks_3.

Brooks, Tyrone. "Moore's Ford Movement Friends and Supporters." *Facebook* ("Moore's Ford Movement" page), 9 Aug. 2016.

Brown, Hayes. "CIA Used 'Rectal Feeding' as Part of Torture Program." *Buzzfeed*, 9 Dec. 2014, www.buzzfeed.com/hayesbrown/cia-used-rectal-feeding-as-part-of-torture-program?utm_term=.ebne7EZ52#.dwBlL09n3.

Brown, Michael Sr., and Lesley McSpadden. "Petition for Wrongful Death." 21st Judicial Circuit Court, St. Louis County, Missouri, 15SL-CC01367, 23 Apr. 2015, *Los Angeles Times*, documents.latimes.com/michael-browns-family-files-civil-lawsuit-against-ferguson/.

Brown, Michelle. "'Setting the Conditions' for Abu Ghraib: The Prison Nation Abroad." *American Quarterly*, vol. 57, no. 3, 2005, pp. 973–97. *JSTOR*, www.jstor.org/stable/40068323.

Brown, Sherronda J. "The Racist Roots of Gynecology & What Black Women Birthed." *Wear Your Voice*, 29 Aug. 2017, wearyourvoicemag.com/identities/race/racist-roots-gynecology-black-women-birthed.

Burke, Kenneth. "The Rhetoric of Hitler's 'Battle.'" *The Philosophy of Literary Form*, Vintage, 1957, pp. 165–89.

———. *A Rhetoric of Motives*. U of California P, 1969.

Burns, Alexander, and Maggie Haberman. "GOP Ponders a Rick Perry 2012 Candidacy." *Politico*, 3 Aug. 2011, www.politico.com/news/stories/0811/60593_Page2.html.

Butler, Judith. *Frames of War: When Is Life Grievable?* Verso, 2009.

Caldwell, Patrick, et al. "'Rectal Feeding,' Threats to Children, and More: 16 Awful Abuses from the CIA Torture Report." *Mother Jones*, 9 Dec. 2014, www.motherjones.com/politics/2014/12/cia-torture-report-abuses-rectal-feeding/.

Caldwell, W. F. "Federal Anti-Lynching Law to Come before Group Jan. 7." *Atlanta Constitution*, 9 Dec. 1933, p. 3.

Carter, Christopher. *Rhetorical Exposures: Confrontation and Contradiction in U. S. Social Documentary Photography*. U of Alabama P, 2015.

Chang, Gordon C., and Hugh B. Mehan. "Why We Must Attack Iraq: Bush's Reasoning Practices and Argumentation System." *Discourse & Society*, vol. 19, no. 4, pp. 453–82. *JSTOR*, www.jstor.org.libproxy.clemson.edu/stable/42889208.

Chaput, Catherine. "Rhetorical Circulation in Late Capitalism: Neoliberalism and the Overdetermination of Affective Energy." *Philosophy and Rhetoric*, vol. 43, no. 1, 2010, pp. 1–25. *Project Muse*, doi.org/10.1353/par.0.0047.

Charland, Maurice. "Constitutive Rhetoric: The Case of the *Peuple Québécois*." *Quarterly Journal of Speech*, vol. 73, no. 2, 1987, pp. 133–50.

Chiang, Emily, et al. "Plaintiffs' Memorandum in Opposition to Defendants' Motion for Summary Judgment." *Salim v. Mitchell*, United States District Court for the Eastern District of Washington, 2:15-CV-286-JLQ, 12 June 2017. *American Civil Liberties Union*, www.aclu.org/legal-document/salim-v-mitchell-plaintiffs-memorandum-opposition-defendants-motion-summary-judgmen-0.

Childers, Jay P. "Transforming Violence into a Focusing Incident: A Reception Study of the 1946 Georgia Lynching." *Rhetoric & Public Affairs*, vol. 19, no. 4, pp. 571–600.

"Chronology of Abu Ghraib." *Washington Post*, 17 Feb. 2006, www.washingtonpost.com/wp-srv/world/iraq/abughraib/timeline.html.

Chumley, Cheryl K. "No Dice, BLM, Michael Brown Was Not Innocent." *Washington Times*, 13 Mar. 2017, www.washingtontimes.com/news/2017/mar/13/no-dice-blm-michael-brown-was-not-innocent/.

Condit, Celeste Michelle. "The Functions of Epideictic: The Boston Massacre Orations as Exemplar." *Communication Quarterly*, vol. 33, no. 4, 1985, pp. 284–98.

Congressional Record. 29 Nov. 1922, pp. 388–437.

———. 25 April 1935, pp. 6344–93.

———. 29 April 1935, pp. 6505–54.

———. 30 April 1935, pp. 6601–50.

Cooper, Brittney. *Eloquent Rage: A Black Feminist Discovers Her Superpower*. St. Martin's, 2018.

Crosswhite, James. *Deep Rhetoric: Philosophy, Reason, Violence, Justice, Wisdom*. U of Chicago P, 2013.

Doss, Erika. *Memorial Mania: Public Feeling in America*, U of Chicago P, 2010.

"A Double Lynching." *Atlanta Constitution*, 30 Nov. 1895, p. 1.

Dray, Philip. *At the Hands of Persons Unknown: The Lynching of Black America*. Modern Library, 2003.

Easley, Joyce Hazzard. Interview with Rebecca Lorins. Texas After Violence Project, 6 Feb. 2013, *Human Rights Documentation Initiative*, av.lib.utexas.edu/index.php?title=TAVP:Joyce_Hazzard_Easley.

Economist Explains. "The Misplaced Arguments against Black Lives Matter." *The Economist*, 18 Aug. 2017, www.economist.com/the-economist-explains/2017/08/18/the-misplaced-arguments-against-black-lives-matter.

Edbauer, Jenny. "Unframing Models of Public Distribution: From Rhetorical Situation to Rhetorical Ecologies." *Rhetoric Society Quarterly* vol. 35, no. 4, 2005, pp. 5–24. *Taylor & Francis Online*, dx.doi.org/10.1080/02773940509391320.

Eligon, John. "Michael Brown Spent Last Weeks Grappling with Problems and Promise." *New York Times*, 24 Aug. 2014, www.nytimes.com/2014/08/25/us/michael-brown-spent-last-weeks-grappling-with-lifes-mysteries.html.

Emanatian, Michele, and David Delaney. "What Message Does 'Send a Message' Send?" *Journal of Language and Politics*, vol. 7, no. 1, 2008, pp. 290–320. *Communication and Mass Media Complete*, 10.1075/jlp.7.2.06ema.

Eng, David L., and David Kazanjian. "Mourning Remains." *Loss: The Politics of Mourning*, edited by David Kazanjian and David L. Eng, U of California P, 2003, pp. 1–25.

Engels, Jeremy, and William O. Saas. "On Acquiescence and Ends-Less War: An Inquiry into the New War Rhetoric." *Quarterly Journal of Speech*, vol. 99, no. 2, 2013, 225–32. *Taylor & Francis Online*, doi-org.libproxy.clemson.edu/10.1080/00335630.2013.775705.

"Executions by Year." *Death Penalty Information Center*, 9 Nov. 2017, deathpenaltyinfo.org/executions-year.

"Far Worse Than Hanging." *New York Times*, 7 Aug. 1890, query.nytimes.com/mem/archive-free/pdf?res=9E06E4D9133BE533A25754C0A96E9C94619ED7CF.

Feinstein, Diane. "Foreword." Senate Select Committee on Intelligence, *Committee Study of the Central Intelligence Agency's Detention and Interrogation Program*, 3 Dec. 2014, www.feinstein.senate.gov/public/_cache/files/7/c/7c85429a-ec38-4bb5-968f-289799bf6d0e/D87288C34A6D9FF736F9459ABCF83210.sscistudy1.pdf.

Fink, Sheri. "Settlement Reached in C. I. A. Torture Case." *New York Times*, 17 Aug. 2017, nyti.ms/2v5gXN5.

Fink, Sheri, and James Risen. "Psychologists Open a Window on Brutal C. I. A. Interrogation." *New York Times,* 21 June 2017, nyti.ms/2sR3niN.

Fleckenstein, Kristie S., et al. "A Pedagogy of Rhetorical Looking: Atrocity Images at the Intersection of Vision and Violence." *College English,* vol. 80, no. 1, pp. 11–34.

Ford, Wayne. "Re-Enactment of 1946 Moore's Ford Lynching Planned." *Athens Banner-Herald,* 22 July 2016, pp. A1–A2.

"Forkscrew-Graphics." *Reframing Photography,* www.reframingphotography.com/content/forkscrew-graphics.

"Former FBI Agent: Torture Doesn't Work." *Al Jazeera,* 3 Feb. 2017, www.aljazeera.com/programmes/upfront/2017/02/fbi-agent-torture-doesn-work-170203153405364.html

Foucault, Michel. *Discipline and Punish: The Birth of the Prison.* Translated by Alan Sheridan, Vintage, 1995.

Fricker, Miranda. *Epistemic Injustice: Power and the Ethics of Knowing.* Oxford UP, 2007.

Galtung, Johan. "Cultural Violence." *Journal of Peace Research,* vol. 27, no. 3, 1990, pp. 291–305. *JSTOR,* http://www.jstor.org/stable/423472.

Garland, David. *Peculiar Institution: America's Death Penalty in an Age of Abolition.* Harvard UP, 2012.

——. "Penal Excess and Surplus Meaning: Public Torture Lynchings in Twentieth-Century America." *Law & Society Review,* vol. 39, no. 4, 2005, pp. 793–833. *Wiley Online Library,* 10.1111/j.1540–5893.2005.00245.x.

Goldsby, Jacqueline. *A Spectacular Secret: Lynching in American Life and Literature.* U of Chicago P, 2006.

Greenberg, Karen J. "Abu Ghraib: A Torture Story without a Hero or an Ending." *The Nation,* 28 Apr. 2014, www.thenation.com/article/abu-ghraib-torture-story-without-hero-or-ending/.

Greenberg, Kenneth S. "The Nose, the Lie, and the Duel in the Antebellum South." *American Historical Review,* vol. 95, no. 1, Feb. 1990, pp. 57–74. *JSTOR,* 10.2307/2162954.

Grinberg, Emanuella. "Why 'Hands up, Don't Shoot' Resonates Regardless of Evidence." *CNN,* 11 Jan. 2015, www.cnn.com/2015/01/10/us/ferguson-evidence-hands-up/.

Gruber, David R. "The (Digital) Majesty of All under Heaven: Affective Constitutive Rhetoric at the Hong Kong Museum of History's Multi-Media Exhibition of Terracotta Warriors." *Rhetoric Society Quarterly,* vol. 44, no. 2, 2014, pp. 148–67. *Taylor & Francis Online,* 10.1080/02773945.2014.888462.

Grusin, Richard. *Premediation: Affect and Mediality after 9/11.* Palgrave McMillan, 2010.

Haag, Matthew, and Richard Fausset. "Arkansas Rushes to Execute 8 Men in the Space of 10 Days." *New York Times,* 3 Mar. 2017, www.nytimes.com/2017/03/03/us/arkansas-death-penalty-drug.html?_r=1.

Hall, Jacqueline Dowd. *Revolt against Chivalry: Jessie Daniel Ames and the Women's Campaign against Lynching.* Columbia UP, 1993.

Han, Suhana S., et al. "Petition for a Writ of Certiorari." *SCOTUSblog,* 3 Nov. 2016, www.scotusblog.com/wp-content/uploads/2016/11/16-602-cert-petition.pdf.

Harding, Luke. "Focus Shifts to Jail Abuse of Women." *Guardian,* 12 May 2004, web.archive.org/web/20161231020355/https://www.theguardian.com/world/2004/may/12/iraq.usa.

Hariman, Robert. *Political Style: The Artistry of Power.* U of Chicago P, 1995.

Hartelius, E. Johanna, and Jennifer Asenas. "Citational Epideixis and a 'Thinking of Community': The Case of the Minutemen Project." *Rhetoric Society Quarterly,* vol. 40, no. 4, pp. 360–84. *JSTOR,* www.jstor.org/stable/27862456.

Hartman, Saidiya. *Scenes of Subjection: Terror, Slavery, and Self-Making in Nineteenth-Century America*. Oxford UP, 1997.

Hartnett, Stephen John. *Executing Democracy, Volume 1: Capital Punishment and the Making of America*. Michigan State UP, 2010.

Haskins, Ekaterina. "Between Archive and Participation: Public Memory in a Digital Age." *Rhetoric Society Quarterly*, vol. 37, no. 4, pp. 401–22. *Taylor & Francis*, doi-org.libproxy.clemson.edu/10.1080/02773940601086794.

———. *Popular Memories: Commemoration, Participatory Culture, and Democratic Citizenship*. U of South Carolina P, 2015.

Hassan, Carma, et al. "Sandra Bland's Family Settles for $1.9M in Wrongful Death Suit." *CNN*, 15 Sep. 2016, www.cnn.com/2016/09/15/us/sandra-bland-wrongful-death-settlement/index.html.

Hauser, Gerard A. "Aristotle on Epideictic: The Formation of Public Morality." *Rhetoric Society Quarterly*, vol. 29, no. 1, Winter 1999, pp. 5–23. *Taylor & Francis Online*, dx.doi.org.libproxy.clemson.edu/10.1080/02773949909391135.

Hawkins, Derek. "Michael Brown's Parents Settle Wrongful Death Suit against Ferguson." *Washington Post*, 21 June 2017, www.washingtonpost.com/news/morning-mix/wp/2017/06/21/michael-browns-parents-settle-wrongful-death-lawsuit-against-ferguson/?utm_term=.6bbf104a165a.

Haynes, Cynthia. *The Homesick Phonebook: Addressing Rhetoric in the Age of Perpetual Conflict*. Southern Illinois UP, 2016.

Hennessey-Fiske, Molly. "Walking in Ferguson: If You're Black, It's Often against the Law." *Los Angeles Times*, 5 Mar. 2015, www.latimes.com/nation/la-na-walking-black-ferguson-police-justice-report-20150305-story.html.

Hesford, Wendy S. *Spectacular Rhetorics: Human Rights Recognitions, Visions, Feminisms*. Duke UP, 2011.

Hesford, Wendy S., et al., editors. *Precarious Rhetorics*. The Ohio State UP, 2018.

Hodge, Roger D. "Weekly Review." *Harpers*, 18 May 2004, harpers.org/blog/2004/05/weeklyreview2004-05-18/.

House of Representatives. House Session Transcript for 11 Apr. 2012. Connecticut General Assembly, www.cga.ct.gov/2012/trn/H/2012HTR00411-R00-TRN.htm.

Hunn, David, and Kim Bell. "Why Was Michael Brown's Body Left There for Hours?" *St. Louis Post-Dispatch*, 14 Sep. 2014, www.stltoday.com/news/local/crime-and-courts/why-was-michael-brown-s-body-left-there-for-hours/article_0b73ec58-c6a1-516e-882f-74d18a4246e0.html.

Jacobs, Ben. "Donald Trump on Waterboarding: 'Even if It Doesn't Work They Deserve It.'" *Guardian*, 23 Nov. 2015, www.theguardian.com/us-news/2015/nov/24/donald-trump-on-waterboarding-even-if-it-doesnt-work-they-deserve-it.

Jaffe, Alexandra. "Huckabee: Michael Brown Acted like a 'Thug.'" *CNN*, 3 Dec. 2014, www.cnn.com/2014/12/03/politics/ferguson-mike-huckabee-michael-brown-shooting-thug/index.html.

Jain, Sarah S. Lochlann. *Injury: The Politics of Product Design and Safety Law in the United States*. Princeton UP, 2006.

Jean, Susan. "'Warranted' Lynchings: Narratives of Violence in White Southern Newspapers, 1880–1940." *American Nineteenth Century History*, vol. 6, no. 3, 2005, pp. 351–72. *Taylor & Francis Online*, dx.doi.org.libproxy.clemson.edu/10.1080/14664650500381058.

Kaba, Mariame. "Transformative Justice." *Prison Culture*, 12 Mar. 2012, www.usprisonculture.com/blog/transformative-justice/.

Kahlon, Rajkamal. "Autopsy No.: ME04–38, pp. 1–11: the teeth appear natural and in good condition." *Did You Kiss the Dead Body?*, www.didyoukissthedeadbody.com/drawings?lightbox=image11z1.

———. *Did You Kiss the Dead Body?* www.didyoukissthedeadbody.com/drawings.

———. "Did You Kiss the Dead Body?" *Comparative Studies of South Asia, Africa, and the Middle East*, vol. 34, no. 2, pp. 336–63.

———. Untitled Image (Autopsy of Abbas Alwan Fadil). *Did You Kiss the Dead Body?*, www.didyoukissthedeadbody.com/drawings?lightbox=image11wg.

———. Untitled Image (Autopsy of Mullah Habibullah). *Did You Kiss the Dead Body?*, www.didyoukissthedeadbody.com/drawings?lightbox=image11z1.

Kaplan, Carl S. "Execution Debate Is Broadened by Photos on Web." *Cyber Law Journal, New York Times*, 29 Oct. 1999, partners.nytimes.com/library/tech/99/10/cyber/cyberlaw/29law.html#1.

Kaufman-Osborn, Timothy V. *From Noose to Needle: Capital Punishment and the Late Liberal State*. U of Michigan P, 2002.

Kelly, Amita. "Does It Matter That 95 Percent of Elected Prosecutors Are White?" *NPR*, 8 July 2015, www.npr.org/sections/itsallpolitics/2015/07/08/420913118/does-it-matter-that-95-of-elected-prosecutors-are-white.

"A Kentucky Lynching: A Negro Murderer Swung to a Tree Near Newcastle." *Atlanta Constitution*, 29 Aug. 1893, p. 1.

Lantigua-Williams, Juleyka. "Are Prosecutors the Key to Justice Reform?" *Atlantic*, 18 May 2016, www.theatlantic.com/politics/archive/2016/05/are-prosecutors-the-key-to-justice-reform/483252/.

Lopez, German. "Trump's First 100 Days Have Been a Criminal Justice Callback to the 1980s and '90s." *Vox*, 28 Apr. 2017, www.vox.com/policy-and-politics/2017/4/28/15457902/trump-criminal-justice-100-days.

"Lynching, Whites and Negroes, 1882–1968." *Tuskegee University Archives Repository*, 192.203.127.197/archive/handle/123456789/511.

Marchant, Bristowe. "3 Years Later, Confederate Flag Casts Shadow Again over SC State House." *The State*, 10 July 2018, www.thestate.com/news/politics-government/article214555950.html.

Markman, Keith D., et al. "'It Would Have Been Worse under Saddam': Implications of Counterfactual Thinking for Beliefs Regarding the Ethical Treatment of Prisoners of War." *Journal of Experimental Social Psychology*, vol. 44, no. 3, pp. 650–54. *ScienceDirect*, doi.org/10.1016/j.jesp.2007.03.005.

Mays, Chris. "From 'Flows' to 'Excess': On Stability, Stubbornness, and Blockage in Rhetorical Ecologies." *Enculturation*, 2015, enculturation.net/from-flows-to-excess.

Mbembe, Achille. "Necropolitics." Translated by Libby Meintjes, *Public Culture*, vol. 15, no. 1, 2003, pp. 11–40.

McDonald, Kelly M., and Christina M. Smith. "The Mundane to the Memorial: Circulating and Deliberating the War in Iraq through Vernacular Soldier-Produced Videos." *Critical Studies in Media Communication*, vol. 28, no. 4, pp. 292–313. *Taylor & Francis*, doi-org.libproxy.clemson.edu/10.1080/15295036.2011.589031.

Medina-López, Kelly. "Rasquache Rhetorics: A Cultural Rhetorics Sensibility." *Constellations*, 2018, constell8cr.com/issue-1/rasquache-rhetorics-a-cultural-rhetorics-sensibility/.

Merica, Dan. "Trump Says Both Sides to Blame among Charlottesville Backlash." *CNN*, 16 Aug. 2017, www.cnn.com/2017/08/15/politics/trump-charlottesville-delay/index.html.

Middendorf, Jeffrey T., et al. "Brief for Respondents." *American Bar Association*, 3 Dec. 2007, www.americanbar.org/content/dam/aba/publishing/preview/publiced_preview_briefs_pdfs_07_08_07_5439_Respondent.authcheckdam.pdf.

Milbank, Dana. "Bush Seeks to Reassure Nation on Iraq." *Washington Post*, 25 May 2004, www.washingtonpost.com/wp-dyn/articles/A52711-2004May24.html.

Mitchell, Koritha. *Living with Lynching: African American Lynching Plays, Performance, and Citizenship, 1890–1930*. U of Illinois P, 2011.

Monberg, Terese Guinsataio. "Like the Molave: Listening for Constellations of Community through 'Growing Up Brown' Stories." *Enculturation*, no. 21, 20 Apr. 2016, enculturation.net/like-the-molave.

Morgan, Danielle Fuentes. "Stop Telling Me to Get over Slavery . . ." *Al Jazeera*, 17 Aug. 2017, www.aljazeera.com/indepth/opinion/2017/08/stop-telling-slavery-170817061717353.html.

Moten, Fred. *In the Break: The Aesthetics of the Black Radical Tradition*. U of Minnesota P, 2009.

NAACP. "NAACP History: Dyer Anti-Lynching Bill." *NAACP*, naacp.org/naacp-history-dyer-anti-lynching-bill/.

Nixon, Rob. *Slow Violence and the Environmentalism of the Poor*. Harvard UP, 2013.

NPR Staff. "Sam Cooke and the Song That 'Almost Scared Him.'" *NPR*, 1 Feb. 2014, www.npr.org/2014/02/01/268995033/sam-cooke-and-the-song-that-almost-scared-him.

"Number of Executions by State and Region since 1976." *Death Penalty Information Center*, www.deathpenaltyinfo.org/number-executions-state-and-region-1976.

"Offender Information: Brooks, Charlie Jr." *Texas Department of Criminal Justice*, www.tdcj.state.tx.us/death_row/dr_info/brookscharlie.html.

Ohlheiser, Abby. "The Creator of Godwin's Law Explains Why Some Nazi Comparisons Don't Break His Famous Internet Rule." *Washington Post*, 14 Aug. 2017, www.washingtonpost.com/news/the-intersect/wp/2017/08/14/the-creator-of-godwins-law-explains-why-some-nazi-comparisons-dont-break-his-famous-internet-rule/?utm_term=.56c434412300.

Oral Argument, *Baze v. Rees*. *Oyez*, 7 Jan. 2008, www.oyez.org/cases/2007/07-5439.

Oral Argument, *Glossip v. Gross*. *Oyez*, 29 Apr. 2015, www.oyez.org/cases/2014/14-7955.

Owen, A. Susan, and Peter Ehrenhaus. "The Moore's Ford Lynching Reenactment: Affective Memory and Race Trauma." *Text and Performance Quarterly*, vol. 34, no. 1, pp. 72–90. *Taylor & Francis*, ttp://dx.doi.org/10.1080/10462937.2013.856461.

Parks, Miles. "Confederate Statues Were Built to Further a 'White Supremacist Future.'" *NPR*, 20 Aug. 2017, www.npr.org/2017/08/20/544266880/confederate-statues-were-built-to-further-a-white-supremacist-future.

Penny, Laurie. "No, I Will Not Debate You." *Longreads*, Sept. 2018, longreads.com/2018/09/18/no-i-will-not-debate-you/.

Perelman, Chaïm, and L. Olbrechts-Tyteca. *The New Rhetoric: A Treatise on Argumentation*. Translated by John Wilkerson and Purcell Weaver, U of Notre Dame P, 1969.

Pérez, Kimberlee. "Embodying 'I Can't Breathe': Tensions and Possibilities between Appropriation and Coalition." *Precarious Rhetorics*, edited by Wendy S. Hesford et al., The Ohio State UP, 2018, pp. 82–104.

Pinter, Harold. "Nobel Lecture: Art, Truth, & Politics." *Nobelprize.org*, www.nobelprize.org/nobel_prizes/literature/laureates/2005/pinter-lecture-e.html.

"Preponderance." *Wex Legal Dictionary,* Legal Information Institute, Cornell Law School, www. law.cornell.edu/wex/preponderance.

"The President's News Conference with King Abdullah II of Jordan." *The American Presidency Project,* 6 May 2004, www.presidency.ucsb.edu/ws/index.php?pid=72619.

Puar, Jasbir. *The Right to Maim: Debility, Capacity, Disability.* Duke UP, 2017.

——. *Terrorist Assemblages: Homonationalism in Queer Times.* Duke UP, 2007.

"Punishment for the Crime of Lynching: Hearing before a Subcommittee of the Committee on the Judiciary." United States Senate, 14 Feb. 1935.

Reinhold, Robert. "Technician Executes Murderer in Texas by Lethal Injection." *New York Times,* 7 Dec. 1982, www.nytimes.com/1982/12/07/us/technician-executes-murderer-in-texas-by-lethal-injection.html.

Rejali, Darius. *Torture and Democracy.* Princeton UP, 2009.

"Reward Offered in Lynching Case: Judge Orders Tennessee Grand Jury to Make a Complete Investigation." *Atlanta Constitution,* 19 Dec. 1933, p. 7.

Rhem, Kathleen T. "Bush Shows 'Deep Disgust' for Apparent Treatment of Iraqi Prisoners." US Department of Defense, 30 Apr. 2004, archive.defense.gov/news/newsarticle.aspx?id=26781.

Rivers, Nathaniel A., and Ryan P. Weber. "Ecological, Pedagogical, Public Rhetoric." *College Composition and Communication,* vol. 63, no. 2, 2011, pp. 187–218. *NCTE,* www.jstor.org/stable/23131582.

Roberts-Miller, Patricia. "Conspiracy Bullshit." *Rhetoric Society Quarterly,* vol. 4, no. 5, 2015, pp. 464–67. *Taylor & Francis Online,* dx.doi.org.libproxy.clemson.edu/10.1080/02773945.2015.1088341.

——. *Demagoguery and Democracy.* The Experiment, 2017.

——. *Fanatical Schemes: Proslavery Rhetoric and the Tragedy of Consensus.* U of Alabama P, 2009.

Romero, Anthony D. "Pardon Bush and Those Who Tortured." *New York Times,* 8 Dec. 2014, nyti.ms/20mTwNB.

"Rumsfeld Apologizes to Iraqis Abused by U. S. Soldiers, May 7, 2004." Internet Archive, 7 May 2004, web.archive.org/web/20060927035551/ italy.usembassy.gov/viewer/article.asp?article=%2Ffile2004_05%2Falia%2Fa4050713.htm.

Sanburn, Josh. "All the Ways Darren Wilson Described Being Afraid of Michael Brown." *Time,* 14 Nov. 2014, time.com/3605346/darren-wilson-michael-brown-demon/.

Sands, Jon M., et al. "Petition for Writ of Certiorari." *SCOTUSblog,* 13 Jan. 2015, sblog.s3.amazonaws.com/wp-content/uploads/2015/01/2015.01.13-Cert-Petition.pdf.

Sarat, Austin. *Gruesome Spectacles: Botched Executions and America's Death Penalty.* Stanford UP, 2014.

——. *When the State Kills: Capital Punishment and the American Condition.* Princeton UP, 2002.

Scarry, Elaine. *The Body in Pain: The Making and Unmaking of the World.* Oxford UP, 1985.

Schilb, John. *Rhetorical Refusals: Defying Readers' Expectations.* Southern Illinois UP, 2007.

Schilling, Dave. "A Brief History of Rectal Feeding." *Vice,* 10 Dec. 2014, www.vice.com/en_us/article/qbe5jd/a-brief-history-of-rectal-feedings-120.

Senate Select Committee on Intelligence (SSCI). *Committee Study of the Central Intelligence Agency's Detention and Interrogation Program,* 3 Dec. 2014, www.feinstein.senate.gov/public/_cache/files/7/c/7c85429a-ec38-4bb5-968f-289799bf6d0e/D87288C34A6D9FF736F9459ABCF83210.sscistudy1.pdf.

Shapiro, Emily. "Charleston Victim's Mother Tells Dylann Roof 'I Forgive You' as He's Sentenced to Death." *ABC,* 11 Jan. 2017, abcnews.go.com/U. S./charleston-victims-mother-tells-dylann-roof-forgive/story?id=44704096.

Sharpe, Christina. *In the Wake: On Blackness and Being.* Duke UP, 2016.

Shermer, Michael. "We've Known for 400 Years That Torture Doesn't Work." *Scientific American,* 1 May 2017, www.scientificamerican.com/article/we-rsquo-ve-known-for-400-years-that-torture-doesn-rsquo-t-work/.

Siemaszko, Corky. "Nevada and Nebraska Executioners Are Turning to Fentanyl." *NBC News,* 12 Dec. 2017, www.nbcnews.comstoryline/lethal-injection/nevada-nebraska-executioners-are-turning-fentanyl-n828796.

Smiley, CalvinJohn, and David Fakunle. "From 'Brute' to 'Thug': The Demonization and Criminalization of Unarmed Black Male Victims in America." *Human Behavior in the Social Environment,* vol. 26, no. 3–4, 2016. *Taylor & Francis Online,* 10.1080/10911359.2015.1129256.

Smith, Roberta. "Botero Restores the Dignity of Prisoners at Abu Ghraib." *New York Times,* 15 Nov. 2006, www.nytimes.com/2006/11/15/arts/design/15chan.html.

Sontag, Susan. *Regarding the Pain of Others.* Picador, 2004.

———. "Regarding the Torture of Others." *New York Times Magazine,* 23 May 2004, www.nytimes.com/2004/05/23/magazine/regarding-the-torture-of-others.html?_r=0.

Sparks, Laura. "Re-Seeing Abu Ghraib: Cynical Rhetoric as Civic Engagement." *Present Tense,* vol. 5, no. 3, www.presenttensejournal.org/volume-5/re-seeing-abu-ghraib-cynical-rhetoric-as-civic-engagement/.

"State by State Lethal Injection." *Death Penalty Information Center,* deathpenaltyinfo.org/state-lethal-injection.

Stein, Rob. "Company to Stop Making Drugs Commonly Used in Executions." *Washington Post,* 21 Jan. 2011, www.washingtonpost.com/national/company-to-stop-making-drug-commonly-used-in-executions/2011/01/21/ABfoQLR_story.html?utm_term=.eb9e04fa418c.

Stern, Jeffrey E. "The Cruel and Unusual Execution of Clayton Lockett." *Atlantic,* June 2015, www.theatlantic.com/magazine/archive/2015/06/execution-clayton-lockett/392069/.

"A Sunday Lynching: Joe Lewis, a Negro, Hanged by Masked Men . . ." *Atlanta Constitution,* 10 Feb. 1896, p. 2.

Supreme Court of Florida. *Provenzano v. Moore,* 1999 WL 756012 (Fla.), 24 Sep. 1999, users.soc.umn.edu/~samaha/cases/provenzano%20v%20moore.htm.

Taylor, Diane. *The Archive and the Repertoire: Performing Cultural Memory in the Americas.* Duke UP, 2003.

The Texas After Violence Project. texasafterviolence.org.

Tolnay, Stewart E., and E. M. Beck. *A Festival of Violence: An Analysis of Southern Lynchings, 1882–1930.* U of Illinois P, 1995.

Tompkins, Christopher W., et al. "Defendants' Response to Plaintiffs' Motion for Partial Summary Judgment." *Salim v. Mitchell,* United States District Court for the Eastern District of Washington, 2:15-CV-286-JLQ, 12 June 2017. *American Civil Liberties Union,* www.aclu.org/legal-document/salim-v-mitchell-defendants-response-plaintiffs-motion-summary-judgment.

Towns, Armond R. "That Camera Won't Save You! The Spectacular Consumption of Police Violence." *Present Tense,* vol. 5, no. 2, www.presenttensejournal.org/volume-5/that-camera-wont-save-you-the-spectacular-consumption-of-police-violence/.

"A Triple Lynching: Takes Place up in the Hills of Habersham . . ." *Atlanta Constitution,* 18 May 1892, p. 1.

"Two States Probe Lynching in Florida: Authorities Meanwhile Consider Withdrawal of Guardsmen." *Atlanta Constitution,* 30 Oct. 1934, p. 6.

US Supreme Court. *Arthur v. Dunn,* Sotomayor, J., dissenting. 580 U. S. ___, 21 Feb. 2017, www.supremecourt.gov/opinions/16pdf/16-602_n758.pdf.

———. *Atkins v. Virginia.* 536 U. S. 304, 20 June 2002, *Justia,* supreme.justia.com/cases/federal/us/536/304/.

———. *Baze v. Rees.* 553 U. S. 35, 16 April 2008. *Justia,* supreme.justia.com/cases/federal/us/553/35/opinion.html.

———. *Baze v. Rees,* Ginsburg, J. dissenting. 553 U. S. 35, 16 April 2008. *Justia,* supreme.justia.com/cases/federal/us/553/35/dissent.html.

———. *Farmer v. Brennan.* 511 U. S. 825, 6 June 1994, *Justia,* supreme.justia.com/cases/federal/us/511/825/.

———. *Ford v. Wainwright.* 477 U. S. 399, 26 June 1986, *Justia,* supreme.justia.com/cases/federal/us/477/399/.

———. *Furman v. Georgia.* 408 U. S. 238, 29 June 1972, *Justia,* supreme.justia.com/cases/federal/us/408/238/case.html.

———. *Glossip v. Gross.* 576 U. S. ____, 29 June 2015, *Justia,* supreme.justia.com/cases/federal/us/576/14-7955/.

———. *Glossip v. Gross,* Syllabus. 576 U. S. ____, 29 June 2015, *Justia,* supreme.justia.com/cases/federal/us/576/14-7955/.

———. *Gregg v. Georgia.* 428 U. S. 153, 2 July 1976, *Justia,* supreme.justia.com/cases/federal/us/428/153/.

———. *In re Kemmler.* 136 U. S. 436 23 May 1890, *Justia,* supreme.justia.com/cases/federal/us/136/436/case.html.

———. *Louisiana ex rel. Francis v. Resweber.* 329 U. S. 459, 13 Dec. 1947, *Justia,* supreme.justia.com/cases/federal/us/329/459/.

———. *Roper v. Simmons.* 543 U. S. 551, 1 March 2005, *Justia,* supreme.justia.com/cases/federal/us/543/551/.

———. *Trop v. Dulles.* 356 U. S. 86, 31 March 1958. *Legal Information Institute,* www.law.cornell.edu/supremecourt/text/356/86.

———. *Wilkerson v. Utah.* 99 U. S. 130, 1878, *Justia,* supreme.justia.com/cases/federal/us/99/130/case.html.

Vicaro, Michael P. "A Liberal Use of 'Torture': Pain, Personhood, and Precedent in the US Federal Definition of Torture." *Rhetoric and Public Affairs,* vol. 14, no. 3, 2011. *Project Muse,* 10.1353/rap.2011.0015.

Vitale, Alex S. "The New 'Superpredator' Myth." *New York Times,* 23 Mar. 2018, www.nytimes.com/2018/03/23/opinion/superpredator-myth.html.

Wagner, Robert F. Statement to the Senate Subcommittee on the Judiciary, Punishment for the Crime of Lynching, Part 1, Hearing, 20 and 21 Feb 1934, 73rd Cong., 2nd sess.

Walker, Jeffrey. *Rhetoric and Poetics in Antiquity.* Oxford UP, 2000.

Walmsley, Roy. "World Prison Population List (Tenth Edition)." *International Centre for Prison Studies,* University of Essex, www.prisonstudies.org/sites/default/files/resources/downloads/wppl_10.pdf.

Weise, Jillian. "Common Cyborg." *Granta,* 24 Sep. 2018, granta.com/common-cyborg/.

Wells, Ida B. *Southern Horrors: Lynch Law in All Its Phases. Project Gutenberg,* www.gutenberg.org/files/14975/14975-h/14975-h.htm.

Wenger, Yvonne, and Mark Puente. "Baltimore to Pay Freddie Gray's Family $6.4 million to Settle Civil Claims." *Baltimore Sun,* 8 Sep. 2015, www.baltimoresun.com/news/maryland/freddie-gray/bs-md-ci-boe-20150908-story.html.

Wexler, Laura. *Fire in a Canebrake: The Last Mass Lynching in America.* Scribner, 2003.

Whaley, Natelege. "Michael Brown's Mother on Forgiving Darren Wilson: 'Never.'" *BET,* 5 Aug. 2015, www.bet.com/news/national/2015/08/05/michael-brown-s-mother-on-forgiving-darren-wilson-never.html.

White, Josh. "FBI Interrogators in Cuba Opposed Aggressive Tactics." *Washington Post,* 24 Feb. 2006, www.washingtonpost.com/wp-dyn/content/article/2006/02/23/AR2006022301813.html.

Whites, LeeAnn. "Rebecca Latimer Felton and the Wife's Farm: The Class and Racial Politics of Gender Reform." *The Georgia Historical Quarterly* vol. 76, no. 2, pp. 354–72. *JSTOR,* www.jstor.org.libproxy.clemson.edu/stable/40582540.

Wolters, Wendy. "Without Sanctuary: Bearing Witness, Bearing Whiteness." *JAC,* vol. 24, no. 2, pp. 399–425. *JSTOR,* www.jstor.org.libproxy.clemson.edu/stable/20866631.

Wood, Amy Louise. *Lynching and Spectacle: Witnessing Racial Violence in America, 1890–1930.* U of North Carolina P, 2009.

Woodall, George N. "Recommends Emergency Trial Law as Remedy for the Lynching Evil." *Atlanta Constitution,* 28 Jan. 1934, p. 5C.

Wright, Jennifer. "When Men Demand Your Attention, It's OK to Ignore Them." *Harper's Bazaar,* 22 Aug. 2018, www.harpersbazaar.com/culture/politics/a22776619/alexandria-ocasio-cortez-ben-shapiro-debate-response/.

Yuhas, Alan. "Controversial 'Rectal Feeding' Technique Used to Control Detainees' Behaviour." *Guardian,* 9 Dec. 2014, www.theguardian.com/us-news/2014/dec/09/cia-report-rectal-feeding-detainees.

Zernike, Kate. "Soldiers Testify on Orders to Soften Prisoners." *New York Times,* 13 Jan. 2005, www.nytimes.com/2005/01/13/us/soldiers-testify-on-orders-to-soften-prisoners-in-iraq.html.

INDEX

NEW DIRECTIONS IN RHETORIC AND MATERIALITY

BARBARA A. BIESECKER, WENDY S. HESFORD, AND
CHRISTA TESTON, SERIES EDITORS

Current conversations about rhetoric signal a new attentiveness to and critical appraisal of material-discursive phenomena. New Directions in Rhetoric and Materiality provides a forum for responding to and extending such conversations. The series publishes monographs that pair rhetorical theory with an analysis of material conditions and the social-symbolic labor circulating therein. Books in the series offer a "new direction" for exploring the everyday, material, lived conditions of human, nonhuman, and extra-human life—advancing theories around rhetoric's relationship to materiality.